Foundations of Morality

By the same author:

THE END OF WAR OR THE END OF MANKIND (1955)

THE FAILURE OF THE SEXUAL REVOLUTION (1974)

ARCHAEOLOGY OF THE MIND (1992)

CIVILISATION: UTOPIA AND TRAGEDY (1992)

THE UNKNOWN SELF (1993)

EXPLORING THE UNCONSCIOUS (1994)

FOUNDATIONS OF MORALITY

AN INVESTIGATION INTO THE ORIGIN AND
PURPOSE OF MORAL CONCEPTS

GEORGE FRANKL

OPEN GATE PRESS
incorporating Centaur Press
LONDON

First published in 2000 by Open Gate Press
51 Achilles Road, London NW6 1DZ
This new paperback edition published 2001
by Open Gate Press

Copyright © 2000 and 2001 George Frankl
All rights, by all media, reserved.

British Library Cataloguing-in-Publication Programme
A catalogue reference for this book is available from the
British Library.

ISBN: 1 871871 52 2

Quotations from the *Evening Standard* and *The Observer*
are © the *Evening Standard* and © *The Observer*
and reproduced by kind permission.

Cover illlustration is *Venus and Cupid*, c. 1830
by William Etty (1787-1849)
York City Art Gallery, North Yorkshire,
UK/Bridgeman Art Library

Printed in Great Britain by
The Bath Press, Bath

Frankl examines the role of moral concepts in the life of societies, pointing to the interaction between neurotic and psychotic disturbances in individuals and the pathologies which periodically overwhelm societies. He then asks why morality is necessary in the human species and examines its neurological, biological and psychological origins. In the philosophical section of this book Frankl attempts a rational reconstruction of moral ideas based on an understanding of man's emotional needs.

George Frankl was born in Vienna, where he studied philosophy and psychoanalysis. The Nazi invasion of Austria forced him to emigrate and he continued his studies in England and then in Canada. Towards the end of the war he came back to England and eventually settled in London where he has been in psychoanalytic practice for some forty years.

He has lectured on psychoanalysis and philosophy, as well as on prehistoric cultures and architectural psychology, and has written several books.

While actively engaged in writing, lecturing and his work as a psychotherapist, he was concerned with the social neurosis and determined to find an explanation for the compulsions which drive nations to pursue irrational and all too frequently self-destructive goals. He is now convinced that the most important achievement of psychoanalysis will emerge in its applications to the social pathologies.

Contents

Prologue	1
Chapter 1	3
The End of Civilisation?	
1. Voices of Disenchantment and Foreboding	3
2. An Illusion Buried not with Respect but with Anger	8
3. The Breakthrough of the Repressed	14
4. Regressive Disintegration of the Arts	27
Chapter 2	32
The Philosophical Vandals	
1. Wittgenstein and the Analysis of Words	32
2. The Vienna Circle	41
3. Background: The Philosophy of the Enlightenment	47
4. The Dilemma of the Vienna Circle: Theory and Practice Divided	56
5. From Logical Positivism to Linguistic Analysis in England and America	60
6. The Tower of Babble: Postmodernism and Deconstruction	65
Chapter 3	79
The Physical Basis of Consciousness and Morality	
1. The Instinctual Void	79
2. The Structure and Function of the Brain	85
3. The Ancient Areas of the Brain	89
4. The Hypothalamus: Hormones and Homeostasis	93
5. Consciousness and Intelligence	97
6. The Neurons of Morality	101

Chapter 4 105
The Origins of Consciousness and Morality
1. A Psychoanalytic Anthropology 105
2. Tool-making and Intelligence 107
3. Tool-making and the Origins of Culture 108
4. The Evolution of Hominids to Humans 111
5. Totems, Ghosts and Spirits 117
6. Big Game Hunters and Homemakers 119
7. The Primal Community 122
8. Myths, Gods and Morality 125
9. Worship and Rituals of Propitiation 126
10. Matriarchy: The Original Culture of
    Homo Sapiens 134
11. The Art and the Culture of the Cave Temples 138
12. The Crisis of Matriarchy: The Goddess
    becomes a Witch 142

Chapter 5 145
. . . and God was born in the Minds of Men
1. The Revolt against Matriarchy and the
   Beginnings of Agriculture 145
2. Patriarchy emerges 148
3. The Divinity of Kings 152
4. The Culture of the Oedipus Complex:
   Patriarchal Paranoia 154
5. The Emergence of Monotheism 157
6. The Birth of Philosophy 159

Chapter 6 166
Towards a Rational Morality
1. Some Basic Questions 166
2. The Need for Morality 170
3. Kant's Categories of Cognition 174
The analytic and synthetic *a priori* 178
4. The Equivalence between the Categories of
   Cognition and the Categories of Morality 179
The Categorical Imperatives 184
5. Reconstructing God 185
6. The Origins of Thanatos 188

Chapter 7 195
Towards the Good Society
1. The Maxims of Moral Aims 195
2. Work as Creativity 197
3. Training and Education 200
4. The Humanisation of Machines and the
    Dehumanisation of Man 202

Bibliography 207

Index 215

Connect, always connect.
Goethe

But if this one hope [of universal love] cannot be at least partly realised, if in the course of evolution we don't learn to divert our instincts from destroying our own kind, if we continue to hate one another for minor differences and kill each other for petty gain, if we go on exploiting the great progress made in control of natural resources for our mutual destruction, what kind of future lies in store for us?
Freud to Romain Rolland, 4th March 1923

Prologue

There is a growing awareness that mankind is facing a crisis of morality. It is a difficult thing to admit, for we want to hold on to a conviction that we know what is right and wrong, good and bad, but in view of what has happened in the twentieth century we can no longer be certain.

While it is true that we have seen stupendous advances in the natural sciences, exploring the vast recesses of the universe both in time and space as well as the origins of life on this planet, our explorations into the recesses of the mind have, despite some initial advances remained disappointing in the end. In fact we are left with the impression that we are far less sure than people of previous ages why we behave the way we do and what values and goals we are meant to believe in. It is true that as inheritors of the Enlightenment and the beneficiaries of scientific knowledge, we know that the moral certainties of past ages, directed as they were by religious belief, the worship of gods and the glorification of kings, were motivated by emotional needs which we now consider to be irrational. Our rational and scientific orientations have undermined the ancient views of the world, which, as we understand now, have led mankind to endless wars, oppression and prejudice, and left large parts of the population trapped in poverty; but we have not arrived at a clarification of the values and purposes to which we could devote ourselves with a sense of conviction and security. We have undermined the old beliefs but we have not created new goals and purposes to replace them.

Our supposedly rational critiques, as exemplified by the various schools of philosophy, psychology and the diversity of social studies, undermine any sense of conviction about the essential nature of our humanity. We are not even sure any more what distinguishes us from the higher animals, when even pigeons and rats are taken as models for the study of human reflexes and behaviour. We have not discovered a rationally valid meaning and purpose that defines humanity. While mankind has existed for a long time immersed in its conflicts and irrational pursuits, humanity is still waiting to be born.

The twentieth century started with great promises and assurances about the advance of science which would at last provide convincing insights into the biological, psychological and cultural meaning of mankind's existence as the highest form of evolution, but after a short moment of optimism we experienced a renewed eruption of national, religious and racial hatreds, savagery and bloodshed unparalleled in its extent and brutality. We had to learn that science could become the tool of fanaticism and prejudice, and that the progress of scientific technology has led to an intensification of man's destructive capacity. The great expectations have turned into disenchantment, with a disbelief that there is anything worthy of belief, and we stare into a moral vacuum, the offspring of a great deception. The twentieth century turned out to be the testing ground of the Enlightenment and exposed its failures.

The sense of disenchantment and cynicism felt by most people is often clearly articulated by our intellectual leaders who have seen their aspirations and their beliefs and hopes crumble around them.

Chapter 1

The End of Civilisation?

1. Voices of Disenchantment and Foreboding

'What is the point of presenting another book to the public in face of the flood of books clamouring for our attention? Anyone who writes books nowadays ought to be shot,' declared R. D. Laing, the prophet of the *new psychiatry* of the hippie period of the 1960s and 1970s, in his later years of distress and confusion. This does not prevent me and others from writing more books with the intention of contributing something to the improvement of the world, but we address ourselves to a world which finds it difficult to believe that anything is really true or certain.

Perhaps the most influential critic of philosophical concepts, Ludwig Wittgenstein, exclaimed in his later years, when he began to be preoccupied with psychology: 'Where is the science of psychic phenomena? Answer: One observes what goes on in one's soul. How? By means of introspection. But if one observes the processes which occur in one's soul, then one changes them and produces new ones. But this should not happen in observation. He who observes should not change the observed. The science of psychic phenomena therefore presents the following puzzle: in the strict sense of the word, it is impossible for me to observe the psychic processes which occur in others, nor can I observe them in myself. Where do we stand then? The answer is: We are in a fog, in a state of helpless confusion.'

A similar question was asked a long time ago, in 1813, by the philosopher Hegel: 'When laws and conventions which are meant to provide the firm foundation and certainty for changing situations are in themselves subject to change, then what would provide firm foundations in a changing world?' Hegel could provide a reassuring answer to his unsettling question: 'Even while the general conventions and laws are subject to change and development, these changes are slow: a single year, or even a man's lifetime, is not affected by them. Developments only occur in the course of long periods.' We might add, they are not sufficiently noticed to cause a sense of confusion. But it is precisely this which cannot be said any more in our time; the political and social changes, as well as the radical transformations of our view of the nature of the universe, happen with a speed which tends to make us psychologically and intellectually quite dizzy, producing a sense of confusion, where nothing can be taken as certain, where nothing can be seen as a firm basis for our values and convictions.

Nothing now is certain; nothing is eternal, there is no unchanging essence behind the torrent of changes. The 'grand theories' of earlier times are deeply mistrusted. The ideas of Hegel and Marx, which claimed to have discovered the laws which govern changes and the transformations of society, have been exposed both intellectually and socially as justifications for totalitarian dictatorships, and, instead of discovering the synthesis and the resolution of social conflict, have been the cause of an intensification of conflict and misery. Now we 'know' that the future is subject to chance events which we can neither anticipate nor control.

The writer who perhaps more than any other has been the prophet of hope, proclaiming the great achievements which his century would witness, H. G. Wells, saw his Utopias collapse and the 'mind of man at the end of its tether'. After the horrors of the two world wars he gave expression to utter disenchantment, and he despaired of the future of mankind. In 1945 he wrote: 'Reality declares coldly and harshly upon any of those who can wrench their minds from the comforting delusions of normality to face the unsparing question which has overwhelmed the writer and mankind. They discover a frightful queerness has come into life. Even quite unnoticing people now are betraying, by fits and starts, a certain wonder, a shrinking and fugitive sense that something is happening so that life will never be quite the same again.' In the course of a long and intellectually supremely productive life, he did his utmost to pursue the trends, the upward spiral towards this convergence in a new phase in the story of life, but the more he weighed the realities before him, the less was he able to detect any convergence whatever. Changes have ceased to be systematic, and the further he estimated the course they were taking, the greater their divergence. Hitherto events had been held together by a certain logical consistency, as the heavenly bodies, as we know them, have been held together by the pull of the golden cord of gravitation. Now it is as if that cord had vanished and everything was driving anyhow to anywhere at a steadily increasing velocity. There is now no pattern of things to come, the attempt to trace a pattern of any sort is absolutely futile.

At the end of his life H. G. Wells was convinced that there is no way out or round or through the impasse – it is the end. He wrote *The Mind at the End of Its Tether* in 1945, and died in 1946.

Another writer who found that his lifelong exposition and love for the values of European civilisation were shattered and ended his life in a state of utter disenchantment was the Austrian, Stefan Zweig. His suicide in 1942 can be seen as a reflection of the suicide of Western civilisation, the end of a world destroyed by the eruption of brutality that overwhelmed and perhaps forever defeated the aspirations of civilisation.

In his last book, written in 1941, he writes: 'We, who are sixty today and who, *de jure*, still have a space of time before us, what have we not seen, not suffered, not lived through? We have ploughed through the catalogue of every conceivable catastrophe back and forth, and we have not yet come to the last page. I myself was a contemporary of the two greatest wars of mankind, and even passed through each one of them on a different front, the one on the German, the other on the anti-German. Before the war I knew the highest degree and form of individual freedom, and later its lowest levels in hundreds of years; I have been celebrated and despised, free and unfree, rich and poor. All the livid steeds of the Apocalypse have stormed through my life – revolution and famine, inflation and terror, epidemics and emigration. I have seen the great mass ideologies grow and spread before my eyes – Fascism in Italy, National Socialism in Germany, Bolshevism in Russia, and above all else that arch-plague nationalism which has poisoned the flower of our European culture. I was forced to be a defenceless, helpless witness of the most inconceivable decline of humanity into a barbarism which we had believed long since forgotten, with its deliberate and programmatic dogma of anti-humanitarianism.

'It was reserved for us, after centuries, again to see wars without declarations of war, concentration camps, persecution, mass robbery, bombing attacks on helpless cities, all bestialities unknown to the last fifty generations, things which future generations, it is hoped, will not allow to happen . . . In those hours I frequently spoke with Freud about the horror of Hitler's world and the war. The outburst of bestiality deeply shocked him as a humanitarian, but as a thinker he was in no way astonished. He had always been scolded as a pessimist, he said, because he had denied the supremacy of culture over the instincts; but his opinion that the barbaric, the elemental destructive instinct in the human soul was ineradicable, had become confirmed most terribly.'

And in his last message, the day before his suicide, Zweig wrote: 'After one's sixtieth year unusual powers are needed in order to make another wholly new beginning. Those that I possess have been exhausted by long years of homeless wandering. So I think it better to conclude in good time and in erect bearing a life in which intellectual labour meant the purest joy and personal freedom the highest good on earth.

'I salute all my friends! May it be granted them yet to see the dawn after the long night! I, all too impatient, go on before.'

Let those few quotations suffice as examples of the disenchantment of great minds who believed that mankind was at last on the threshold of realising the great potentials of wisdom and understanding proclaimed by Isaiah and Jesus, Plato, Aristotle, Pico della Mirandola, Shakespeare, Voltaire, Goethe, Spinoza, Kant, Schopenhauer, Galileo, Newton, Darwin, Freud and Einstein, whose inheritors they felt themselves to be. We had to recognise that civilisation is but a thin veneer unable to contain the periodic eruptions of brutality which overwhelm and defeat the aspirations of morality and reason. The apparently innate savagery of the species could no longer be hidden from consciousness. The achievements of science were shown to be not, as hoped, the tools for the liberation from man's irrationality but its servants. Bows and arrows were 'improved' and made into machine guns, and now nuclear powers of destruction have achieved the feat of harnessing the energies of the cosmos into the service of human aggression and stupidity. The stupendous discoveries of nuclear physics have been crowned (or degraded) by making it possible not only to defeat and destroy an enemy but to destroy the life-supporting biosphere of this planet. Reason itself has shown its impotence to guard us from the dark side of our nature. No wonder that the defeated hopes of the Enlightenment have produced an ideology of disbelief, which goes under the name of post-modernism; for the end of the Enlightenment is really the end of belief. Those who consider themselves the promoters of the Enlightenment and have recognised no moral or spiritual authority outside human reason, have now come to the conclusion that 'reason', in the words of Roger Scruton in his review of *Enlightenment's Wake* by John Grey, 'cannot fill the god-shaped hole which reason itself created and therefore nothing matters'.

We are no longer sure how to evaluate things and how to respond to them, how to judge what is right and wrong, particularly as we are told by our philosophers that there is no scientific basis for moral concepts, that they have no cognitive significance and that therefore everything is relative.

'What is happening to the world?' is the instinctive reaction of most people. It is not only the traumatic memory of two world wars, the unspeakable horrors of Auschwitz and the continuing killing orgies which have re-erupted in many parts of the world and in the centre of Europe, but also the brutalisation of civic life, which have made us realise that civilised values are only a thin veneer, frequently unable to protect us from savagery. It seems we are no longer allowed to hope for a better future; indeed the future now inspires a feeling of dread and apprehension. This civilisation, and in particular the moral and intellectual framework of the Enlightenment, which has been its chief credo for some two hundred years, arouses not only a deep sense of disappointment but anger. We want to attack this collective superego, this father-figure which promised so much and failed so miserably. The intellectuals produce philosophical systems which attack the cognitive and moral certainties of the Enlightenment; post-modernism, post-structuralism, hermeneutics and deconstructionism combine their voices in a far-reaching critique of our concepts of reality. In a language which is largely incomprehensible they exemplify the impossibility of anyone being sure about the meaning of what is being said. Deconstructionism, in particular, aims at the destruction of confidence in the pursuit of knowledge. The cognitive interest, or rather purpose, of deconstruction leads to the knowledge that we can have no knowledge; it is a persistent enterprise to make us see diverse works as an interminable freeplay of indeterminable meanings. In other words, we cannot trust our judgements or even our perceptions because we cannot trust the concepts of our civilisation which have determined our judgements.

2. An Illusion Buried not with Respect but with Anger

Just as millions of people who experienced or heard about the mass killings in the trenches of the first world war or the horrors of Auschwitz, asked, 'Where was God when these things happened?' so we ask again, 'Where was reason, where was morality, to allow the orgies of savagery and sadism to overwhelm our culture and continue to do so?' Where is this era of peace and co-operation which we were led to expect among the nations of Europe and beyond? Nationalistic and religious fanaticism would give way to the rational and humanistic ideals of the Enlightenment, with a readiness to resolve conflicting interests through tolerance and mutual understanding. The twentieth century was expected to witness a great leap forward in the sciences, which would revolutionise our concept of the universe and of life, and of the evolution and origins of mankind. A new consciousness of the common heritage of our species would make the old obsessions with our national and religious identity which have separated mankind into opposing factions viewing each other with mistrust and fear, obsolete – a thing of the past. Social anthropology and the social sciences would advance our understanding how nation states with their hierarchic structures, the authority of kings, priests and rulers came into being, and psychology would make us understand the reasons for our subservience and how we came to tolerate their coercive powers. Reason would come to rule and under its guidance science would bring innumerable benefits to mankind.

It was considered merely a matter of decades before the last vestiges of hatred and violence would finally be overcome, and this faith in an uninterrupted and irresistible progress acquired the force of a religion. Sociologists and philosophers, those who were drawn to the prophecies of Marx as well as those of the liberal persuasion, competed with one another to find ways of making healthier and happier living conditions for the working masses.

The application of scientific knowledge to the means of production – scientific technology – would produce an abundance of commodities beyond the imagination of previous ages. New forms of transport and communication, railways, motor cars, steamships and aeroplanes, telegraph, telephone and radio, would not only make it possible to gain free access to distant parts of the world but would also make it possible to distribute commodities wherever they were needed to make them available to all men. A new age of prosperity would open before us and defeat the Malthusian law according to which every advance in productive capacity would cause humans to multiply, keeping the level of deprivation and scarcity of available supplies more or less constant, thus annulling any progress. With the new machines, the scientifically organised mass production would, it was thought, easily outstrip population growth. The dreams of universally-shared prosperity would move towards fulfilment, would make the economics and politics of scarcity and with it the inevitability of an impoverished underclass, unnecessary and produce new economic and political concepts. The dehumanising drudgery of labour to which the majority of mankind was enchained would be replaced by a world of machines, which would perform the menial tasks, and universal education would enable workers to control modern technology and enable them to fulfil their human potential as rational and free persons; their improved level of education would enable them to participate in the decision-making processes of society.

Socialism would create the political and economic conditions to put an end to the ancient division of classes between the owners of machines and the workers who serve them, the rich and the poor, and the common ownership of the means of production would herald a new world community of creative persons, no longer enslaved to hierarchic rule but capable of creating a social order and an environment fit for free men to enjoy.

Psychoanalysis would investigate the reasons for our deep-seated awe of authority and our fear of freedom, our mistrust of our own instincts and of our fellow men, the irrational drives which prompt nations to wage war against each other and commit the most dreadful cruelties. To quote Freud: 'The fateful question for the human species seems to me to be whether and to what extent cultural developments by it will succeed in mastering the derangements of communal life caused by the human instinct of aggression and self-destruction. In this connection, perhaps the phase through which we are at this moment passing deserves special interest. Men have brought their powers of subduing the forces of nature to such a pitch that by using them they could now very easily exterminate one another to the last man. They know this – hence arises a great part of their current unrest, their dejection, their mood of apprehension. And now it may be expected that the other of the two "heavenly forces", eternal Eros, will put forth his strength so as to maintain himself alongside of his equally immortal adversary.' (*Civilization and its Discontents*)

Freed from his ancient repressions, Eros, the life-affirming power, the source of love and empathy with one's fellow humans, would emerge triumphantly, if not immediately then progressively, and defeat Thanatos, the life-negating drive, the source of aggressiveness, sadism and the destructive and self-destructive urges, both in the life of individuals and in society.

But now we look back at the proclamations of the Enlightenment which were meant to find fruition in the twentieth century, the promises of rationality, of science, of socialism and liberalism, and psychoanalysis, with the bitter taste of disillusion. No one with a modicum of sensibility can forget the two world wars, the transformation of socialism into the tyranny of Stalinism, the horrors of Nazism which were the ultimate betrayal of European culture, the economic recessions and mass unemployment of the inter-war years which have discredited the pretensions of capitalism; and even now large parts of the population in the capitalist countries remain trapped in poverty, not to speak of the corruption and economic decay of former communist countries. And once again we experience the obscenities of nationalistic, racial and religious fanaticism and their terrorist movements. At this moment there are many wars going on in the world, frequently conducted with the utmost brutality, and famines, with widespread starvation and death in their wake. So much for the wonders of modern technology to provide the commodities needed to satisfy man's material needs. And then there is the spectre of environmental ruination, the poisoning of the air, the seas and the rivers, the exhaustion of the raw materials needed for human as well as animal survival, the global warming due to the so-called greenhouse effect, and the depletion of the ozone layer.

There are many other factors which contribute to our sense of disenchantment and foreboding. For instance, the one science which was always considered to be life-enhancing, medicine, has shown its double-edged character by interfering with the balance of human ecology and natural selection, thus contributing to the population explosion. A vast number of children being born due to the advances of modern medicine are destined to become the victims of famine and starvation in many regions where the rape of natural resources due to population pressure produces an ecological catastrophe. Not only humans but countless animal species are being exterminated. It seems that Malthus is having the last word, as once again we are helplessly falling victim to his laws.

As the culture of the Enlightenment, this divinity of reason and science, has betrayed itself and betrayed our faith in it, we turn against it with anger and are determined to prove that its premises have been worthless. We defy its rules and mock its pretensions as it has made a mockery of our hopes. A cult of cynicism has emerged, and a belief which rejects all belief, a cynicism which is an act of revenge against the God who has failed us. In our anger we tear this God to pieces and only recognise the disconnected bits left in a world no longer governed by a culture that gives meaning and a sense of direction to our existence; we are left prone to the accidents of events which are no more than apparently unconnected happenings. The concept of the random universe of physics has invaded man's life in society which is subjected to random events without any recognisable pattern or meaning.

So we lower our gaze to the here and now with nothing beyond, and cut ourselves off from the past and the future; for the past is a tale of horror, a story of betrayals and shame, and the future fills us with dread. No wonder that so many children no longer believe in education, for they do not see a future worthy of being educated for, and many women consider pregnancy a nuisance or a catastrophe which disrupts the pursuit of pleasure or success in the here and now world. Children see their parents as the representatives of a past world which has betrayed us and they can no longer be respected and act as a role model for the young generation; religion and ideology no longer inspire young minds and are seen as discards on the rubbish heap of failed promises which litter the records of history. But if the vision of a higher, a spiritual meaning of the world ceases to act as a guide and no longer stimulates our minds, then the more primitive areas of the psyche will find a way to the surface. While in the past we repressed our primitive, aggressive-sexual and ego-centred drives and attempted to find sublimation for them in culturally approved forms, we now repress the culture and serve those primitive drives. Those primitive areas of the mind will now find entry into consciousness, dominate it and feel free to assert themselves without guilt, and they will not disturb our conscience. We can thus speak of the breakthrough of the repressed, not only in individuals but in the collective life of society. As the integrative forces of a culture have disappeared, social life is split into separate entities of the here-and-now experience, and the here-and-now experience is greed that excludes compassion or empathy with our fellow men –

everyone for himself as in a sinking ship – the frantic search for satisfaction in a short-term universe.

The culture of the Enlightenment has failed to give us the sense of security and moral guide which a culture is meant to provide, and we are left without a valid meaning or value, with no reference to a universal concept that guides our judgement, and we can neither emotionally nor rationally be sure of what it is that constitutes right or wrong, good or bad. We are all 'specialists' now, pursuing our own specific interests without a sense of identification with the past or the future, the values taught by a common history, its traditions and customs, the kings, rulers, adventurers, the conquerors and merchants who made our country what it is; nor do we seem to gain much inspiration from the great writers, poets and dramatists who have illuminated our spiritual horizon, proclaiming the virtues of liberty, justice and equality, the real legislators, according to Shelley.

But now Shakespeare, Byron, Shelley, Mozart and Beethoven and other heroes of the human spirit are accused of an elitism that contravenes the rule of racial and ethnic equality and of political correctness, and are being hounded out of the educational curriculum. And the music of Beethoven and Mozart is presented on CDs in small extracts as 'mood music' in no way superior or qualitatively different from African or Indian, Tibetan or Chinese music. Similarly, a belief in the future, which would inspire a sense of hope and achievement to look forward to and give meaning to our present existence, has disappeared from our view and we are left with an egocentric and cynical world where only short-term gratification and 'success' matter, separated from each other and from nature as we have cut our links from a culture which was meant to speak for humanity and for life.

In his *Negative Dialectic* Theodor Adorno declares that after Auschwitz the belief in metaphysical ideas is shattered, because what has happened makes metaphysics and large-scale ideas irreconcilable with experience: 'After Auschwitz the failure of our culture is incontrovertibly proven.'

But as we lower our gaze to the here-and-now and can no longer experience the higher visions and they no longer stimulate our minds, then the primitive 'lower' areas of the psyche – which were held in check and their energies sublimated to serve the moral aspirations of our culture – emerge to the surface and dominate our consciousness. What we have called the breakthrough of the repressed acquires the form of a culture of anti-culture, a new realism whose goals will be seen as virtuous and our devotion to them an obsession.

3. The Breakthrough of the Repressed

'Greed is Good'

The breakthrough of the repressed can take many forms. We can easily recognise three main aspects: the liberation of greed, selfishness and sadism from their moral restraints. Indeed they become a new morality, a commanding goal to be pursued.

To speak in psychoanalytic terms: in its urge to defy and to annihilate the superego, the ego will align itself with the primitive drives of the id, and they will acquire dominance over the ego functions. When Freud hoped that where id was there shall ego be, now we find that where ego was there shall id be. While traditionally the aggression towards the own superego is repressed and projected outwards, to be directed against the alien superego, the gods and kings of the enemy, as in fanatical nationalism with its paranoid fantasies and its collective myths frequently leading to wars, now the aggression is directed to the own superego, the own culture.

We can with Herbert Marcuse characterise this process as regressive desublimation or, even more succinctly, as regressive identity-seeking insofar as we identify ourselves with the id forces – the 'lower instincts'. We may mention three manifestations: the liberation of narcissism from its cultural restraints which had emphasised a measure of selflessness in the service of a common goal; the emergence into dominance of greed, and on an even more primitive level, of sadistic-destructive aggression. The first of these drives, namely narcissism, focuses upon the ego, the love of the self, as the main concern of satisfaction. It transforms the ego regressively into a primitive narcissistic ego, and this is usually recognised as selfishness or egomania. It will be dominated

THE END OF CIVILISATION?

by status-seeking in order to receive the attention and admiration of the world. However, in what form such a person will expect to be admired and to admire himself will largely depend upon the values which the world appears to uphold. And in our world we find images of greed and its pursuit as a dominant goal.

Greed is an expression of the oral-incorporative drive which if it experiences deprivation and denial turns into a devouring, aggressive and what Karl Abraham has called oral-cannibalistic drive. It expresses itself in a ruthless pursuit of the acquisition and possession of commodities. Wealth signifies the successful pursuit of these drives, the ability and the power to give them fulfilment by filling oneself up with the objects of desire, and to possess them and to overcome any obstacle that stands in one's way. The profit motive provides the incentive, the satisfaction and the justification. Thus the uninhibited pursuit of wealth becomes a virtue and at the same time serves a narcissistic need for recognition and status. It is no exaggeration to call it oral-cannibalism, which sees the world as an object to be attacked and devoured, without any regard for its feelings or needs. It is an aggression aligned with sadism that provides pleasure in the act of aggression, and is devoid of any sympathy for the attacked object.

We should remark here that in the traditional cultures of the West, dominated by the moral constraints of its superego, individuals who are driven by the oral-aggressive urges have to repress them and will find outlets in neurotic symptoms. However, in a culture which, like ours, has dismissed its superego, the aggressive and oral-cannibalistic drives will find expression in social behaviour and be considered a virtue if they serve the pursuit of profit. So one will feel completely justified in polluting the rivers and the seas, in destroying the forests and poisoning the earth, the utmost cruelty to animals if it serves the profit motive. The point here is that the environment is seen as an object upon which one can vent one's aggression as one depersonalises it, so to speak, without any awareness of its feelings and with a complete denial of the animistic sentiments. However, we must notice that what we may call a displacement or secondary sublimation leads individuals to identify themselves with the business corporations and financial organisations which pursue those aims.

It is those organisations who represent the all-devouring dinosaurs (and will without a doubt suffer the same fate, and so will humanity if it continues to identify with them). They sharpen their technological teeth to attack and devour the natural resources and the animals of the world, and fill their bellies with the profits they make and discharge the waste product upon the world and pollute it. They not only attack nature but they also attack each other in the great hunting competition and devour each other in a relentless pursuit of dominance by means of take-overs, amalgamations and other aspects of financial wizardry. And the individuals who belong to these organisations and direct them receive vicarious pleasure in their aggression and their success and identify themselves with their power and also fill their bellies with the wealth acquired. The mega-companies are their teeth, their mouths and their bellies, and as they act for these companies, the companies also act for them.

These gigantic organisms of commerce spend vast resources and ingenuity in the manipulation of the market, which entails the art of persuading the public that the good offered for sale are not only desirable but necessary. This is euphemistically called 'serving the market forces'.

In his book *The Philosophy of Money* (published in 1912) Georg Simmel describes the cynical character of money in its power to transform goods which are not commodities into commodities. 'It is the purchaseability of everything and everybody which involves capitalist society in ever deeper cynical corruption. The more money becomes the sole centre of interest, the more will honour and truth, talent and virtue, beauty and the healthy mind become a marketable commodity, and a cynical, mocking and frivolous attitude will develop towards them. Their value will be considered akin to wares on the street market. The cynical function of money is manifest in its power to transform the higher values into dirty business.'

Everything is marketable and the value of everything is determined by its marketability, to the point that anything that does not produce profit on the market is not worth anything. This leads to the power of money to seduce people of talent, honour and creativity, who wish to gain recognition and recompense for their labour, into selling themselves to the market. When universal seduction prevails, when those who allowed themselves to be seduced consider the word 'corruption' to be merely an expression of moralistic posturing motivated by envy, it becomes a cultural climate. Then people are resigned to its inevitability, as if it were a universal law; indeed, we see that the so-called higher values of truth, beauty and intellectual honesty are considered practically useless, merely self-indulgence. 'And the market is determined by the lowest common denominators of taste and desire which can be most readily manipulated by the advertising industry.'

These practitioners of the id justify themselves by a concept of human psychology which can be summed up in the phrase 'human nature being what it is . . .'

> It was Ivan Boesky, the celebrated Wall Street dealer, who coined the phrase 'Greed is good'. Each day seems to bring news of 'fat cat' salaries, mind-boggling pay-offs, or other examples of what pass for sleaze or corporate disfigurement. We may still argue that the excesses are confined to a minority, whose antics receive disproportionate publicity. But we cannot deny that this minority is growing, and behaving in such a way that it threatens to overwhelm the corporate culture of the whole country. Too many of Britain's executives have lost their moral touchstone. The paradox of the last fifteen years is that the more Britain's executives are paid, the more they seem to want. The bigger the salary, the more they clock up other perks as well – the performance-related bonus, the share options, the pension scheme. Share options are granted in such quantities that even a small upward tick in share prices, the kind of rise which is almost bound to come in a stock market bull cycle, can guarantee huge profits regardless of how the individual company is performing.
>
> Finally, and all too frequently, if the executive pension seems inadequate to keep top men in the style to which they have become accustomed, their salary is topped up even more dramatically a couple of years before retirement, at a true cost to the pension scheme which can run into millions, to make sure they have a comfortable old age.
>
> This brings us back to the ego. Executives look at the size of the businesses they run, at the hours they work and the responsibilities they carry and the profits they make and they think they are worth it.

British business is currently embroiled in an orgy of euphemism. It is called re-engineering, focusing, downsizing, restructuring, or a host of other words disguised to avoid the unpleasant reality of what is happening. What this restructuring always means is that companies are being closed down and people sacked, at a time when there are already millions out of work. There are many who find it morally repugnant that the executives responsible for these cuts should be awarding themselves massive bonuses on the back of the profits which result. (Anthony Hilton, City Editor, *Evening Standard* 3rd April 1996)

****

This year, the cumulative value of bids and deals inside Britain will top £100 billion, double that if cross-border deals are included. With fees averaging 5% on most deals, that's a cool £10billion directly to share between a few thousand directors and partners, and indirectly with the other 200,000 who work in the City. The fees paid by Royal Bank of Scotland and Bank of Scotland, for example in their current takeover bids for NatWest, along with the fees paid to the bank's defending advisers, will exceed £500million, to be shared between three investment banks with a total staff of less than 2,000. These are riches beyond the dreams of avarice.

Some bonuses for top investment bankers, lawyers and other advisers will top £3m; up to another 1,000 will qualify for a cool £1m, while most of the rest of the City will pick up bonuses of at least a few thousand. On some estimates, the value of bonuses to be declared this Christmas 1999 could exceed £1billion, which is probably an underestimate considering the current profitability of most City firms . . .

Every six months or so, there is a flurry of interest in top people's pay as some fresh news breaks, reminding the country of the stunning imbalance between the incomes of the rich and poor. The defenders of the status quo rehearse the same arguments – that there is no bucking the market, whose iron logic must be obeyed, and that British executives will leave the country, as will the business in the City of London, if any restraint or taxation is proposed, We don't condemn footballers for making millions, so why do we condemn investment bankers? The City is a private sector wealth creator; jobs and wealth cascade all over London as a consequence of its efforts. Let's get real and stop carping at hard-working 30-year-olds taking home millions. (Will Hutton: *It's tax-free. That's the real bonus – Blair and Brown are determined to defend the City's privileges in a multi-billion pound bonanza – The Observer*, 12th December 1999)

It seems unbelievable that men in positions of eminence and responsibility and who are known to be in the public eye show no embarrassment and are untroubled by their conscience when receiving huge salaries and bonuses, while at the same time ordering the closure of branches and the dismissal of thousands of employees. However, the practitioners of the id justify themselves with a concept of human psychology which can be summed up by the phrase 'Life is nasty, brutish and short, and one has to make the best of it; one has to overcome this impediment imposed by nature which has been confirmed by Darwin's law of the survival of the fittest in the struggle for self-preservation', and it is the fittest who succeed by making as much money as possible to enjoy the advantages of wealth as well as the exercise of power. These are the good things of life and show the superiority of those who are able to acquire them.

Crime and Violence

But this is only one side of the contemporary situation. The aggressive processes occur even more strikingly in those sections of the population which do not share the excitement and satisfaction of money-making as members of the big corporations or as lawyers, accountants, public relations experts or members of the advertising industry, where greed is legally sanctioned. Those who cannot identify with the commercial dinosaurs express their defiance of the superego, the conventions and the traditional norms of behaviour by a rebellion which finds expression in personal aggressiveness and violence. They are the people who have no vision or hope for the future, when the future confronts them as useless and without any meaning. They defy the future and see no point in repressing the primitive urges of the id, for they see no real promise of rewards beyond the here and now, and therefore there is no reason why they should repress their anger and defiance.

While the working classes of old had a hope of transforming society, either by democratic means or by revolutionary struggle, they felt themselves as the insiders in the political and ideological movements devoted to the making of the future. Their anger and aggression were aligned with a rational and moral aim that could be articulated and heard, and they knew that the intellectuals, the philosophers and scientists, were on their side. But now that the intellectual and moral justification of the political struggle for social justice, for the ideology of socialism is everywhere in doubt and ridiculed, the framework of sublimation, which not only justified their collective aggression against the oppressors but made it into a virtue, has disappeared and their aggression has lost its moral justification.

They no longer see themselves as the vanguard in the fight for justice, and their attack upon the social system is seen as antisocial and repugnant, devoid of any dignity or honour. They no longer have a vision of the future, either for themselves or for humanity. They are not seen as the vanguard of history but as its failures and its rejects, and their attack upon the social system is reduced to a personal confrontation with what they consider a hostile environment, and deprived of the sublimatory processes which an ideology provides. Indeed, they owe nothing to the traditions and norms of the past, and feel themselves free from any obligation to contribute anything to society or to the making of a better world. All these things are perceived by them as deceits and the impertinence of false promises, a mockery to their commonsense; and they respond with mockery to any lectures about duty and responsibility. Many of them come from working-class backgrounds, whose fathers and grandfathers, and their mothers as well, have been victims of society, subject to unemployment or had to spend their lives in labour for which there was little reward, barely knowing how to feed their families. It is the injustice done to their ancestors which frequently is in the minds of these rebellious and defiant outsiders, and particularly in the mind of ethnic minorities, such as the Afro-Asians and West Indians who are not allowed to forget that their ancestors have been slaves.

THE END OF CIVILISATION?

So now they are not going submit to the same fate and are going to revenge themselves upon the society they live in.

This sense of alienation from the norms and traditions of the past and from any ideological purpose affects not only the working class, now labelled as underclass, the poor and socially deprived, the losers and defeated, but is shared by a growing section of the population who are disenchanted with the ideals and expectations of our own culture. A defiance of what used to be considered civilised manners has become the norm, particularly among the young, in the way they dress, behave and the persona they adopt. In the arts we see an explosion of angry, violent and sadistic imagery which is designed to offend and outrage the innate perceptions of reality and insult good taste; disruptive, disharmonious, infantile sounds of rage masquerade as music, and jagged, aggressive, spastic movements in dance. We find a worship of defiance of civilised virtues not only in the arts but also in literature and biographies of famous people, where only muckraking of the most ruthless kind, and exposés of perverse sexuality, of dishonesty and of criminal traits arouse the interest of the general reader and serve the profit motive of the publishers. To be fashionable means to be free from the restraints of a defunct culture and to expose the dirt that lurks underneath. There is a kind of psychological warfare against the role models of society, who are the successful and the respected who are seen to perpetrate all kinds of humbug and swindle, and 'liberated' people declare their hostility against them and the culture which promotes them.

As there is no vision of a better future and the political and ideological protest movements of the radical left have been discredited and the ideologies of the hippie sixties have led nowhere, they level their sights to the here and now of instant gratification, and instant gratification is the personal discharge of anger and violence, the theft of the goodies which the law withholds from them. While the respectable members of the commercial and legal establishments seem to be justified in pursuing their short-term gratifications, teenagers have their gangs which defy the law and proclaim themselves to be its enemies. Their greed will find expression in the acquisition of luxuries, such as expensive trainers or smart clothing which enables them to show off their spending capacity and their ruthlessness by any means whatsoever, which includes robbery, burglary, personal violence such as mugging or attacking and injuring and killing people, to rob them of whatever they may possess. This often leads them to inflict extreme violence and severe injuries on complete strangers, and frequently leads to killing. In the week I wrote this, an eighty-eight year-old woman was attacked in her home, savagely beaten, kicked on her head, robbed of her £50 pension and left dying.

What is particularly shocking and beyond the comprehension of normal people is the complete lack of any sign of conscience or remorse among the perpetrators of these acts, as they dehumanise their victims and see them merely as objects without any empathy or feeling for their suffering, and as enemies upon whom violence can be perpetrated as if by right. It is not merely greed or a sense of revenge but a worship of sadism, the excitement of causing injury or even death to anyone who stands in the way of their greed. Nothing personal, you understand, you don't know the victim from Adam, but the expression of an infantile tantrum, a spasm of rage discharged, as they would say, 'for the buzz' which it provides.

We encounter an epidemic of robbery, violence, murder and rape, not merely in the inner-city deprived areas, but even among the very young, down to ten years old. We are shocked by daily reports in newspapers of the violence and cruelty in our society, and most people have at one time or another been mugged or suffered the experience of having their homes and their cars broken into.

The increase in violence can be gauged by some statistics. Between 1993 and 1994 violent offences were up by 17,300 to 311,500 and violence against the person by 7% to 219,270. Serious violent offences causing permanent and serious injuries to the victims increased by 8% to 19,498. Since then there has been a further dramatic increase of violence, particularly among the very young.

From the *Evening Standard*, Thursday, 24th October 1996:

THE END OF CIVILISATION?

If the crime wave were to be measured in bicycles, it would make frightening reading.

In 1934, when public concern was growing about the increase in crime in London, 791 bicycles were stolen in a year – 2.1 a day. Last year, when police were congratulating themselves because the 40-year-long rise in general crime had begun to level off, thieves helped themselves to 19,219 bikes in London: 52 a day and a rise of 2,376 per cent.

The depressing message of this admittedly somewhat quirky measure of the increase in crime in London over the past six decades is echoed by the overall statistics: the number of recorded offences rose from 86,863 in 1934 to 822,596 in 1996.

The types of crime that are most prevalent have, however, changed in their nature. The figures for 1934 show the main offences committed were drunkenness, disorderly behaviour and prostitution.

Today, it is violent crime, house burglaries, car theft and break-ins, street mugging – much of it fuelled by the need for drugs – as well as white-collar fraud, which cause the most concern to the public and police alike. Since 1950 the average rate of increase in crimes of violence has been an extra 3,000 a year. But in the eight years since 1987, there have been, on average, 12,000 more violent crimes each year.

The rise of recorded offences of violence against the person in London jumped by 26% in the six months to September 1999, compared to the same period in 1998. Sexual crimes increased 20.1%, and robberies were up by 34.7% in the same period. Many older people today speak of the good old days of their youth, and there is some evidence for this: after a rise in crime towards the end of the Second World War, there was a lull in the early fifties when the number of offences dropped to pre-1938 levels. It was only in the late fifties that crime began its continuing surge.

Offences in London: all crimes

1934:	1945:	1956:	1995:	1999:
86,863	128,954	108,582	817,082	over 1m.

One of the disturbing aspects of the increase of violence which has become part of the daily life of people in our society is the intimidation of witnesses to such crimes to the point of indifference. Young women are raped outside an underground station in full view of the passers-by, and nobody takes any notice or tries to save the victims.

I shall in the following pages quote some newspaper reports, as their journalists were able to make direct contact with the victims and their dependants and provide us with a first-hand insight of their experiences and those who witnessed the crime with apparent indifference and refusal to protect the victims.

Every day we read of incidences of deeply shocking cruelty and murder which have no obvious motivation other than the robbery of quite paltry sums from pensioners and old people who are killed in the act. The complete lack of any moral qualms amongst these criminals, indeed their sense of puzzled outrage for being accused and condemned was shown by the twelve-year old boys who abducted and killed a boy of four years, but simply did not register that they had done anything wrong, or by a man who killed a young shop manager and told the police after his arrest that any have-a-go hero deserved what he got.

On June 5th 1996 the *Evening Standard* reported on schoolboys mugging a woman of 72:

> The family of a frail 72-year-old pensioner fighting for her life after being mugged by two 12-year-old schoolboys said today they were praying for her to pull through.
>
> Ellen Fresquez, known as Nellie, was violently attacked from behind, spun around and pushed over a metal barrier by the pupils who stole her handbag which contained a packet of cigarettes, a lighter and a pen but no cash. Mrs Fresquez' invalid husband, Frank, 78, who has already suffered one stroke, yesterday suffered a second minor stroke after hearing that his wife of 50-years had been injured. The victim's family has been keeping vigil at her bedside at St Thomas' Hospital. Mrs Carina Scott, 50, one of Mrs Fresquez's ten children said today: 'We've been staying with her all night and all day yesterday. She is very, very ill in a critical condition on a life-support machine. We are just praying at the moment and we are having hourly updates on her condition.'
>
> Mrs Scott's brother John Fresquez, 48, added: 'This has devastated this family. We need all the help we can get on this one. My father

is on a knife-edge, we haven't told him what has happened to Nellie and we will tell him gradually. I can't believe that a 12-year-old would want to do this to a lovely old lady like my mum. There must be something wrong somewhere in society. She spent all her life looking after us and this is not fair, it really isn't.'

Since then incidents of unbelievable brutality and violence have been reported practically every day and more than once.

As I have indicated earlier the defiance of the superego and the attack upon the cultural authority, with its release of pent-up aggression, has many other aspects, manifest in the behaviour of schoolchildren, in popular entertainment, films, music, dancing and in art.

The eruption of violence, particularly amongst the young, is all too evident in schools. Many teachers are finding their tasks reduced to maintaining a modicum of discipline in their class and gaining their pupils' attention in their task of teaching. But beyond that they confront a pandemic of violence. A twelve-year-old boy is charged with raping an eleven-year-old girl; a boy of thirteen shoots his teacher in the back with a gun; a gang of girls are involved in the killing of another girl; gangs of ten-year olds carry out organised muggings of elderly women. Young children are committing many more violent crimes than ever before. The statistics of attacks upon teachers by young children, often causing grievous injury and even permanent disabilities, have increased in recent years. A teachers' union held conferences on how to protect their members from violent children without being able to find a solution. They made it clear that teachers cannot be blamed for the violence, bullying and truancy and the disobedience in the classroom. By the time teachers get their new classes a minority of young pupils who are already out of control will begin to set the tone for the whole form. And all too often this minority of disruptive children fall into a pattern. As Christopher Hudson writes in the *Evening Standard* of 14th May 1996:

> If not physically brutalised at home, they will have been emotionally brutalised – unacknowledged, left to their own devices, typically, with a TV and video-recorder in their rooms where they can watch the violent films handed on to them by an elder brother. Herein lie the

seeds not just of classroom disruption and bullying but of the whole cycle of violence which leads to street gangs, knife fights, murder and government enquiries. It seems to be an unassailable truth that the constant visual battering of shooting, rape and murder on TV contributes to a culture of tolerance of violence in real life. Not merely that one-off violent programme, but the constant flow of violence on TV, right across the channels. A society such as ours which allows films of unremitting violence to be beamed down twenty-four hours a day to the television screens of adults, who have nothing better to do with their lives, and children who haven't formed the power of judgement, is bound to engender moral confusion and despair.

The truth is that in millions of homes across Britain, television has become the primary educator of the young. It can hardly be a coincidence that during the 1950s–1960s when violence among ten- and twelve-year olds was virtually unknown, television was far less violent than today – and what violence there was on screen (mostly cowboys and Indians) tended to be given an inescapable moral dimension. Can it really be so difficult to check this constant flow of screen violence and return, at least for most of the day, to the more upbeat television of the past, which dramatised moral issues rather than shoot-outs? If we want a future in which our schools don't need wire-netting and security guards, we should be looking back at the lessons of the past.

There is no doubt that television and films play a very considerable role in the brutalisation of children, and are themselves manifestations of a culture which attacks its own values. The teacher's authority and his leadership in the classroom has been denied and children are supposed to acquire skills and knowledge either by themselves or in association with their peers. This has deprived a large proportion of children of basic numerical and literary abilities and exposed the shortcomings of the 'new teaching methods' and their underlying libertarian and anarchistic theories.

4. Regressive Disintegration of the Arts

If we look at contemporary paintings we behold a thundering emptiness, an overwhelming confusion of aggressive forces and dark forebodings, images of explosive powers and spooky apprehension of doom.

Already in the early part of the last century, the expressionists warned of the threat to the human personality. They saw the danger of the growing regimentation, the cold mechanisation of life imposed by the authority of the state and industrial mass production. Expressionism was the outrage of the artist against the cold logic of machine technology and the mathematical calculations of the profit motive, which takes no account of the native skills and intuitive responses of the human being. In their work these artists aligned themselves with the socially deprived, with the masses who become the victims, outcasts of industrial society. Their forms were exaggerated, sharp and sudden, decidedly aggressive, not by any means realistic or natural. Many among the expressionists showed humanity squashed, distorted, horror-struck and confused by the modern world. They aimed for unrestrained self-expression and impulsiveness, and spontaneity was their most widely used word and taken as their slogan. Empathy was considered to be of a higher order than knowledge or accuracy, for only through empathy and exaggeration could the deeper feelings be expressed, could the vibrancy and excitement of nature and of man find adequate presentation.

Ludwig Kirchner, Erich Heckel, Munch, Gauguin, Otto Mueller, August Macke, Egon Schiele and Kokoschka were just a few of the artists who followed this school. But their humanistic endeavours to reaffirm the human self-image in an increasingly alien and threatening environment were swamped by the very forces which prevailed in that environment. The world which no longer sees the human being as its central and dominant figure, either in nature or in the affairs of society, found reflection in an art which obliterates the human being. The schools which had dominated during the early part of the twentieth century more or less merged and succumbed to a common imagery of chaotic disintegration of reality.

Wassily Kandinsky, the founder of abstract painting, expressed his views about the role of art in the modern world not only in his paintings but also in his writings: 'New images have to be found, a new kind of language of artistic communication, which reflects a radical break with tradition.' Many abstract painters presented a reality in which object form was seen in its atomic particles, vectors and trajectories, lines of tension and strain. Form in the sense of solid substance has melted away and resolved itself into its elemental forces.

We might ask whether the artists of the beginning of the twentieth century anticipated the conceptual revolution of modern science or whether they reacted to it. There can be no doubt that the disintegration of the superego images of Western civilisation provided an important emotional and intellectual impetus for the development of the new sciences, and that the most sensitive artists both anticipated and responded to it.

While the abstract painters, cubists, futurists, constructivists and other schools of modernism reflected the impact of the physical sciences, there was another science, namely psychoanalysis, which revolutionised our view of the world and of man.

The discovery of the fourth dimension of the mind, the unconscious, paralleled the discoveries of the fourth dimension of the physical world, of relativity theory and quantum mechanics. The world of the unconscious, which has its existence in the hidden and unknown regions of the mind below the level of consciousness but which emerges in our dreams, became the chief subject of surrealist painting.

André Breton worked in the Psychiatric Institute of St. Dizier near Paris and made drawings of the fantasies and dreams of schizphrenics and analysed them. He also analysed and drew dreams of children, whose mental processes he recognised to be closer to the deep layers of the mind than those of normal adults. He wanted to discover an inner world which is usually hidden and repressed from consciousness but determines a man's life without him having any knowledge of it. In his *Manifesto of Surrealism* (1924), he wrote: 'Surrealism is based upon the belief in a higher actuality, in forms of association which have up till now been largely neglected, in the importance of dreams as the aimless game of thought. It is the aim of surrealism to dissolve or destroy all those psychological mechanisms which have hitherto hidden from us our unconscious processes in order to arrive at the solution of the fundamental problems of human existence.'

In other parts of his *Manifesto*, Breton declares that the domination of rationalism, civilisation and progress has thwarted man's imaginative capabilities, and that it is therefore the task of surrealism to mobilise the powers of the unconscious in order to re-establish an equilibrium of all human faculties.

Chirico, Miro, Max Ernst, Yves Tanguy, Dali and Man Ray presented a dream world where the categories of time and space, of form and substance, are in abeyance: a juxtaposition of object relationships, of memories of things past appearing in things present, of undefinable tranquillity and undefinable terror in a general breakdown of organised perceptions. Images of childhood or schizophrenia characterise their paintings; however, by penetrating through the veils of repression, they challenged the dominance of the ego, they allowed the world of the id to appear on the stage of their paintings. To some extent, we may say that they were willing servants of the id clamouring to find expression in the real world and in consciousness; they opened gates which had been kept locked and well-guarded by the ego's defences. In Salvador Dali's brilliant presentation of unconscious and dreamlike images, we encounter many aspects of sado-masochism, anal-eroticism and paranoia in a clarity and sharpness unparalleled since.

Surrealism and abstract art in general created a new dynamism and excitement, an eruption of colours and sensations, a degree of self-expression, on a depth and scale never before attempted. These movements occurred not only in painting but also in music and architecture, in literature and drama; they had an impact on human relationships and behaviour. Everywhere old boundaries were broken, traditions were rejected, and modernism meant informality in manners, in conversation and in thought: the hidden was to be revealed!

Alban Berg, Stravinsky, Picasso, Strindberg, Wedekind, the second generation of pioneers, continued and consolidated the spirit of modernism, a celebration of the libido set free. 'The morning sun of a new freedom', a discovery of new worlds of the mind and an exposition of its oppression flurried the artistic consciousness of Europe before and after the First World War.

But just as Einstein, having discovered the stupendous energies locked up in matter, could not have foreseen the consequences of his discovery and came to regret it when he saw that these cosmic energies were used for nuclear bombs, so the originators of modernism could not foresee the consequences of their art.

A curious thing happened. The vision of a free and expansive humanity, liberated from the strait-jacket of convention, gave way to a vision of a world in which the human being had disappeared; the individual dissolved into a world of random particles and chance eruptions of energy in a cauldron of dissociated sensations and impulses. In other words, the discovery of primeval forces in nature and the energy of the id had led not to an expansion and enrichment of the human self-image but to a loss of identity. The integrative functions of the ego succumbed to the onslaught of id forces and gave way to dissociation; purpose-direction gave way to confusion.

While the early modernists, followed by abstract expressionists and tachists gave visual expression to ego disintegration, retreat from reality and chaotic aggressiveness, the process of regression goes further.

As the ego finds it increasingly difficult to integrate the manifold drives from the unconscious, the repressed breaks through its old boundaries and begins to dominate consciousness. We can in this way speak of the normalcy of madness. We must expect an eruption of anal defiance and of sadistic, masochistic and destructive drives. They do not merely declare war on the norms and values of our culture, they glory in images of self-destruction. And the artists give public expression to these fantasies: bodies are torn apart, revealing visions of blood, skeletons, pieces of skin and intestines, excreta paraded defiantly, human beings presented in grotesque forms of catatonia, pain and terror – all our defences are deliberately shocked and our senses outraged.

Oral-sadistic images, skulls with threatening teeth, claws ripping at bodies, bodies torn open, drenched in blood, figure prominently; skeletal, emaciated bodies, lobsters with fangs intermingled with human figures, huge bloody vaginas with teeth, self-portraits with horrifying aggressive skulls symbolising the dominion of sadism superimposed upon the conscious ego, can be found in a multitude of themes in very many paintings. Jannis Kounellis' shows exhibited very large canvases, ten of them covering the walls of an exhibition hall, with entirely identical paintings of numberless skulls executed in primitive style; and Francis Bacon became an expert exponent of human horror and despair shown in a sadistic manner. There is little compassion to be found in these paintings – rather an exploitation of human tragedy and suffering for the sadistic pleasure they provide to the artist and, presumably, to the onlooker.

In contemporary exhibitions of young artists such as Tracey Emin, Damien Hirst and others, we are shown images of decay and disintegration which are meant to show the disintegration and death of our culture. They appear to be meaningless, just as there is no real meaning left in the world, and the onlooker can interpret them in any way he wants to.

Chapter 2

The Philosophical Vandals

1. Wittgenstein and the Analysis of Words

What the artists began with their attack upon the perceived reality the philosophers continued by their intellectual attack upon the perceived moral order. They set out to prove that all metaphysics and the concepts of morality based upon them contradict the evidence of our senses and therefore are non-sense. They considered themselves the spokesmen of the disillusionment with the morality that has failed, and by their attack upon it as a chimera that has no basis in rational thought have played a significant role in the promotion of the moral vacuum that has spread across Europe.

The various and confusing arguments of the logical positivists, linguistic analysts, postmodernists and deconstructionists, all expressed with an air of dogmatic finality, have gradually percolated down to the common understanding, and provided the ammunition for the murder of the superego, the metaphysical and moral framework of Western civilisation. They did not, and still do not, seem to understand that it is in the very nature of human beings to create a framework for their perception of reality and their orientation in it, and that it is the task of the philosopher to subject the metaphysics which dominate their culture to a rational critique, not merely to deny its significance but to pave the way to a rational understanding of the world and of a rationally based morality. In the first part of this book we have observed some of the consequences of the erosion of moral convictions and the defiance of its guidelines. We have observed the development of the moral vacuum in the civilisation of Europe leading to the breakthrough of primitive, aggressive and ruthlessly self-assertive drives when – in psychoanalytic terms – the ego, having lost its trust in the superego, rebels against its command, turns towards impulses of the id, and succumbs to its promptings. We have found that this has led to an uninhibited and ruthless pursuit of wealth in the name of the profit motive that transforms nature into a soulless commodity, to be exploited and conquered without any regard for the damage done to our natural environment upon which we depend, an erosion of empathy with animals upon whom we commit acts of appalling cruelty and cause the death of thousands of species; at the same time business and finance corporations as well as the growing body of bureaucrats reduce humans to inanimate figures in their statistics, without much regard for their identity and dignity as persons. While this is bad enough we find another manifestation of the loss of a collective moral consensus in the brutalisation of civic conduct of the last few decades, and what is perhaps most disturbing, an absence of a sense of guilt or conscience, particularly among young offenders who commit the most appalling acts of cruelty and resent being condemned for their crimes. This attitude of 'innocence' among the wrongdoers exasperates and baffles most people. There is a widespread concern about the 'moral crisis' and a growing understanding that moral values are important, for we can all too plainly see what happens in their absence.

We can no longer simply blame capitalism, poverty and social deprivation for the discontent, anger and violence that pervades so many areas of society, nor can we blame the disruptive influence of Marxist movements with their cry for revolution. We face the paradox that in our time, when the revolutionary movements with their disruptive and confrontationalist propaganda have lost their influence and democracy has made great advances in our political institutions and poverty as it was known in earlier times has been significantly reduced, antisocial behaviour has reached unprecedented dimensions. While economic inequality and particularly status deprivation continue to blight our social life, we cannot hold them entirely responsible for the pandemic of violent behaviour which has no discernible purpose, and the rebellion without a cause is not confined to the oppressed classes. Drug addiction, for instance, and the crimes related to it are widespread not only amongst the poor but also among the affluent sections of society.

Many people are beginning to think that we need some moral principles to guide our judgement and instil a sense of responsibility in our dealings with our fellow men, but then we are reminded that the commands of religious authority have lost their credibility, of the duties imposed by feudal rulers and more recently by dictatorships, all proclaiming that it is our duty to submit to their commands. And they all upheld a metaphysical concept about the meaning of life, in order to convince us that it is not their self-interest or their pursuit of power but the very nature of the universe and men's destiny which justifies their rule.

There are of course certain duties we have to obey in our work and in our various activities, but they can be termed instrumental duties, insofar as they are the means to promote our livelihood or our urge to succeed in whatever activities we are engaged in. The entrepreneur has duties to meet the demands of the market and to organise his business in accordance with the rules of commerce. He has to be aware of what he can get away with in his quest for profit without overtly breaking the laws. This does not necessarily prevent him from cheating and circumventing the laws of taxation and fair competition, but he has a duty to do so in a clever and calculating manner. Even the criminal has a duty to conduct his activities in a manner which will minimalize the chances of being caught by the police. Such duties demand cleverness, in order to avoid bankruptcy and the stigma of corruption or police prosecution. In other words, one has to learn the rules which govern whatever activity one is engaged in to assure its success.

But these cannot be considered moral duties which aim at the 'general good', the protection of life and goodwill to our fellow men, and, we may say, give expression to the instincts of altruism. What had started at the turn of the last century as a hopeful attempt to apply the ideals of the Enlightenment turned after the First World War into a frenzied attack upon its philosophical pretensions. The horrors of the war, and the subsequent poverty and large-scale unemployment produced not only a deep revulsion against a society which seemed indifferent to the sufferings of its citizens but also a widespread sense of disillusion with the hypocrisies of a morality which brazenly nullified its own credo.

The pundits of the 'new philosophy' declared that only the evidence of our senses, combined with the rules of logic, can have any truth value, and moral concepts, which have their foundation in metaphysics and claim to have universal validity, were declared to be nonsense; or as they put it, morality is no more than smoke and exhaust of the emotions, no more than delusion and deception.

The Vienna circle of logical positivism based their philosophy – or rather, philosophical anti-philosophy – upon Ernst Mach, Frege and Bertrand Russell, with Wittgenstein, Schlick, Carnap, Neurath, Feigl, Waismann and Popper as the most prominent members of this movement of brilliant and revolutionary thinkers. Wittgenstein led the war upon the propositions of the Enlightenment, as he considered it based upon metaphysical assumptions, by which everything can be explained: 'The whole modern conception of the world is founded on the illusion that the so-called laws of nature are the explanation of natural phenomena.' And in the same way as he considers all metaphysics as an illusion, so he considers ethics as a metaphysical concept above the world of objects and facts: 'The world is independent of my Will, and thus it has an existence, whose observation has to be independent of human psychology and human motivations.' He does not realise that all observation of the phenomena of the world depend upon the direction of our interest, what we look at and what we see, what we are looking for. (Even Popper came to accept this.) He maintains that, as ethics is transcendental and above observable facts, it cannot be put into words: 'The meaning of the world must lie outside the world. In the world everything is as it is, and everything happens as it happens. There is no value and no meaning in the world and in the facts of the world. Any value which does have value must lie outside what happens in the world, for everything that happens and what is the case is merely accidental, and therefore it is impossible to have any proposition of ethics.' It follows, therefore, that ethics cannot be put into words and thus cannot be spoken of. 'It is therefore equally impossible to speak of the Will (as it is purely subjective), and the foundation of the ethical. Therefore the Will as a phenomenon is of interest only to psychology.'

It is worthwhile to point out here that Kant considers that any investigation of ethics must take psychology into account. But Wittgenstein said that 'the Will – good or bad – cannot alter the facts nor that which can be expressed in words. The way the world is is a matter of complete indifference for what is beyond it, the higher – for that is beyond our world of morality. God does not reveal himself in the world.' I should mention here that in Jewish philosophy God is beyond our perceptions, he is a noumenon beyond our understanding but he reveals himself in the world and he gives words to the prophets to communicate his purpose and to speak to his people. The world of facts is a manifestation of his will and his purpose. Wittgenstein counters this by maintaining that 'we feel that even when all possible scientific questions have been answered, the problems of life remain completely untouched. Obviously then, there are no questions left. There is indeed the unspeakable, that which transcends the world of facts, it is the mystical, the higher, and of that we cannot speak.' He goes so far as to say that 'anyone who understands my propositions, therefore, must recognise that in the end they are non-sensical. He must transcend these propositions, but of the higher world – the metaphysical – one cannot speak. And of that of which we cannot speak, we must remain silent.'

After his tortured, often quite banal statements, he arrives at the conclusion that we can only know the world of facts, whereas of the real, higher world, which transcends the senses, we cannot have real understanding, because we have no words for them. He believes that what we cannot know one cannot speak of. From this it follows that knowledge is in the words and confined to the words, therefore the analysis of language replaces the analysis of the mind. The mind only exists insofar as it is manifest in words.

I remember many many years ago hearing Einstein speaking on the radio about his philosophy, when he said that he did not understand what the linguistic philosophers are all about, 'for have we not all experienced that sometimes we have an idea in our mind but cannot find the words to express it?' It does take a genius to put a very complex philosophical problem into straightforward and simple words. Wittgenstein, on the other hand, is determined to deny the mind of man its ability to strive for an understanding of the nature of the world beyond the manifest world of our senses. We are, as he says, confined to science, which he believes only deals with phenomena available to our senses, and any attempt to go beyond them is quite useless. He ends with the assertion that things beyond the senses and in particular metaphysics are non-sense and cannot be known and spoken of. For it is the business of language to assert or deny facts, as Bertrand Russell has said. Wittgenstein and his followers obviously did not understand that scientific theories are usually born out of some metaphysical concept about the nature of the world, and aim to justify it. They did not understand the synthesizing functions which underlie our understanding, what Kant has called the synthetic *a priori*.

It is the fundamental function and goal of the mind to co-ordinate the manifold of sensations or impressions into a unified, general theory in order to understand the world and why it is the way it is, to relate the temporal to the eternal. It is of course true that this frequently produces fantasy images about the world or the human condition, which can be irrational and devoid of empirical evidence or logic, as we find it in many religions and ideologies. It is also true that the language we use to express those beliefs can be entirely irrational. But the irrationality is not in the words but in the ideas which are expressed in words. It is, therefore, the proper task of philosophy to analyse the mind which gives rise and meaning to words.

An investigation into the nature and the origin of words and of language is certainly of great interest. Social anthropology as well as brain neurology has in the last fifty years made great advances in our understanding of how this particular human ability has evolved, but Wittgenstein knew nothing about them. For him, the mind remains in the words, which can be examined as objects, whereas what goes on in the mind and the processes which give rise to the formation of words he considers too elusive for logical or scientific explorations. We can say that in this respect, he and his followers are the precursors of a behaviouristic psychology which also proclaims that only the external manifestations of the psyche, namely a person's behaviour, is the proper subject of scientific investigation, and what lies behind it, the nonobjective, has to be ignored by a scientific psychology. It is a kind of vandalism, an attack upon the mind as a mysterious entity which we cannot know and therefore cannot speak of. This fatalism behind the posturings of logical necessity, frequently interspersed with mathematical formulae drawn from Frege and Russell, shows itself in Wittgenstein's conclusion of his introduction to the *Tractatus Logico-Philosophicus*: 'It seems to me that the truth of the thoughts which are expressed here is unassailable and definite. I therefore believe that on all essential points I have found the solution of the problems. And, if I am not mistaken, then, secondly, the value of this work consists in that it shows how little is achieved when the problems are solved.'

It seems that Mr Wittgenstein, after his unbelievably meticulous and often tortured analysis of words, managed to prove that they are unable to bring us any nearer to 'the higher things', but only show their illusionary pretensions of doing so. This, of course, particularly pertains to any possibility of arriving at any moral concept that we can be sure about, so any philosophising about it is useless. Therefore, the mind as such is impotent before its real task, and reason itself has to admit this.

Wittgenstein can be considered to be a prime example of the psychological motivations of a person's philosophical approaches. We can recognise some overwhelming conflicts which largely determine his way of looking at things, and what one has to prove or to hide. In view of our much more enlightened attitudes, I do not think that I am indulging in a vulgar exposition of Wittgenstein's secret, which he had to hide, when I mention that he was homosexual and deeply ashamed and disturbed by this 'terrible affliction'. He was compelled to hide it in his overt behaviour, and did not want anyone or himself to speak about it. What he wanted to be known about himself was his overt manifest behaviour, which, while eccentric, did not reveal this secret of his libido – his inner (or 'higher') essential self. His language only related to facts, with what can be perceived by the senses, with manifest appearances, which he proclaimed to be the only source of real knowledge of what is the case (as he proclaimed: 'The world is the sum of what is the case'). Anything beyond that is a metaphysical construction, based on belief and guesswork and, therefore, nonsense. But of course there is something beyond the manifest appearance of things, what he calls 'the higher, the true driving force of life and of the universe', and what must not be known was love, his love for young boys. We can say that he set up a barrier between his inner world and the world outside.

Wittgenstein brings us face to face with the psychological and particularly the unconscious foundations of philosophical ideas. I think it would be wrong to judge a philosopher's ideas, or an artist's productions, by his psychological problems, or to 'psychologise' a person's artistic or philosophical productions, for I believe that they should be judged on their own merits. But if a philosophy is dominated by confusing and self-contradictory statements, which in the name of logic or science contradict the rules of logic and of empirical evidence, then it would be interesting to find how a brilliant mind came to arrive at such statements. There is much evidence that Wittgenstein's philosophising reflects a psychological turmoil, an obsessive self-questioning which he found difficult to resolve. In his lectures and in his later work *Philosophical Investigations* he ruminates obsessively about the conflict between how one can feel or know something instinctually and what one can present consciously to one's self and to the world. In one lecture he talked about the notion of an explanation: 'In supposing that the colour red (and also the phenomenon of thinking something to oneself) is something specific and indescribable, one supposes that one could learn what red is as simply seeing a red image. But what if I hit you on the head, and therefore you are able to see the word "red" correctly? Would this be an explanation of what "red" is? Of course not. An explanation is not anything that produces understanding. A key is not anything which opens a door.' And he continues: 'An explanation cannot be something private. It must be public. An explanation must provide a technique for getting somewhere. It must show the way. It must provide a method for using the word. So if someone says "I can show myself what thinking is, although I can't show anyone else", we reply that he may do something which makes it possible for him to use the word correctly, but this may not be at all what we call explaining or showing.' By his tortured obscurantism he intended to hide the truth about 'what is the case'.

He came to be acutely retentive of his secret self, the treasure that was inside him, which he was not going to squander upon an indifferent or even rejective world which could not understand or appreciate it. Professor Norman Malcolm, who knew him intimately, reports many instances when he could be very sensitive to any apparent indifference towards him, when he clammed up and adopted a hostile attitude, only loosening up, as it were, if Malcolm assured him that he understood what Wittgenstein was saying. His mistrust about showing his feelings or his ideas to others even extended to his questionings about whether one can know or understand one's own feelings or even bodily sensations. In one of his lectures Wittgenstein discussed our knowledge of our bodily posture and the position of our limbs: 'In order to move my arm voluntarily, I must know what position it is in and whether I have moved it. Now, how do I know what the position of my hand is when I am not looking at it, or feeling it with the other hand? How do I know that my fingers are bent? For do you always have a certain feeling when your fingers are bent in that way? Have you always noticed that feeling, and what feeling is it?'

The notes from another meeting read as follows: 'There is a philosophical question as to what one *really sees*. Does one really see depth, or physical objects, or sideness, or a face, etc? There is a temptation to say that all of this is *interpretation*, *hypothesis*, etc., and that what one really, really sees is a flat surface of coloured patches. But if I am required to describe what I see, I do it with physical-object expressions: I see the top of a tile-covered table and on it is an ink bottle towards the right end, etc. I would not be able to describe it by referring only to coloured patches. It might be thought that, although I cannot describe it in words, at least I could paint it. But the fact is that I can hardly paint at all unless I know what physical *objects* I am painting.' His obsessive self-questioning, even about sensations and feelings of his own body, and how one can actually know them and communicate them in words or in paintings, show the profound split in his ego, between holding on to the reality of his feelings and how to put them into words and to communicate them: 'Only that which can be expressed in words has objective – i.e. public reality', and that which cannot be expressed in public remains behind a barrier imposed by his narcissistic defences, in order to safeguard himself against the danger of being judged, misunderstood and condemned.

One of the abiding impressions left in his students during his sessions was the deep silence. They would find Wittgenstein sitting in prolonged silences in his canvas chair, greeting no one, his face apparently engrossed in serious reflection and a kind of self-torture. No one dared to break the silence with some idle remark. Norman Malcolm relates how he had the impression of a Quaker prayer meeting. Any form of spontaneous self-expression had to be carefully scrutinised or censored. His tortured ruminations, many reported by his students to be incomprehensible and disturbing, nevertheless evoked a profound resonance, a kind of empathy with his students, and produced a large following. It would, I think, be true to say that he appealed to many sensitive young men who had been deprived of the guidance and responsiveness of their fathers, or in a sublimated manner, of the fathers of religion and the ideals of the Enlightenment. They had lost their sense of direction which gives meaning to the future and could not find a cultural community which would take notice of what they felt. How to communicate, how to find the correct language, the right words to express what one thinks, became an obsession among philosophers. Like all obsessions, it led nowhere, and nowhere became the ultimate wisdom, the answer to despair. And that is the end of philosophy – philosophy denies itself. The psychological and intellectual turmoil of that time which led many to question the meaning of what is being said was perfectly represented in the person of Wittgenstein, and he became a role model for a generation that had lost its directions.

2. The Vienna Circle

In the years following the First World War, which had shown the bankruptcy and the hypocrisy of the old certainties, the Vienna circle of logical positivism determined to subject all metaphysical statements and the language they used to an uncompromising critique in order to clear the ground for the creation of a rational society. They were determined to subject any statement or proposition to two central questions: 'What do you mean, and, how can you know this?' By persistently asking these questions, they thought that one could clarify the relevance and truth value of all philosophical or political propositions. Such questions inevitably point to the verification principle, according to which a statement can be considered to be meaningful if there is empirical evidence for it.

The Vienna circle of logical positivists were to a large extent inspired by Wittgenstein and Russell (if not always in agreement with them on all counts), and were deeply aware of the dangers of metaphysical irrationalism, as it held sway not only in the dogmas of the Church but also in the totalitarian philosophy of Hegel and its influence upon the thinking of Karl Marx. They considered all metaphysics as theoretical constructs which by their lack of reference to a logical or empirical evidence allow and even encourage all kinds of fantasies to parade as eternal truths. However, Schlick repeatedly warned that critical philosophy, whose aim it is to clarify and analyse statements in their cognitive as well as moral dimensions and subject them to a ruthless analysis, may not directly be concerned with the day to day social and political issues, but with the principles of knowledge. As Schlick put it: 'Philosophy belongs to the centuries and not to the day. She is not directly concerned with actualities.' Carnap, who was a socialist, wrote that 'all of us in our circle were strongly interested in the social and political progress, but affirmed at the same time that the purely logical-philosophical investigations have to be neutral towards political aims, whether they concern moral purposes of individuals or political aims for society.'

While they were committed to a democratic socialism, they determined to clarify once and for all the epistemological question of the nature of knowledge, and how we come to believe in the truth of our ideas; particularly how a metaphysical concept like the laws of history could make it possible for a dictator like Stalin to assume the role of the representative and defender of the movement of history towards the classless society, with the working class under the guidance of the communist party as its agents. Through the class struggle and the revolutionary consciousness of workers and intellectuals, the Communist Utopia, as the culmination of history, would be fulfilled, even if it needed the dictatorship of the working class and a dictator to promote men's final emancipation from serfdom and exploitation, even if it turned out that he had to oppress and enslave the workers in the cause of their liberation, to abolish men's freedom in order to fight for their freedom. Unprecedented cruelties and mass-murder would not divert the believers in the historic mission of this Communist movement, as long as they were convinced of the truth of a metaphysical fantasy, of which Stalin was seen as the embodiment and defender, with the help of the NKVD, of course.

The Viennese philosophers were profoundly concerned about the horrible degradation of the ideals of socialism and the rise of Nazism with its metaphysical fantasies of the racial superiority of the German people and its assumed destiny to establish the 'thousand year Reich', even if it entailed the annihilation of all 'inferior' races. The members of the Vienna circle considered themselves as the philosophical wing in the fight for a rational and humane society, unencumbered by the phantasmagorias of the laws of history ('historicism' as Popper called it), which clearly were projections of manic-sadistic drives whipped up among the population who came to believe in them in defiance of all reason and commonsense. We can see here the distortion of a perception of reality by the force of myths. It is understandable that the philosophers were determined that their epistemological enquiries should be set on secure foundations and they declared them to be the scientific method, the purely objective view, which was to be entirely founded upon data provided by the senses.

I should like to quote here a key sentence written by Ernst Mach (1838–1916), physicist, psychologist and historian of science, from his fundamental [*elementarisch*]-rational programme: 'The view that science has to restrict itself to the presentation of matters of fact leads inevitably to the exclusion of all concepts which cannot be controlled by experience, above all the metaphysical.

If one keeps to this point of view which embraces the physical as well as psychological domain, then it follows that "sensations" are the foundation of all possible physical as well as psychic experiences, and theoretical concepts merely the connections between them. Metaphysical concepts are merely a series of disturbing pseudo problems and are shown to be irrelevant.' All members and supporters of the radical positivist movement, including Wittgenstein, Schlick, Neurath, Carnap, Waismann and Popper accepted this statement as fundamental to their philosophy. However, it seems to me that they did not understand that if you deny any possible rational justification for metaphysical concepts, if you declare them to be without any rational significance and dismiss them categorically as being nonsense, then we deny reason the opportunity to subject them to a rational investigation. Indeed, we encourage the construction of all kinds of irrational metaphysical concepts and deny that philosophy has any business to make rational judgements about them. We leave the door wide open to a regressive process and the breakthrough of unconscious fantasies of paranoic and manic drives which then come to dominate metaphysics. This flies in the face of the fundamental task of philosophy; indeed you castrate the whole philosophical endeavour and reduce the quest for understanding to the collating of sense impressions, where they parade as ultimate knowledge and understanding. We deny reason its role in the shaping and elaboration of moral ideas, and morality will inevitably feel free to acquire irrational and philistine modes of thought, and primitive fantasies will come to dominate it.

It is a tragic illustration of this truth that Schlick, the paragon of strict empirical and logical philosophising, was killed by the Nazis, who had no need for a rational examination of their irrational and brutal morality, and the rest of the Vienna circle had to emigrate and disperse before the ultimate obscenity of hate and violence overtook Europe.

If we examine their epistemological efforts, we find that they did not show much understanding of the role of sensations in the formation of knowledge, a process which was clearly pointed out already by Locke, and then by Kant and Schopenhauer. Sensations are the trigger for the evocation of *a priori* concepts, or, as Locke called them, innate ideas, which transform sensations into perceptions. As Kant has put it very succinctly: 'There can be no doubt that all our knowledge begins with experience. For how should our capacity of knowledge be awakened into exercise otherwise than by means of objects which affect our senses and transform them into perceptions (mental presentations). In respect of time, therefore, no knowledge of ours is antecedent to experience, but begins with it. However, while all our knowledge begins with experience, it does not by any means follow that it all arises out of experience. For, on the contrary, it is quite possible that our empirical knowledge is a co-ordinate of sensory impressions with our innate cognitive faculty.'

Perceptions (mental presentations of objects) arise from sensations which are interpreted by our innate mental faculties (the *a priori*), and perceptions in turn are co-ordinated and combined with other perceptions which have a common characteristic and enable us to make generalisations, theories, and beyond that grand theories, from which we arrive at the meaning of facts. Thus we arrive at an understanding of facts by means of a synthesising process which is innate to the human mind and which Kant called the synthetic *a priori*. The human mind attempts not only to understand the facts of our experiences but to interpret them by concepts about the nature of the universe and the meaning of life. This attempt to gain an image of the universal is called metaphysics which is by its nature synthetic, i.e. the co-ordination of all given experience into a unified whole.

It must be recognised that this type of reasoning is a natural need for humans, such as the question, 'What is the origin of the universe, how was it created, and what is the purpose of life?' These, I believe, are questions which are innate characteristics of human beings and, as I shall show in the next chapter, inevitable in the development of the human brain. While Kant recognised the human need to arrive at metaphysics, the miserable progress it has hitherto made as far as 'truth content' is concerned can make one doubt whether metaphysical concepts have any rational significance, or whether they are merely an aberration of the human mind hardly worth taking any notice of. Yet metaphysics must be considered by any philosopher, if not as a science, nevertheless as a natural disposition of the human mind. For human reason increasingly progresses towards such questions as cannot be answered by the empirical application of reason, and furthermore there has always existed in every man some system of metaphysics which he believes in, and it will always exist as soon as reason is aware of its powers of speculation. But if we decide in view of the irrationality of metaphysical concepts simply to ignore them in our philosophical investigations, we make it impossible to subject them to a critical and rational investigation, and allow them to exercise their commands over our minds unchallenged, and open the doors to a proliferation of irrational and childish fantasies.

It is of course perfectly true that metaphysical concepts arise out of a psychological as well as a cognitive need (Kant speaks of 'natural metaphysics'), and we can easily recognise that men project all kinds of emotional images onto metaphysical concepts, as we find them in myths, religions and ideologies, and that, moreover, our perceptions and judgements of what is the case are influenced by them. Equally, concepts of morality are more responsive to our emotional needs than the criteria of reason.

We must, therefore, recognise a difference between men attempting to arrive at metaphysical concepts either by the greatest possible exercise of their rational faculties or by subordinating their understanding to dominant or fashionable metaphysical construction, without exercising their faculties of reason. As we know, the Enlightenment set itself the task of promoting mankind's progress from its childish dependency and subordination to dogmatic myths imposed by some superhuman authority, to a state of maturity where each person exercises his rational faculties and relies upon them for his evaluation of what is the case, and he subjects any metaphysical constructs imposed by an authority to a fearless critique.

While the philosophers of the Vienna circle were determined to reduce all cognition to sensory perception, they left themselves in a strait-jacket by rejecting all metaphysics, all general concepts and in particular all morality, considering them to be non-sense, not worthy of any rational investigation.

What 'scientific' philosophers seem to forget is that their concepts of science as the only possible source of all knowledge is itself based upon an universalised set of values which we would be justified in calling metaphysic. They took it for granted, to the extent that they were not even conscious of it, and considered it as the inevitable and necessary form of all valid cognition. But, as I have said before, our perceptions are determined not only by *a priori* (before experience) categories such as causality, mass, extension and others, but also by dominant myths, religious or ideological views of the world which give meaning to our various experiences and the way we perceive them. For instance, if some misfortune befalls us in a religious culture, we will seek to understand it as the will of God or as some divine punishment and make efforts to propitiate the God who has punished us. In this respect we will be justified in speaking of a cultural *a priori*.

3. Background: The Philosophy of the Enlightenment

The religious view of the world had spiritualised nature and our perceptions of it as the creation of God once and for all and therefore eternal. The cosmos, the stars, the sun and the moon with our planet at the centre, as well as all the life of the earth, were seen as the permanent and eternal expression of God's will and purpose. God was pleased with his creation, and at the end of his labours on the sixth day considered it perfect; and he embraced humanity, the crown of his labours, as well as all his creations with his love, and in his embrace men would experience his protection and his forgiveness for their transgressions, for the sins of the body and the temptation of disbelief. Men had to admit their innate disposition to sin and submit in gratitude to the eternal father in obedience and humility, to gain his blessing and their salvation by prayer and worship. The Church eternal – the consecration of the divine spirit on earth – and those who belonged to it are the community of the faithful and receive God's blessing, and partake in his love and in his power, privileged above others who do not know him or question him.

When men began to take God out of the universe and of nature, and refused to acknowledge him as the creator of all things, and no longer wanted to submit to the unchanging, eternal order of nature and of the human condition, they were obliged to investigate what made the world the way it is and the origin of social institutions and their values. Curiosity replaced faith and worship, and men began to feel free to exercise their rational faculties in an organised scientific manner. The mysteries and insecurities which confront men in their exposure to the world around them, as well as the complexities and confusions of their own mind could be investigated. The new sciences were governed by the belief that the study of phenomena can lead to an understanding of universal laws and theories concerning those general laws; that theories, in turn, can be tested by observation in order to show whether they are congruent with the observed data. Already in the sixteenth century Giacomo Zabarella (1533-1589) explained how theories are formed by investigating phenomena: 'When we form some theory about the matter, we are able to search out and discover something else in it; where we form no theory at all, we shall never discover anything.'

Whereas the Christian Middle Ages had split the world into a number of separate compartments and was concerned with the process of separation and the fixation of separates into isolated units, the new approach also used the method of classification and separation, but as a first step in the process of unification. The natural order was seen by medieval philosophers as God's museum of things and creatures, eternally divided into their kinds and alienated from the process of evolution, insofar as they were finished products. Theologians had avoided investigation, which aimed to arrive at general or universal principles, as this would have asserted the primacy of human reason over the dogmas of the Church. Pope Innocent III in 1219, and Gregory IX in 1228 declared that: 'Theology must exert its power over each separate faculty – as the mind over the flesh – and it must be explained solely according to the traditions tested by the saints and not through the use of the "carnal arms" [that is, observation by the senses]'. Statements of authority, or reasons deduced from authority, are advanced for each topic, and all things that exist remain static and isolated from each other forever.

The Renaissance transformed the static universe of the Middle Ages into a developing universe, and the tyrannical God into a reasoning and creative being whose intentions and activities became intelligible to man. Man's emerging powers of self-determination were reflected and encouraged by the image of a rational deity who created man and intended him to become rational also.

The new intellectuals who were encouraged by the Renaissance assumed that there is harmony and unity behind the manifold of appearances, and they devoted themselves to the search for the unifying principle through the observation of phenomena. Thus classification of phenomena and their separation was no longer an end in itself but a first step in the process of unification, i.e. induction, in order to arrive at the general principle that lies behind things. 'The truth of philosophy,' writes Roger Bacon, 'is to derive axioms from particulars, rising by a gradual and unbroken ascent so that it arrives at the most general axiom last of all.'

Copernicus, like many of his contemporaries, was guided by a vision of a world that was both monotheistic and Platonic, a world order expressing a universal purpose characterised by harmony and founded on orderly, rational, mathematical relationships. Medieval astronomers had been content with any astronomical models that would 'save the phenomena', that is, 'grind out' models roughly in accordance with observation. Copernicus maintained that all such models were inadequate, and that the true geometry of the heavens would be known by the 'unalterable symmetry of its parts' and by the contrast between the evident necessity of its relationships and the arbitrary character of false systems.

Copernicus had two outstanding merits which are not necessarily, and even rarely, found together: immense patience of observation and great boldness in framing hypotheses. These two qualities were much encouraged by the renewed influence of monotheistic theology and Platonic philosophy. Few among the ancients possessed both merits together, and no one in the Middle Ages possessed either: Copernicus possessed both.

Descartes based his epistemology on the theory of *veracitas dei*: what we clearly and distinctly see and know must be true, for otherwise God would be deceiving us. We can find the roots of this theory in Plato's theory of anamnesis which grants to each man in some measure the possession of the sources of knowledge. For Descartes it is, to be sure, the sensible world about which philosophising goes on, but the method of correct procedure must not rest on sense experience. In truth, we perceive no object as it is by sense alone, but only by our reason exercised upon sensible objects: 'We must seek the "certain principles" of material things not by the prejudices of the senses but by the light of reason, and which thus possess so great evidence that we cannot doubt of their truth.'

The mind that thinks is for Descartes the very source of human experience and the core of his existence. 'The truth, "I think, therefore I am", is so solid and so certain that all the most extravagant suppositions of the mystics are incapable of upsetting it. I judged that I could receive it without scruple as the first principle of the philosophy that I sought' (R. Descartes: *Discourse on Method*; also his *Meditations*).

This passage is the kernel of Descartes' philosophy of knowledge and contains what is most important in his philosophy. Most philosophers since Descartes have attached importance to the theory of knowledge, and their doing so is largely due to him. 'I think, therefore I am' makes mind more certain than matter, and gives the ego's intellect a supremacy that goes beyond anything earlier thinkers have dared to do.

Spinoza, perhaps the most lovable and most notable of all great philosophers, upheld that the wise man, so far as human finiteness allows, endeavours to see the world as God sees it, under the aspect of eternity.

We shall see that, by drawing God from His heavenly existence and bringing Him into the world, Spinoza paved the way to a deification of nature; it was not long before nature herself became the object of worship as well as of enquiry, as the philosophy of nature and as science, and God disappeared into the world.

Newton was perhaps the last of the great scientists who had not forgotten God in his worship of nature; indeed, his scientific activity was a worship of God who made everything and created the laws which Newton endeavoured to observe and reveal. Like Descartes, he intended to discover the logic and mathematical laws which guide the mechanics of nature by means of reason and scientific experiment as substantial proof for the existence of God.

Newton was confident that empirical facts implied unqualifiedly the existence of a God of a certain definite nature and function. God was not detached from the world that science seeks to know: indeed every true step in natural philosophy brings us nearer to a knowledge of the First Cause, and is for this reason to be highly valued. It will enlarge the boundaries of moral philosophy also, inasmuch as, 'so far as we can know by natural philosophy what is the First Cause, what power he has over us and what benefits we receive from him, so far our duty towards him as well as towards one another will appear to us by the light of nature' (Isaac Newton: *Optics*). So, although religion and science are fundamentally different ways of approaching the universe, each valid in its own way, yet for Newton, in the last analysis, the realm of science was dependent on God and led the reverent mind to a fuller assurance of His reality and a readier obedience to His commands. 'The main business of natural philosophy,' Newton maintains, 'is to argue from phenomena without feigning hypotheses, and to deduce causes from effects, till we come to the very First Cause, which certainly is not mechanical. . . . Does it not appear from phenomena that there is a being incorporeal, living, intelligent, omnipresent, who in infinite space, as it were, in his sensory, sees the things themselves intimately and thoroughly perceives them, and comprehends them wholly by their immediate presences to Himself?' (*ibid*).

We witness here a transformation of men's relationship to God: the superego authority which had previously been perceived as forbidding and aloof, unfathomable and awesome, changes into a friendly god, who loves man and is pleased with the universe He has created. He wants men to understand Him, and is close to them as a guide and teacher. Secure in the thought that they are acknowledged and protected by the omnipotent father, His sons feel free to develop their intellectual and moral faculties. The reconciliation between God's omnipotence and the confident expression of man's ego faculties eventually led to the expansion of the ego into the universe, and men began to take over from God.

With Spinoza and Newton, God was expanded throughout all space and time, and there was still something spiritual in the world; the superego was still present, all-powerful and recognisable. However, Newton's conception of the world was gradually shorn of its divine foundation. The categories of rational thought invaded the universe until it was conceived in terms of mathematics and geometry and experimentally proven causal relationships. Space, time, motion and causality needed no further explanation by the existence of God, and seemed capable of exact and final formulation by the laws of mechanics, geometry and mathematics. The process of eliminating the providential elements in the world-order reached its climax in the work of Laplace, who believed himself to have demonstrated the inherent stability of the universe by showing that all its irregularities are periodical and subject to an eternal law which prevents them from ever exceeding a stated amount.

While God was thus being deprived of His duties by the further advancement of mechanical science, and men were beginning to wonder whether the self-perpetuating machine thus left stood in need of any supernatural beginning, Hume questioned whether the concept of a First Cause was as necessary an idea as it appeared, and Kant was preparing the penetrating analysis which removed God from the realm of knowledge altogether, and some time during the eighteenth century, God disappeared from men's view; he got lost in a mechanistic universe. What then happened to the superego? What happened to its image that had for millennia been projected from its habitation in the mind upon the heavens in the same way as a projector throws the pictures inside it onto the cinema screen and men watch the shadowy reflections, pretending them to be reality. Two things happened: one was that, with the advance of science, the material universe assumed the dynamics, the reverence and the awe previously vested in God; the second was that men began to recognise that the seat of reason and the images of power are located inside the brain. God, the ancient projection, was returned to where He came from – to men's mind.

The humanists of the Enlightenment were, above all, concerned with freeing the human ego and its rationality from dependence upon the divine superego, and they declared man to be the measure of all things, the source of knowledge, the *causa prima*, the creative agent.

The idea of the Enlightenment was beautifully described by Kant: 'Enlightenment is the emancipation of man from a state of self-imposed tutelage... of incapacity to use his own intelligence without external guidance. Such a stage of tutelage I call self-imposed if it is due not so much to lack of intelligence but to lack of courage or determination to use man's own intelligence without the help of a leader. Dare to use your own intelligence! This is the battle-cry of the Enlightenment.' The struggle for spiritual freedom represents the quest for man's maturation, his emancipation from childish dependency upon an omnipotent and omniscient father-figure. In order, however, to achieve maturity and the capacity to make rational and correct judgements, he must be equipped with the necessary tools and the skills to use them. On the intellectual level, this means that man is equipped with reason and that he can acquire the skills of rational thought to obtain knowledge. 'Cogito ergo sum,' said Descartes, but equally, 'Cogito ergo est,' meaning, I think, therefore I create the truth about the universe, as Bishop Berkeley declared.

Kant connected the concept of the centrality of the human mind in the processes of cognition with the activity of the senses, and showed that they must necessarily interact in rational thinking. Although confirmed by observation, scientific theories are the result not of these observations merely, but of our own ways of thinking, of our attempts to order our sense data and understand them. It is not these sense data but our own intellect which is responsible for our theories. Nature as we know it, with its order and with its laws, is largely a product of the assimilating and ordering activities of our mind: 'Our intellect does not draw its laws from nature, but imposes its laws upon nature.'

Men's independence from a divine authority placed a new

obligation on them, which the great minds of the time grasped with alacrity. In the same way as in the great period of Greek culture men had to discover how the mind works, both in order to acquire knowledge and also to formulate the principles of right conduct in order to create an ideal society, so the men of the Enlightenment had to discover the principles by which they themselves, without reliance on God, could create a society that reflected the principles of reason and morality.

In their enthusiasm for the new-found freedom, men lost their eternal ruler; they became fatherless in the universe and had to brace themselves to acquire for themselves the powers and wisdom previously ascribed to God. Pascal, Bayle, Voltaire, Rousseau, Hobbes, Locke, Hume and Kant, among others, saw new gates of knowledge and freedom opening up before mankind, and they announced their visions to a fascinated public. New scientific academies were set up all over Europe. The maturation of the European ego and its struggle for independence was beset by many conflicts and complexities which characterise cultural and personal development. Old primacies, fixations and traditions, and vested interests in the preservation of an ancient establishment, the defenders of orthodoxy and dogma, continued to protect their positions against the innovators.

However, nothing could for long stifle the development of the new spirit that spread over the intellectual landscape. The controversies, the exchanges of information, the borrowings and recoveries, only served to uphold the new sciences as an example to intellectual life as a whole. They all contributed from different angles to lay down the co-ordinates of a new society and a new world that was going to be built. Many dreamt of a changed mankind and even of a changed world of nature created by experiment and calculation. They won the attention of their contemporaries because they fulfilled deeply held desires for a better knowledge of nature which would enable men to dominate it more fully, and for a better understanding of themselves.

Man no longer faced God primarily, but nature herself, and he approached it with that sense of awe and wonder previously reserved for God. His prayers were transformed into study and experiment and the answers to these prayers were to be attained by his control over nature. At the same time man faced himself and his reason had to direct itself to an investigation of the capabilities, conditions and limitations of his mind. Epistemology (the theory of knowledge) became the focus of philosophical enquiry, with Locke, Hume and Kant as its most profound exponents.

At the same time, man took a new interest in the world of political and economic reality, and above all in that supreme organisation of society, the state. Institutions of state, no longer accepted as an expression of God's will and thus permanent for all time, became the object of rational investigation. The intellectuals responded to the challenge of the new-found freedom to decide what kind of world men wanted to live in.

The discovery that nature has her own laws by which she has created all the things, all the facts, 'everything that is the case' in the process of evolution over millions of years, transformed the static universe into a creative universe, and inspired men with a sense of their own creativity. It gave men the freedom to define and pursue their own purposes and their goals, and opened their eyes to the vision of a new future. Evolution thus became associated with progress towards a more healthy, more just and more beautiful form of existence. The idea that nature follows its own laws, and is thus endowed with its own creativity opened the doors to a new vision of human creativity by which it can transcend its ancient limitations and burdens. As Francis Bacon remarked: 'The improvement of men's lot and the improvement of men's minds are one and the same thing.'

The optimism which characterised the Enlightenment movement nevertheless gave way to periods of pessimism, when philosophers, poets and dramatists proclaimed the virtues of resignation and submission to what seemed to be inevitable, while others dramatised the constant conflict between the awe of authority and the aspirations of freedom, between pessimism and optimism, between man's inherent creativity and his enslavement to 'the facts of life'. The rationalism of the Enlightenment, which Napoleon intended to spread across Europe by his wars of conquest, was not only defeated militarily but evoked a resurgence of nationalistic passions, not only among the public but also by philosophers such as Fichte, Hegel and Heidegger. (I have mentioned earlier that Hegel considered the Prussian State to be the fulfilment and realisation of the dialectic process. Marx does not seem to have been aware of this nationalistic aspect of Hegel's philosophising, whereas Schopenhauer recognised it and subjected it to a withering attack.)

The First World War and its aftermath of confusion and despair betrayed the hopes for an enlightened world order and gave way to a resurgence of nationalistic passions, particularly among the defeated nations intent upon revenge. Stalin under the guise of communism promised the victory of Russia over the capitalist West, and the Germans welcomed Hitler to lead them to victory over the capitalist Jewish communists who had defeated and insulted their national pride. Optimism betrayed produces a reaction of outrage that clamours for discharge by aggression and a dictatorship which will rally the people in the struggle for victory and the rehabilitation of the nation's pride.

The Viennese socialists, however, resolved to rekindle the spirit of optimism by creating a new socialist order in the spirit of the Enlightenment, and their philosophers were determined to defeat the old metaphysical fantasies which had poisoned the mind of Europe.

4. The Dilemma of the Vienna Circle: Theory and Practice Divided

Vienna, once the sparkling cultural capital of central Europe with the brilliance of its intellectual and artistic innovations, lost its nerve with the advent of World War I and the collapse of the monarchy. The stage was set for the socialist party to inaugurate a far-reaching experiment not only to abolish the old class structure by radical economic and social changes but by a transformation of values. They went beyond the piecemeal social reforms of other capitals by promoting a sense of community and aesthetic ideals, thorough-going innovations in public health and social services and the radical reform of education. But they went even further, as Otto Bauer, one of the intellectual leaders of the socialist movement, declared: 'It is our aim to bring about a revolution in the soul of man.' One of the first articles of the socialist constitution related to 'the woman question', and the determination to affirm the equality and the standing of women in society, assuring equal opportunity, both in education as well as in the professions. Another paragraph of the constitution emphasised that no young person should be thrown onto the labour market without acquiring a diploma or a degree. Those children who had a talent for craftsmanship would be trained to receive a diploma of being skilled craftsmen and, after some years of experience, of masters in their trade, or, if their talent was of the academic kind, they would be given the opportunities to acquire a university degree as doctor, barrister or architect. A high proportion of women became doctors and lawyers. They were also the first to set up a national health service and social security system.

An enormous array of publications appeared in order to stimulate people's intellectual interests, and excellent 'workers libraries' were set up in all districts. The socialist movement of Vienna took Lenin's dictum to heart that the workers could only succeed in overthrowing the old regime and become the effective legislators of the new society if they equalled and even surpassed the educational and intellectual level of the bourgeoisie.

Of course they had considerable opposition from the old middle and upper middle class, aided and encouraged by the clerics, who feared that their status in society as well as their wealth would be diminished, and would have needed more years than they were granted to fully accomplish their aims. But despite the short spell of time available to them, less than fifteen years before they were cut down by the counter-revolution of the semi-Fascist Dollfuss regime and shortly afterwards by the Nazi invasion, they achieved much.

At the time when the belief in progress and the necessity for change and transformation of values and social systems pervaded the atmosphere, it is quite pathetic to hear Wittgenstein declare (and I am quoting again from the *Tractatus*): 'In the world everything is as it is, and everything happens as it happens. There is no value and no meaning in the world, and in the facts of the world, for everything that happens and what is the case is merely accidental and therefore it is impossible to have any proposition of ethics – it is therefore clear that ethics cannot be put into words, and thus cannot be spoken of. It is therefore equally impossible to speak of the will, as it is the foundation of the ethical, as the will is a phenomenon of interest only to psychology.'

As Professor Norman Malcolm remarked: 'It was Wittgenstein's character to be deeply pessimistic, both about his own prospects and those of humanity in general.' Anyone who was on an intimate footing with Wittgenstein must have been aware of the feeling in him that our lives are ugly and our minds in the dark – a feeling that was often close to despair. And we might add that his pessimism was profoundly influenced by the feeling that there is nothing one can do to transcend and transform reality – the state of affairs of the world.

The logical positivists were determined to create a philosophic system by which all statements and propositions can be judged for their truth value, by asking whether they are based upon solid empirical foundations, and that meant upon the evidence provided by the senses. They identified facts with sensory experience independent of values, interests or normal concepts. Any theory or proposition which did not fulfil these conditions had to be dismissed, not analysed or investigated for its meaning, but dismissed.

Bertrand Russell maintained that a science-based philosophy cannot prove that it is bad to enjoy the infliction of cruelty. This is in keeping with Wittgenstein's declaration that 'someone is being robbed of his wallet' is a moral statement which is outside the realm of scientific thinking, which can only describe sensory perception and observe that someone reaches into another person's pocket and is removing his wallet. Whether this is right or wrong is a moral inference which has nothing to do with scientific observation. Whatever can be known, Russell says, can be known by means of science; but things which are legitimate matters of feelings, of the will, of value and morality lie outside its province. While it was recognised that as persons they might have some view about the evils of society and stand on the side of progress, as philosophers they felt constrained to ignore such things. Most members of the Vienna circle were in sympathy with the left and considered themselves supporters of social democracy, and felt considerable unease about the split between theoretical and practical thinking, and the barriers which their philosophy upheld between them. At the height of the confrontation between social democracy and Nazism as well as communism, Carnap wrote an essay entitled *Theoretical Questions and Practical Action*, where he intended to make it clear that there is a strict division between theoretical questions and practical activity: 'What the Vienna circle wanted to achieve on the political level lies outside the theoretical area of science. While one can prove that philosophic and religious metaphysic frequently represents a danger, a narcotic of the people, which we reject, we cannot prove this by empirical philosophy. We can hope to influence the public by appeals and propaganda, and in particular through education, but we have to be clear that these influences lie outside the theoretical field of science.'

But by that time these explanations and justifications of the logical positivist project had become irrelevant, and we might even say that they contributed in some measure to the paralysis of the left. The fanatics of the Nazi as well as the communist movements were not in the least burdened by the painstaking analysis of the empirical foundation of their ideologies, but felt free to express their beliefs in action. The Fascists smashed the socialist government, and this was soon to be followed by the Nazi invasion which buried any trace of rational philosophy and denied the humanity of those whom they thought stood in the way of the thousand year Reich. Reason and intellect and any debate about the merits or demerits of their belief was seen as a threat to the 'German spirit'.

In 1936 Schlick was killed by a Nazi and his murder justified by the Catholic church of Austria. Before then Feigl could see that in the increasingly anti-semitic climate there was no opportunity for the pursuit of his profession, and he left Vienna and emigrated to the United States. In 1934, when the Schuschnigg regime took over, Neurath escaped to Holland, Carnap emigrated to the United States in 1935, Popper fled Vienna in 1937 and found a position in New Zealand, and Waismann was offered a professorship in Oxford. The last remaining member of the Vienna circle, Gödel, emigrated; he managed to escape in 1940, and via Manchuria found his way by ship to San Francisco.

The disintegration of the Vienna circle was accompanied by an increasing internationalisation of their ideas. While the logical empiricists had to leave their original spiritual home or were killed, their publications gained international recognition and influence. Particularly in the United States they encountered considerable interest, and were a decisive influence upon American philosophy. The foundation of a widely-acclaimed journal, *Philosophy of Science*, edited by Carnap and Feigl, is evidence for the spread of logical empiricism in America. New institutes of research and increasingly positions at universities were opened with the theory of scientific philosophy established at universities.

While they had to flee their original home they were enthusiastically welcomed in England and the United States.

5. From Logical Positivism to Linguistic Analysis in England and America

In their home town, the Viennese philosophers had confronted a tidal wave of irrational fantasies and they tried to rescue the visions of a rational culture by a merciless analysis of language. Theology and the politics of the ruling class had employed linguistic phraseology, which they claimed to present the eternal truth about the nature of life but which contradicted the rules of logic and empirical evidence; and at the same time they paraded as the defenders of a moral world-view which used immoral aims and had their apotheoses in the worst manifestations of immorality the world has ever known. The logical positivists hoped to defend democracy by their critique of the uses and misuses of language by means of philosophical rules. They were good-naturedly accused of establishing a language police. This pun ceased to be amusing in the later development of linguistic analysis, particularly as expounded by Austin in his lectures and writings at Oxford University after the war.

When they arrived in England and America the Viennese philosophers found a very different situation in those countries. They were welcomed as important contributors to an already established and widely accepted philosophical atmosphere. Those countries had their revolution against metaphysical systems, and unlike the Austrians and the Germans had long ago defeated the politics and ideology of feudalism. The bourgeois revolution in America with its proclamation of the rights of man based upon the ideas of the Enlightenment, with its concepts of the freedom of individuals, had provided the foundation for a liberal democracy. In England the aristocracy managed to survive as the symbol of national identity, as it had the wisdom to embrace the entrepreneurs who amassed large fortunes. In this way they secured the continuity of the class system, with the aristocracy on top and capitalists fully acknowledged as important and valuable members of the nation, together with the military and the Church, which was no longer a threat to the new bourgeoisie and therefore could be tolerated. Indeed, the three estates, Church, the military and the capitalist were seen to uphold the virtues of democracy and civilisation across the world.

In America the break with the metaphysics of Church and feudal hierarchy was more radical. After all, people of the North American continent had escaped the religious persecution and poverty which were endemic in Europe, and they saw new opportunities in the land of freedom opening up before them. It was natural for them that a scientific view of the world, unencumbered by fear of authority and religious dogma would help them to achieve a measure of prosperity. They had a vision opening up before them where every citizen was to be free to express his talents and gain recognition for his efforts to raise his standard of living and achieve honour and prestige among his fellow men.

However, their view of science was different from that of European philosophers. The labourers and farmers of the new continent embraced the philosophy of the bourgeoisie, and many of them managed to become bourgeois, members of the middle class, whose values came to dominate the thinking and the political character of the common people. They saw fresh opportunity for making a decent living, and gave powerful support to the new freedom of thought, of self-expression and the pursuit of wealth; and many, if not all, entered the class of the bourgeoisie and passionately upheld its values. They became the uncompromising enemies of all forms of totalitarianism and resisted the lure of transcendental beliefs with their claim to direct men's destiny. They were going to control their own destiny, and if some invoked the help of God they did not want Him to do it for them. They wanted to improve the effectiveness of their labours, to improve productivity and increase the reward in terms of profit and the acquisition of wealth. And the one thing that would guarantee success was technical innovation with the employment of science. This new bourgeoisie resolved to apply science and scientific technology for the improvement of the means of production, for the pursuit of wealth and the power and confidence that came with it.

The two great Yankee philosophers, William James (1842–1910), and John Dewey (1859–1952) gave the most systematic expression of American optimism. William James is generally acknowledged as the founder of pragmatism – truth consists in useful ideas, and the truth of an idea is proven by the practical fulfilment of its propositions; or in other words, that its propositions are congruent with the result they produce. Pragmatism held out the promise of resolving the old opposition between philosophical idealism, where ideas stay in the head, and the realists, who assume that ideas are a reflection of facts encountered by the senses. James saw the correspondence between reality and the way we judge it based upon our intentions. In other words, our search for truth and understanding serves to promote our interests and our survival instinct. We might notice that many of William James' concerns with practice foreshadowed Nietzsche's understanding of the political dimension of language use: 'By naming and categorising we do not do something in a practically neutral manner, but to follow social attitudes and structures.'

John Dewey developed a systematic pragmatism which he considered as a philosophy which is deeply involved in social issues. His philosophy was concerned with the question how life should be lived, and intended to bridge a gap between morality and scientific knowledge. His writings on logic were a general account of how thought operates, not in an abstract or purely formal mode but in the pursuit of science, and how the problems of ordinary lives should be solved. He thus gave further impetus to the concept of intentionality, and the primacy of the will as upheld by Schopenhauer and Nietzsche. But he insisted that the study of facts had to orientate the direction of men's purposes.

In England practically all linguistic analysts were professors or lecturers at universities, particularly at Oxford and Cambridge, with their rather aloof devotion to ancient tradition, however radical they thought themselves to be. They did not want to change the world, for after all, democracy had been fought for and won long ago, and successfully defended, often with support from the American allies. They fought for freedom and democracy, and emerged victorious in the two world wars of this century, and saw no need to jeopardise their victories by any major transformation of society. In 1945 the Labour prime minister Attlee declared a few days after the victory celebrations that the Labour party was not going to abolish the aristocracy, nor in any significant way interfere with its privileges. Continuity was the watchword even while considerable reforms were to take place within the established order. While they admired the achievements of the Austrian socialists and in many ways were inspired by them, they rejected the need for a radical transformation of society.

The Oxbridge philosophers were determined to examine the use of language by which we interpret reality and the world in which we live, but not to change it. In keeping with their statist views they maintained that intentions have nothing to do with the truth and have to be kept out of philosophical discourse. They were only concerned with the correct interpretation of the way things are, 'of what is the case'. While the Austrian philosophers imagined that by clearing the decks from the pressures of irrational metaphysical assumptions they would prepare the ground for a rational society, the English philosophers did not intend their work to be a preparation for change but an end in itself. In order to prevent students from losing interest and being overcome by boredom, lecturers tried to start an argument about 'What would you have done in certain problem situations which you encounter and why?' But as Professor Mandel has pointed out, this method ignores the fact that such dilemmas are moral dilemmas because they involve a conflict of rules as to how people in general ought to behave. (C.W.K. Mandel: *A Critique of Linguistic Philosophy*, 2nd edition, 1979.)

In their painstaking, meticulous and, we may say, compulsive investigations into how people use words, they resurrected Wittgenstein and he had considerable influence upon English philosophy. Their method fostered a preoccupation with classifying word uses in a prim and authoritarian set of rules for how we should employ words and what we ought to say and what we must not say. Whatever we may say is subjected to a legalistic system, and puts taboos upon what they call the incorrect use of language.

One of the most influential members of this group of Oxbridge philosophers was J. L. Austin, who from 1945 to 1960 was professor of philosophy at Oxford University. He made important contributions to linguistics and added a new dimension to grammar, which he considered decisive in the use of what he called word tools. He provided a painstaking analysis of the many jobs that we do with words and of their different uses, and introduced new ways of classifying the functions of language. But behind his many contributions to linguistic philosophy, both in writing and above all in his lectures, which were collected and edited by J. O. Urmson and G. J. Warnock, there is the basic assumption that our perception of reality and our knowledge of it is determined by the words we use. He held that the wrong use of words would produce mistaken perceptions of the phenomena transmitted to us by our senses, and therefore the meticulous analysis of language would be a major contribution to clear thinking. He maintained that when we examine what we should say and when, we are not looking merely at words but also at the realities for which we use words to talk about them, and we acquire a sharpened awareness of words to sharpen our awareness of phenomena. (J. L. Austin: *The Meaning of a Word*, 1940). He taught his students that knowing what a thing is is to an important extent knowing what the name for it is, and the right name. He suggested the term *linguistic phenomenology*, which means the correct study or description of phenomena (appearances), as Professor Mandel has pointed out, not so much of reality outside us but of apparent facts as expressed by the words we use.

Austin took his cue from Russell who claimed that grammar can be a guide to the structure of reality and the correct application of grammatical rules would enable language to acquire, or at least approximate its truth function. What we have to do, Austin taught his students, is to unpick one by one a mass of seductive verbal fallacies. In this way we may hope to learn something positive. And indeed, he was remorseless in the unpicking of 'verbal fallacies', both in his books as well as in his lectures. He and his fellows used millions of words to analyse words, till his students became intimidated by this flood of verbal analysis of words and became inhibited to express their ideas by what they must have felt to be a censorship upon the way one could express oneself, till many felt confused and disorientated and could not trust their own thought. To use a pun, too much and unremitting analysis leads to paralysis. This has led many students to adopt a cynical attitude towards the possibility of ever arriving at a valid understanding of the world, or indeed, about the nature of the mind, and in particular, how we can possibly know what moral conduct means. The cynicism of which I have spoken earlier found its representation in this philosophical vandalism and has contributed to it.

6. The Tower of Babble: Postmodernism and Deconstruction

While their Anglo-Saxon cousins almost, but not quite, put an end to philosophy (as Wittgenstein intended), French philosophers, not to be outdone, have drawn attention to their own effort of confusing the public. They did it by the pyrotechnics of brilliant words, trapeze artists in the philosophical circus whose performance dazzles the audience. In fact they seem to make a special effort to obscure any meaning behind their sentences. They brought the art of obscurantism to a new level hardly ever approached before, not even by Hegel. But what does it mean? How can a philosophical movement led by obviously intelligent and educated people succumb to the temptation of deliberately confusing people and leave them baffled? Can it be that they simply can't write properly and don't understand the basic arts of communication? This cannot be the case, or if it were we would still have to ask how this became an acceptable and promising form of doing philosophy, particularly in a nation which was the founder of the Enlightenment and proud of its rationality. The exponents of this movement, which has for some forty years dominated the French intellectual scene, goes by the name of post-modernism, post-structuralism and deconstructionism, and they trace their direct ancestry to hermeneutics, which means the art of interpretation.

Hermeneutics was introduced by the Greeks, whose education was extensively based upon the study of poetry and drama, and became a subsidiary discipline of theology throughout the Christian era, because so much depended upon the interpretation of the scriptures. With the emergence of the rationalist movement, Schleiermacher and Schelling attempted to bring the process of interpretation into the new philosophy, and Dilthey gave hermeneutics a prominent place in the rational world-view. All forms of communication such as written statements, verbal exchanges, even gestures and actions were considered as texts which are to be subjected to interpretation. It is quite true, as any practitioner of psychoanalysis knows, that a patient's communications have to be interpreted in order to find the hidden meaning behind neurotic symptoms. Thus there is a subjective, usually unconscious, reality which can be made conscious and understood.

In all forms of interpretation there is something there to be interpreted. Even if final, incontrovertible interpretations elude us, we look for better interpretations to get nearer to the truth we are seeking. We do not cross the threshold to complete cynicism. Deconstruction crosses the threshold.

When there is nothing to believe in, when what has been thought of as certain and real is shown to be a delusion, then we can either analyse – take to pieces – the words we use, or we mock them by deliberately talking nonsense, like a child which imitates grown-ups in a mocking manner and says 'boo sucks' to words which mean nothing to it.

The confusion of languages, which had defeated men's attempt to reach heaven and discover its truth, is re-enacted in our time, but the inherent confusion and contradiction of the language we use prevents us from reaching heaven or the certainty of any truth. While the Anglo-Saxons meticulously analysed words, syntax and grammar, the French in their more sophisticated manner used the refinements of the sarcasm of the court jester in order to ridicule the pronouncements of our culture and adopt a meaningless language to make their point. But the trouble is that mockery has become professionalised; the clowns believe in their mockery and have forgotten to laugh – they want to be taken seriously.

The main exponents of this movement are Jacques Lacan, Jacques Derrida, Julia Kristeva, Luce Irigaray, Bruno Latour, Gilles Deleuze and Félix Guattari. Their writings have been exposed as being meaningless, confused and uninformed by Alan Sokal from America, and Jean Bricmont from Belgium, both professors of physics, in their recent book *Intellectual Impostures*.

Perhaps one of the best examples of meaningless verbiage quoted by Sokal and Bricmont is this text published in 1984 and 1991 by Paul Virilio:

> When depth of time replaces depths of sensible space; when the commutation of interface supplants the delimitation of surfaces; when transparence re-establishes appearances; then we begin to wonder whether that which we insist on calling *space* isn't actually *light*, a subliminary, para-optical light of which sunlight is only one phase or reflection. This light occurs in a duration measured in instantaneous time exposure rather than the historical and chronological passage of time. The time of this instant without duration is 'exposure time', be it over- or underexposure. Its photographic and cinematographic technologies already predicted the existence and the time of a continuum stripped of all physical dimensions, in which the quantum of energetic action and the punctum of cinematic observation have suddenly become the last vestiges of a vanished morphological reality. Transferred into the eternal present of a relativity whose topological and teleological thickness and depth belong to this final measuring instrument, this speed of light possesses one direction, which is both its size and dimension and which propagates itself at the same speed in all radial directions that measure the universe. (Virilio 1984, p.77; Virilio 1991, pp.63-64)

The writings of the other philosophers of France are no better, and Jacques Lacan is no exception.

In their determination to impress the general public, in particular the 'intellectual', they manipulate phrases and sentences which are shown upon any closer investigation to be devoid of all meaning. Many of the spokesmen of this tower of babble confuse the reader by the use of esoteric terms and neologisms taken out of any context, pretending to apply scientific terminology which obviously they do not themselves understand and do not expect the reader to understand either. So they feel free to invent scientific concepts, without even the slightest justification or explanation in order to impress their non-scientific readers, unperturbed by the contemptuous criticism from real scientists.

Jacques Lacan is a prime example in this employment of mathematical formulae which he invented in order to 'advance' psychoanalytic theory. Apart from his usual linguistic gobbledegook, his application of mathematics to psychoanalysis is probably the most outrageous attempt to impress readers with the 'scientific evidence' for his theories.

Lacan's predilection for mathematics is by no means marginal in his work. Already in the 1950s, his writings were full of graphs, formulae and 'algorithms'. In a seminar held in 1959, he said:

> If you'll permit me to use one of those formulas which come to me as I write my notes, human life could be defined as a calculus in which zero was irrational. This formula is just an image, a mathematical metaphor. When I say 'irrational,' I'm referring not to some unfathomable emotional state but precisely to what is called an imaginary number. The square root of minus one doesn't correspond to anything that is subject to our intuition, anything real – in the mathematical sense of the term – and yet, it must be conserved, along with its full function. (Lacan, 'Desire and the interpretation of desire in *Hamlet*', pp.28-29, seminar held in 1959)

A year later, he further developed the psychoanalytic role of imaginary numbers:

> Personally, I will begin with what is articulated in the sigla $S(\emptyset)$ by being first of all a signifier...

> And since the battery of signifiers, as such, is by that very fact complete, this signifier can only be a line [*trait*] that is drawn from its circle without being able to be counted part of it. It can be symbolized by the inherence of a (-1) in the whole set of signifiers.
>
> As such it is inexpressible, but its operation is not inexpressible, for it is that which is produced whenever a proper noun is spoken. Its statement equals its signification.
>
> Thus, by calculating that signification according to the algebraic method used here, namely:
>
> $$\frac{S \text{ (signifier)}}{s \text{ (signified)}} = s \text{ (the statement)}$$
>
> with $S = (-1)$, produces: $s = \sqrt{-1}$.
>
> (Lacan 1977b, pp.316-7, seminar originally held in 1960)

Sokal and Bricmont comment:

Here Lacan can only be pulling the reader's leg. Even if his 'algebra' had a meaning, the 'signifier', 'signified' and 'statement' that appear within it are obviously not numbers, and his horizontal bar (an arbitrarily chosen symbol) does not denote the division of two numbers. Therefore, his 'calculations' are pure fantasies. Nevertheless, two pages later, Lacan returns to the same theme:

> No doubt Claude Lévi-Strauss, in his commentary on Mauss, wished to recognize in it the effect of a zero symbol. But it seems to me that what we are dealing with here is rather the signifier of the lack of this zero symbol. That is why, at the risk of incurring a certain amount of opprobrium, I have indicated to what point I have pushed the distortion of the mathematical algorithm in my use of it: the symbol $\sqrt{-1}$, which is still written as '*i*' in the theory of complex numbers, is obviously justified only because it makes no claim to any automatism in its later use.
>
> ...
>
> Thus the erectile organ comes to symbolize the place of *jouissance*, not in itself, or even in the form of an image, but as a part lacking in the desired image: that is why it is equivalent to the $\sqrt{-1}$ of the signification produced above, of the *jouissance* that it restores by the coefficient of its statement to the function of lack of signifier (-1).
>
> (Lacan 1977b, pp.318-20)

By using nonsensical terminology, he arouses his audiences' and his readers' obvious puzzlement, and intimidates them into thinking that they are ignorant and that therefore Lacan must know more than they do, while he himself was unable to differentiate reality from fantasy, and apparently could not recognise the boundaries of reason. At a somewhat later stage of his investigations, he claimed that language is 'the vehicle to express the unconscious' and that 'it is at the level of language that the problem exists. Language is the only communication we know; there is no unconscious except for the speaking being.'

Lacan said many cryptic things which contradict the theories he claimed to represent, but did Lacan, the 'psychoanalyst and founder of the école freudienne', not know that a very important dimension of the unconscious is dominated by the early pre-verbal period of the infant and continues to exercise its influence upon the individual, that the traumas and conflicts of the earliest period of our lives have a profound influence upon the character as well as neurotic and psychic symptoms long before we can speak and express them in words. Man is not all into language, but acquires it gradually, and as everybody knows and certainly psychoanalysts know, that words are often used in order to cover up what we really think, they are both an expression as well as instruments by which we repress these feelings, and thoughts which disturb our ego defences.

Not only in France but also in Anglo-Saxon countries a preoccupation with semantics is seen as the latest fashion in the sharpening of the tools in the psychoanalytic armoury, a sort of obligation for any analyst who would consider himself up-to-date. However, these analysts of language, in their pride at having found the correct tool for the clarification of the meaning behind the patient's words and narratives have become trapped in their own words and have reduced them to verbiage. The researchers into the meaning of words have come to use words without meaning. They have not advanced our understanding of the human psyche, nor have they improved therapeutic methods. What they have done is to draw attention away from the unconscious processes to a study of verbal behaviour, to an investigation of the words which the patient produces in his consulting hour. But the patient's words and his 'narrative' are very inadequate manifestations of his psychic processes. After all, the words we pronounce, particularly under the stress of anxiety and the conflicts imposed by our inhibitions, reveal only a small part of our mental experience, and by taking the words as if they were the full expression of what goes on in the mind, the linguistic analysts flatten the multidimensional complexities and richness of our mental processes. Psychoanalysts, who have followed the fashion of linguistic analysis which has dominated philosophy for too long and has lead to a dead end and practically destroyed philosophy in our time, are threatening to do the same to psychoanalysis.

Paul Ricoeur proclaims:

'Today we are in search of a comprehensive philosophy of language to account for the multiple functions of the human act of signifying and for their interrelationships . . . We have at our disposal a symbolic logic, an exegetical science, an anthropology, and a psychoanalysis, and, perhaps for the first time, we are able to encompass in a single question the problem of the unification of human discourse. The very progress of the aforementioned disciplines has both revealed and intensified the dismemberment of that discourse. Today the unity of human language poses a problem.'

Ricoeur had the title of 'philosopher of integral language' bestowed upon him as the man 'able to achieve a comprehensive philosophy about the human mind as reflected in language'. Not a bad example of mystification parading as exactitude!

But nobody can outdo Lacan, both in the falsification of Freud's ideas as well as in the deliberate obscurantism of language. I cannot resist quoting another passage from one of his lectures entitled *A Love Letter*, where he tries to explain his concepts of 'signifier' and 'signified' and goes to great lengths in tortured arguments to do this: 'I am taking up what Freud expressly left aside, the *Was will das Weib?*, the *What does the woman want?* Freud argues that there is no libido other than masculine. Meaning what? What other than that whole field, which is hardly negligible, is thereby ignored.' (This great analyst of psychoanalysis could not have read Freud to make such a statement.) And he goes on:

> The woman relates to the signifier of this Other, in so far as, being Other, it can only remain always Other. I can only presume here that you will think back to my statement that there is no Other of the Other. As the place where everything of the signifier which can be articulated comes to be signified, the Other is, in its very foundation, radically the Other. Which is why this signifier, with this bracket open, marks the Other as crossed through – S (Ø).
>
> How can we conceive that the Other might, somewhere, be that to which one half – since that is roughly the biological proportion – one half of speaking beings relates. And yet that is what is written up on the blackboard by means of the arrow pointing from the ~~The~~. This ~~The~~ cannot be said. Nothing can be said of the woman. The woman relates to S(Ø), which means that she is already doubled, and is not all, since on the other hand she can also relate to Φ.
>
> Φ is assigned this phallus which I specify as being the signifier which has no signified, the signifier supported in man by phallic *jouissance*. What is it? – other than this, sufficiently stressed by the importance of masturbation in our practice, the *jouissance* of the idiot.
>
> (*Jacques Lacan & the École Freudienne: Feminine Sexuality*, pp.151–152, Macmillan, 1985*).*

Julia Kristeva, who was widely acclaimed as an exponent of linguistic analysis, employs mathematical theory according to Gödel, and is a supporter both of Lacanian analysis of Freudian theory as well as of Marxism. In her book *Revolution in Poetic Language* (1974), she writes:

> 'A discovery of Marx, which has not heretofore been sufficiently emphasized, can be sketched here. If each individual or each social organism represents a set, the set of all sets that the State should be does not exist. The State as set of all sets is a fiction, it cannot exist, just as there does not exist a set of all sets in set theory... The State is, at most, a collection of all the finite sets. But for this collection to exist, and for finite sets to exist too, there must be some infinity: the two propositions are equivalent. The desire to form the set of

all finite sets puts the infinite on stage, and reciprocally. Marx, who noticed the illusion of the State to be the set of all sets, saw in the social unit as presented by the bourgeois Republic a collection that nevertheless constitutes, for itself, a set (just as the collection of the finite ordinals is a set if one poses it as such) from which something is lacking: indeed, its *existence* or, if one wants, its *power* is dependent on the existence of the infinite that no other set can contain' (Kristeva 1974, pp.379–80, italics in the original).

But Kristeva's mathematical erudition is not limited to set theory. In her article 'On the subject in linguistics', she applies mathematical analysis and topology to psychoanalysis:

[I]n the syntactic operations following the mirror stage, the subject is already sure of his uniqueness: his flight towards the 'point ∞' in the signifying [*signifiance*] is stopped. One thinks for example of a set C_o on a usual space R^3 where for every continuous function F on R^3 and each integer $n > 0$, the set of points X where $F(X)$ exceeds n is bounded, the functions of C_o tending to 0 when the variable X recedes towards the 'other scene'. In this topos, the subject placed in C_o does not reach this 'centre exterior to language' about which Lacan speaks and where he loses himself as subject, a situation that would translate the relational group that topology calls a *ring*.
(Kristeva 1977, p.313, italics in the original)

Sokal and Bricmont comment:

'This is one of the best examples of Kristeva's attempts to impress the reader with fancy words that she obviously does not understand. The definition given here of the set of functions $C_o(R^3)$ is not even correctly copied, and the errors stand out to anyone who understands the subject. But the real problem is that the purported application to psychoanalysis is nonsense. How could a 'subject' be 'placed in C_o?' (Alan Sokal & Jean Bricmont *Intellectual Impostures*, pp.45–46).

Alan Sokal and Jean Bricmont (pp.9–10) make the point that half-formulated theory – be it in physics, biology or the social sciences – cannot be redeemed simply by wrapping it in symbols or formulas.

The sociologist Stanislav Andreski has expressed this idea with his habitual irony:

> The recipe for authorship in this line of business is as simple as it is rewarding: just get hold of a textbook of mathematics, copy the less complicated parts, put in some references to the literature in one or two branches of the social studies without worrying unduly about whether the formulae which you wrote down have any bearing on the real human actions, and give your product a good-sounding title, which suggests that you have found a key to an exact science of collective behaviour. (Stanislav Andreski, *Social Sciences as Sorcery*, 1972 pp.129-30)

Andreski's critique was originally aimed at American quantitative sociology, but it is equally applicable to some of the texts cited here, notably those of Lacan and Kristeva.

It is significant that deconstructionists never seem to write about an author upholding certain views expressing a certain personality developing his own ideas, but depersonalise the author by always referring to texts. The death of the author is one convenient device to combat the possibility of meaningful communication, a rejection of distinctions between what is essential and what is marginal, all aim at undermining any central meaning a text may have. Another deconstructionist device to undermine meaning is the often repeated dogma that all texts contain contradictions and therefore deconstruct themselves. Thus Anderson writes: 'Discourse is already caught up within the critical text, the play of differences within the critical text, which guarantees its deconstruction of knowledge and meaning as graspable essences that independently precede or follow expressions.' (Danny Anderson: 'Deconstruction: Critical Strategy, Strategic Criticism', *Contemporary Literary Theory*, Macmillan, 1989, p.150)

In his article *From Hermeneutics to Deconstruction* Prof. Rickman (*New Analysis*, Journal of Psychoanalytic Social Studies, Spring 1998) comments that deconstruction – far from being merely a more exacting and critical method of analysis – aims at the destruction of confidence in the pursuit of knowledge and meaning, and he quotes Goodheart: 'The cognitive interest of deconstruction leads to the knowledge that we can have no knowledge'. (Eugene Goodheart, *The Sceptical Disposition*, Princeton University Press, 1984, p.127). This despair of reason reflects the horrifying encounter with human irrationality in our time. The rejection of established procedures can be seen as a new generation cocking a snook at preceding generations of scholars. Maybe intellectuals in the safety of their classrooms and in their writings want to feel in the vanguard of a revolution against the complacency of a bourgeois society, and want to appear daring and defiant.

It is significant that the deconstructionists and postmodernists no longer speak of writings but only of texts, words without intrinsic meaning, cohesion or purpose; we cannot possibly know what is in the mind of the author, or what his intentions are and what made him write down his ideas. What the author thinks he says appears irrelevant, and he disappears behind the text, and it is only the readers projections and interpretations which make him come alive. The interpretation is much more important than the thoughts and ideas of the author, be he a politician, scientist or philosopher, poet or novelist. There is no unifying spirit behind the words, or as Wittgenstein insisted, 'no higher meaning beyond the words we use'.

In his book *The Death of the Author*, Roland Barthes writes: 'It is the language which speaks, not the author. We know now that a text is not a line of words releasing a theological or philosophical meaning, but a multidimensional space in which a variety of writings, not one of them original, blend and clash.' (Roland Barthes, quoted by Catherine Belsey in *The Future of Theory*, Harvester Press, 1987, p.145.) By denying the author, the man of God or the man of reason, the new philosophers declare war upon the intellectual superego; they attempt to be the intellectual father murderers by declaring that the fathers of our cultural ancestry have nothing useful or original to say to us. But it is particularly interesting that this releases the sons from any constraints of reason, allows them to talk a lot of nonsense, and to uphold the incoherent and incomprehensible babble as a kind of virtue. They invent words which are unfamiliar and meaningless.

In the 'old days' the fathers or the authorities used to say: 'Listen carefully, and do as I say.' This was the approach of the theological or the secular ideology presented as dogma and reinforced by law. The intellectual rebels of the Enlightenment proclaimed: "Listen carefully to what the authorities say, judge it by the exercise of your own reasoning and do what reason tells you to do, in conjunction with your rational band of brothers." But then the rational band of brothers failed reason, they too became dogmatic and authoritarian, unable to fulfil their promise of making the world a better place to live in, and a new rebellion took place intending to kill the betrayers of reason. But being unable to conceive of a new and convincing rationality which would direct our actions, all they can do is to attack reason itself and deny its very existence.

There is a confrontation with the intellectual father figures, an obsession with defeating their power over us. As Derrida describes it: 'One of the two governs the other. To de-construct the opposition is to overturn the hierarchy at a given moment.' (Jacques Derrida, *Positions 1972*, Athlone Press, 1981). And as Roy Boyne wrote: 'Deconstruction means reversing polarities and according privilege to the side of the opposition which was hitherto unprivileged.' (*Foucault and Derrida: The Other Side of Reason*, Unwin and Hyman, 1990, p.125.) One wonders whether in their agonised abstractions they are conscious of their revolutionary intent. When they speak of polarities, decentralising, reversal of centre and margin, and other obscurantist terms, do they really mean the opposition between man/woman, white/black, capital/labour, law/lawlessness, attacker/victim, and the reversal of the traditional supremacies? In their attempt to affirm Nietzsche's call for the revaluation of all values, they merely succeed in confusing, till we don't know how to differentiate between good and bad, true and false, right and wrong.

It is of course common knowledge that words tend to be interpreted from the point of view of our own interests, our own ideas and values. If you were a Nazi, you would understand words like super-race, blood and soil, the power of the will, and the conspiracy of the Jews to poison the pure blood of the German race.

For a non-Nazi or anti-Nazi these were not only meaningless and nonsensical slogans but would have been understood as the paranoid fantasies of a leadership determined to achieve world power. We can see from this example, and there are of course many, many others, that the words of a text are not by themselves completely without meaning and have to be interpreted by the reader or listener to make them meaningful, but it is the intention and the ideas which the speaker or writer upholds which give meaning to their words. It has always been the task of the intellect and its exercise of reason to subject the assumptions, the world-view and the metaphysic that lie beyond the words to a critical analysis, and this is the traditional purpose of philosophy; to understand why we say things and what motivates us to say them, and not merely how we say them. To discover what the Nazi or the racist or the communist, or for that matter the capitalist really mean by their slogans, and what their intentions and purposes are is the task of reason; to investigate the cognitive errors which we harbour and take for granted.

The deconstructionists thus undermine the higher faculties of our minds. That they promote the destruction of our confidence as rational beings is attested by its practitioners and noted by its writers. M. H. Abrams refers to 'the persistent enterprise to make us see their diverse works as an interminable free-play of indeterminable meanings.' (M. H. Abrams in *Modern Criticism and Theory*, Longman, 1988). If we cannot recognise a human mind behind the texts and the statements and the slogans do not appear as an author's intentions and ideas, then they stand before us as an empty space covered by words. We can then attempt to squeeze any meaning out of them by analysing the syntax and verbal relationships if we are linguistic analysts or we are free to interpret them in whichever way we feel satisfactory, but we cannot apply our rational faculties to make them understandable – our rational and ethical judgements become redundant. Not only the author's mind, his reasoning and his values, are irrelevant, but our own is no longer required in the encounter with the written or spoken words. One belief or prejudice will then be regarded as good as any other, and there remains no rational criterion by which we examine their value. The prevailing cynicism of which I have spoken earlier will be encouraged and justified by the meanderings of the new philosophers.

If the authors' rational and ethical values disappear from view and are deemed to be irrelevant, then the higher faculties of our minds atrophy through lack of exercise; we then regress to more primitive levels of cognition, and our minds will succumb to irrational impulses, prejudices, unexamined traditions as well as certain preconscious complexes. And there is no rational criterion by which we can evaluate them. What is left of our rational faculties will be used as an instrument to promote and to justify whatever conviction we uphold or activities we pursue in order to justify them.

Chapter 3

The Physical Basis of Consciousness and Morality

1. The Instinctual Void

We have observed the breakthrough of primitive aggression, ruthless self-assertive and acquisitive drives, when, in psychoanalytic terms, the ego, having lost its trust in the superego, rebels against its commands, turns to the id and succumbs to its promptings.

On the wide spectrum of mankind's social behaviour we witness the extremes of collective sadism intent upon degrading, torturing and killing people who do not belong to one's own tribe, race or religion, to the extent of their extermination; and at the other extreme the conviction that all people, religions and cultures are equal and claims of religious and social supremacy must be rejected. This goes by the name of moral or cultural relativism and more recently political correctness, which has come to dominate many areas of Western democracy. In the name of freedom of self-expression we must not discriminate between different values or even intellectual concepts, so that one truth is considered to be as good as another, and even to be convinced of the truth of an idea or metaphysical concept is a kind of blasphemy. We have seen this in the pronouncements of post-modern or deconstructionist philosophers, whose relentless analysis of words is a kind of torture of reason. They have succeeded in confusing and intimidating our rational faculties.

It is now many years ago since I myself experienced this 'democratic' reaction in a series of lectures I gave to an audience of philosophers and psychologists on the philosophy of Kant and his concept of universal moral imperatives, when members of the audience showed their reluctance to accept anybody's right to tell them how to think, and were nonplussed that I should uphold the ideas of a German philosopher trying to impose universal concepts of right and wrong upon freedom-loving people. At the same time some members of the audience wanted me simply to tell them what is to be done in a practical and realistic manner instead of indulging in this theoretical philosophising which was alien to their ways of thinking. This reaction to Kant's philosophy by highly educated and responsible persons who uphold the right of individuals to choose their own values and arrive at judgements without having them imposed by some higher authority has a particular poignancy, for Kant was without doubt a most profound exponent of the Enlightenment. In his essay entitled *An Answer to the Question: What is Enlightenment?* (1784), he wrote:

> *Enlightenment is man's emergence from his self-imposed immaturity. Immaturity* is the inability to use one's understanding without guidance from another. This immaturity is *self-imposed* when its cause lies not in lack of understanding, but in lack of resolve and courage to use it without guidance from another. *Sapere Aude!* 'Have courage to use your own understanding!' – that is the motto of enlightenment.

But the appeal to man's freedom to use his own understanding, without dependency upon the commands or instructions of a higher authority, implies that it is an ability which is innate to man's nature, and applies both to his rational as well as his moral equipment. In his major work *The Critique of Pure Reason* where Kant analysed the potentials as well as the limitations of rational thought, he propounded innate or *a priori* forms of the understanding which underlie all our perceptions of the world and all cognitive processes. In his books devoted to morality he defines certain *a priori* or categorical imperatives which are common to all sensate beings, meaning all human beings. He is careful to define human rationality, and man's freedom to exercise it, as a capacity which distinguishes man from all other animals, who are dependent to a large extent in their judgements upon instincts, (genetically programmed, to use our modern language). Mankind,

Kant proclaims, is destined to shape his own fate beyond the limitations of his animal existence, and by his unique capacity of freedom to exercise his will according to the dictates of his reason: 'Reason in a creature is a faculty to extend the rules and objectives of the use of all his powers far beyond natural instinct and it knows no limits to its projects.'

But, as he wrote in his essay, *Idea for a Universal History* (1784): 'Since in their endeavours men proceed neither merely instinctively like animals, nor yet according to a plan that is determined by reason, we cannot avoid a feeling of indignation when one sees men's actions on the great stage of the world's history, despite the wisdom of a few individuals, dominated by folly and childish vanity, and often even childish malice and destructiveness.' This certainly rings a bell in our own time, and one has no difficulty in recognising our predicament. There can be no doubt that Kant's theories are profound and convincing, but we live in a scientific age, when a theory in order to acquire truth value (before we can be sure that it is true) has to be verified by empirical evidence. But in order to give empirical, factual evidence for consciousness and a wide range of rational thinking – this most non-material of all human qualities – we have to find physical-physiological evidence for them and what makes them possible.

I shall elaborate upon the fundamental philosophical principles of morality in a later part of this book. But first we must ask whether we can find scientific evidence that the human mind possesses the freedom to determine its actions and his beliefs by rational considerations, whether reason itself is capable of guiding men's behaviour. If we consider the endless examples in human history as well as in the life of individuals when reason failed to guide a person's or a nation's behaviour, it is no wonder that the conviction has gained ground that human nature (being what it is, as they say) lacks the freedom to change its basic nature. It follows therefore that the belief that humanity is not governed by the genetic determinants of instinct and that it is different from animals is merely an illusion to satisfy men's vanity.

The physicalistic concept of cognition which has made a credo of denying that there is anything specific about human forms of thinking and knowledge which sets it apart from animal psychology and transcends biological and genetic conditioning, has provided a philosophical foundation and justification for behaviourism. Behaviourism has become not only the research method but above all a name for physicalistic and mechanistic psychology. The behaviourist pioneer K. S. Lashley in his statement of 1923 laid the foundation for his fundamental faith: 'To me the essence of behaviourism is the belief that the study of man will need nothing except what is discernible in the concepts of mechanics and chemistry.' Such statements can be endlessly quoted and have become the foundation for a sociology, psychiatry and psychology which considers itself to be scientific.

The ideal of establishing a science of human behaviour which can take its full place among the natural sciences and show man as a part of the unity of nature has forced its adherents to explain human thought processes by reductionistic methods, i.e. explaining psychological processes and mental processes by means of physical, chemical and genetic causations. But if science has no place for the specific and central characteristic of humanity to exercise its rational faculties and to modify its genetic endowment, it is the poorer and not the richer for it.

The mechanistic and reductionistic concepts of science have been strongly criticised by the Russian biologist A. I. Oparin, who upheld the view that there is in nature a qualitative change from material to mental phenomena. Under the heading *The Qualitative Change from Natural to Mental Phenomena* he wrote: 'It constrains science to remain ignorant of the specific and central characteristic of humanity, and thereby makes it not merely inadequate for its task but bad science.'

There can be no doubt that man is a biological organism and as such the product of evolution. He is both a physical as well as a psychological organism, he is endowed with mind and intellect, and there is equally no doubt that there is a correlation between his brain and his thinking, his conscious as well as his unconscious processes. All our feelings, perceptions, our thought and our ideas are based upon our brain, and we could not exercise our mental processes without it. It is therefore obvious that there is an inevitable interaction between the organic and the psychic, between the two dimensions of man's nature. In the words of Steven Rose: 'What is needed is a recognition of the interactive nature of the human situation, and hence of human brain states' (Steven Rose: *The Conscious Brain*, Pelican, 1978). Rose agrees with Oparin that with the emergence of consciousness a qualitative evolutionary leap forward has occurred, making for a critical distinction between humans and other species: 'The emergence of consciousness has qualitatively changed the mode of human existence. And this change is also manifest in the structure and function of the human brain.' While in the evolution of the animal kingdom we can observe an increasing emphasis upon cortical activity and expansion of the frontal areas, in the evolution of the human species the expansion of the frontal and particularly the prefrontal lobes has dramatically accelerated and provides the physiological basis for the specific quality of his mind, which has reduced his dependency upon his instincts and sets him apart from all other animal species.

We can say that with the course of his evolution the emergence of the prefrontal lobes has provided the neurological equipment to serve his need for foresight, anticipation and a wide range of choices which were of decisive advantage in his evolution and made his survival possible. By being conscious of his own needs as well as the conditions of his environment and of the dangers around him, i.e. having an internal representation or image, not only of the way things are and how he wants them to be but also of his actions and their likely consequences, he has learned to choose between different possible ways of dealing with reality. While animals needed many generations to establish new biological variations to cope with new conditions, he needs only minutes to reflect, or even seconds, to recognise unforeseen dangers or advantages and to act accordingly. As we shall see this also entails the ability of the higher areas of the brain connected with consciousness and ideas to influence the older areas of the brain, its chemistry and genetically determined instincts, and in some measure to transform their bio-physiological functions. The enormously increased freedom from the determination of his instinctual responses enabled him to make a wide range of adaptations to environmental conditions.

But this new-gained freedom granted by his new brain also produced new problems: he was exposed to an instinctual void, he ceased to react with the certainty of instinctual reactions. Mankind is never quite sure whether its judgements are right or wrong, it has lost that sense of unquestioned necessity for its behaviour, which other animals possess, and man is constrained to think and to provide his own justifications for his judgements and actions. But in order to feel certain that his behaviour was correct and justified according to his own assessment he also needs the assurance and the approval of his fellows; he needs collectively shared memories and values which transcend instinctive responses. In other words, he needs the security of a culture in order to replace the security of his instincts, which he lost when he gained his freedom. There is no individual or society without a culture, even if it only means a culture of anti-culture as we have seen earlier.

However, the paradox that a part of the brain, which after all is a physical organism, can be the source of our higher mental and psychological processes, which moreover provides us with the freedom to transcend and modify our instincts, has been a source of much puzzlement among scientists and philosophers, and has been called 'the astonishing hypothesis' by Francis Crick (*The Astonishing Hypothesis*). He never ceases to be surprised that our psyche, our soul, has a biological basis, and feels that he has to justify his thesis before an incredulous audience apparently still steeped in the Cartesian dualism which implies a separate existence of mind and of matter, an internal and an external reality. The latter is seen from the outside, so to speak, where all material, physical phenomena are objects transmitted by our senses, and the other from the inside where we experience the reality of our own thoughts, our own emotions, of our hopes and anxieties. But if we take the evolutionary view we must recognise that it is the will to survive, the will to live, which is shared by all organic systems, and to respond to the environment in a manner which is advantageous to our survival and our well-being, that it is the internal, subjective world which is itself the agent of biological changes. The enormous transformations which took place in the brain and the body of our species and set it apart from all other animals is probably one of the most astonishing events of biological evolution on this planet. It is not merely the genetic programming of our species which made it dominant among all biological organisms, but the capacity for internal representation of possible events and the capacity to anticipate the future and the consequences of our actions.

2. The Structure and Function of the Brain

The human brain is an incredibly complex organ for receiving, communicating and storing information, issuing instructions to the various internal and external functions of the body, for the reception and interpretation of stimuli, to the formation of abstract concepts regarding the meaning of the world and one's relationship to it.

Brains are probably the most complex structures in the universe. Each human brain contains some hundred billion nerve cells (neurons) interconnected through more than ten thousand times that number of junction points, or synapses. If this phenomenal organ developed – largely over the nine months from conception to birth – at an even rate (which it doesn't, of course), this would mean some 4,000 nerve cells per second being formed throughout the entire gestational period. And if this seems dramatic enough, it is worth contemplating the fact that over the first few years of life some 30,000 new synapses are being created every second under each square centimetre of the brain's surface!

'This huge array develops with impressive orderliness, wiring up the brain in order to perform its manifold functions through the process of ontogenesis – that is, development understood as the product of a continuous exquisite interplay between genes and environment. Because brains must perform routine functions – such as analysing images falling on the retina and transmitted to the brain's visual regions – in as error-free way as possible, while also being able to modify performance as a result of experience, this creation of cells and their intercommunications can best be envisaged as a dialogue between specificity and plasticity. On the one hand, we have the relatively unmodifiable connections that enable sense data to be decoded, motor actions to be performed and even the multiple functions outside normal aware control, such as standing upright, breathing, sleeping and waking. On the other, the subtle changes in cellular connections that form the brain representation of learning and memory enable us to modify our thoughts and actions as a result of experience' (Steven Rose: 'Brains, Minds and the World', in *From Brains to Consciousness – Essays on the New Sciences of the Mind*, edited by Steven Rose, Penguin 1999).

The cortex, which is of particular interest to our study, is by far the largest part of the human brain and according to recent estimates contains between thirty and fifty thousand million neurons (nerve cells) condensed in an area of two hundred and fifty thousand square millimetres, roughly the size of a man's handkerchief. For this reason it has to be extensively folded to fit into the skull. The sheet varies in thickness but is generally between two and five millimetres thick.

There are some hundred thousand neurons in every square millimetre of the cortical sheet and they are all connecting with each other. Most of these connections are local and only extend to a minute fraction of a millimetre, but others are longer and travel some distance to enter another part of the sheet or go into another part of the brain. It is estimated that some thirty per cent are made up of large connections, the axons or dendrites and nerve tracts, which demonstrates how much connection there is between various parts of the brain. It is also the synchronicity of human brain activity which distinguishes it from all mechanical processes like that of a computer, which, however fast, operates in a serial manner. (It may be worth also considering the element of synchronicity which prevails in the world of elementary particles, which not only travel with the speed of light in a serial manner but interact simultaneously, and therefore appear to be in different places at one and the same time.) The cerebral cortex consists of two separate sheets, one on each side of the head, dissecting neatly half way down its mid line. To visual inspection and to microscopic inspection as well, each half is very nearly the mirror image of the other. From a vertical division of the brain one can observe different regions by which the cortex can be divided into a number of major centres or lobes. At the front of the head is the frontal lobe, whose main functions are related to speech, learning, memory, intelligence and willed performance, as well as planning and choice. We shall turn to this area of the brain in more detail, for it represents the physical dimension of consciousness, the so-called higher functions of the mind.

Behind the frontal lobes occupying the upper half of the brain we find the parietal lobe, which contains the centres responsible for the co-ordination and control of sensory input and motor output particularly relating to touch and body sensations.

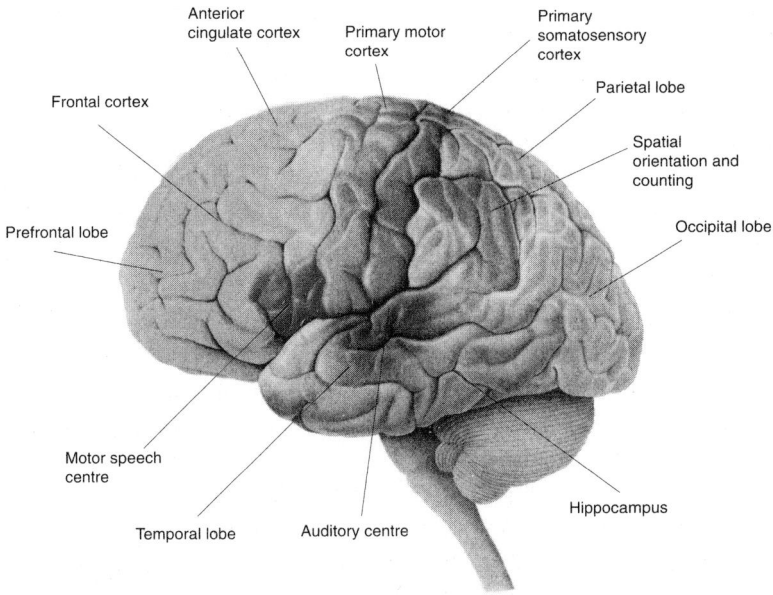

The main lobes of the cortex and the location of the main motor areas and primary sensory areas

In the middle of the cortex, between the frontal and the parietal lobes, going vertically down from the top of the brain towards the temporal lobe below, is the primary motor cortex, and alongside it the primary somatosensory cortex. The latter is the centre for the analysis and interpretation of the sensations of touch and peripheral body sensations, sending its messages to the motor centre in front of it, which controls voluntary motor reactions, that is, the willed instructions to the muscles. It is interesting to note that these two centres connect the frontal lobes with the parietal lobes and interact between them, illustrating the simultaneous feedback between the various cortical centres and beyond that to the other areas of the brain.

The temporal lobe covers the area at the lower part of the cortex and contains the temple region which controls the sensations of hearing and the interpretation of sounds. At the lower back of the brain we find the occipital areas concerned with vision and the analysis of the sensations of light and colour. It also contributes to the analysis of shapes and patterns and spatial orientation. It transforms the optical stimuli of the retina into images and places them into the outside world where they are perceived as representations or perceptions of reality. But these visual images can be directed back to the frontal lobes where they are employed by the 'thinking centres' to produce creative imagination which plays an important role in conceptualisation and abstract thought. We can observe, therefore, that visual imagery plays a significant part in our intellectual ideas as well as in the arts, and they both influence each other.

The interaction between the various parts of the cortex is illustrated by the fact that any object we see has a great many different characteristics, such as form, colour, motion and spatial attributes, which are processed in many different visual areas, and, furthermore, an object seen is also heard, smelled or felt. When we listen to someone talking it is not only the speech centres which interpret the sounds he makes into words; we also interpret the expressions of his face, his gestures and his bodily movements into an integrated understanding of what he is attempting to express. In turn this evokes our reaction and judgement, our sympathy or rejection.

However, the various centres of the cortex not only interact with each other to produce coherent perceptions of the world around us but elaborate them into a continuum of causal relationships, a unity of time – of past, present, and future – and a unity of space beyond the immediate here and now extending to a concept of the world. These integrative processes of the cortex not only serve the cognitive functions but are equally responsible for our values which largely determine how we interpret the cognitive processes and our views about the meaning of the world. The cortex not only has a capacity for visual representation of the reality outside us, but also integrates the thousands of stimuli, drives and urgesfrom within which attempt to gain entry into the forebrain and into consciousness, and transforms what would be a chaos of messages into a coherent sense of self. It is the task of the ego to select and discriminate between the vast number of impulses which demand motor discharge in action, into those which are acceptable and which are not, which promote the interest of the self and which would harm it, and thus has to inhibit the impulses which it considers harmful and unacceptable to the ego. Who has not felt the impulse to hit someone one disagrees with, or to kill someone whom one hates but has had to repress and block it from entry into the motor areas or even from consciousness.

3. The Ancient Areas of the Brain

Inside the cortex, and largely covered over by it, lies the midbrain. This much older part of the brain represents the physical foundations for our instincts and genetically programmed reactions, our feelings, desires and primitive drives. It is the inherited store of the experiences acquired by humanity over millions of years, which, without our being aware of it, influences our behaviour and our thinking. One can say that each human brain contains all the periods of the evolution of our species from its earliest origins to the present. The different ages of our evolution can be seen in the different parts of the midbrain and their specific functions. By dissecting the brain we gain some insight into the neurological equipment of our biological ancestors.

While the forebrain and in particular the prefrontal lobes of the cortex are the latest acquisition of the development of our species, the organic representation of our psychic processes, the midbrain can be considered as an intermediary stage of evolution and a link between the cortex and the oldest areas of the brain, which governed the life of our primitive ancestors and their present surviving representatives such as fish and reptiles, and are largely responsible for the chemistry and physiology of our body and its reflexes. But even these can be influenced by the prefrontal lobes through the mediation of the midbrain which establishes a link between the newest and the oldest areas of our nervous system. Many aspects of language such as the interpretation of words, the quality of sounds, as well as the emotional response which sounds evoke, are provided by the massive tract of the nerve fibres of the corpus callosum which has about half a billion individual nerve fibres with connections running in both directions.

The two halves of the brain appear as a mirror image of each other. However, the left half of the brain is concerned with functions of the right half of the body, and the right half of the brain with the left half of the body. Thus stimulation of the left motor cortex results in movements on the right side of the body. There are exceptions to the statement that every function in our left half of the cerebrum is mirrored in the other, for in a number of brain functions there is only one side of control. This is particularly true for speech. The speech centres of the brain are confined to one side which is generally the left hemisphere, and the other hemisphere, while anatomically identical, is functionally silent. The main agent responsible for the transfer of information from one hemisphere to the other is the corpus callosum which makes it possible for one side of the body to know what the other is doing.

At the centre of the midbrain we find one of the most important subcortical structures, namely the thalamus, sometimes called the gateway to the cortex because the main inputs to the cortex and the connections between its various areas have to pass through it. For instance, the optical centres at the back of the cortex have to connect with the frontal areas in order to be interpreted into visual images, and the messages from the retinal ganglions pass through the thalamus and not only produce integrated imagery but also stimulate the relevant emotional significations. It is generally accepted by neurologists that the thalamus receives incoming stimuli, integrates them to various degrees and then relays them to other subcortical centres or to the cerebral cortex. In this way the crude stimuli received by the peripheral end organs become elaborated, to be presented to the highest hierarchy of the central nervous system, namely the frontal lobes of the cortex.

THE PHYSICAL BASIS OF CONSCIOUSNESS AND MORALITY

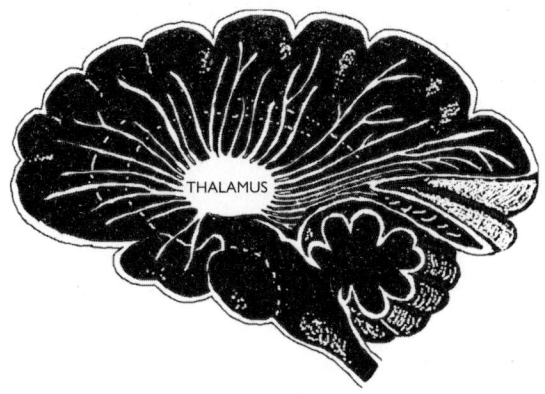

The key position of the thalamus and its axons, with its connections to and from the cerebral cortex

While much is known about the somatic, visual and auditory connections, little is known of the gustatory and the olfactory connections between the thalamus and the cortex. However, in recent years there has been much work done on the very important functions of those centres, and their significance for psychic activity.

I want to mention the innovative researches of the psychiatrist Peter Randell who is paving the way for a new understanding of the importance of the gustatory functions, both ontogenetically as well as phylogenetically. He writes: 'The ancient phylogenetic source of the prefrontal cortex still persists in the contemporary human brain as a strip of old cortex lying at the foot of the - prefrontal lobe, on its underneath, orbital surface. In contradiction to previous teaching, which held that the prefrontal lobe received no primary sensory input, it has now been repeatedly shown that this persistent palaeocortex receives and processes the chemoceptive sensations of smell and especially that of taste. Early in the ontogenesis of the prefrontal system – for instance, the suckling newborn – taste is not merely a minor sensory event localised in the mouth as it is in the adult, producing no more than the occasional gusto-facial reflex response like a smile (sweet) or a grimace (bitter). Rather the continuum of infantile gustation during sucking incorporation at the mother-breast can evoke dramatic (sometimes life-threatening) effects in virtually any or all of the body's physiological systems. So, for example, respiratory disturbances culminating in apnoea, shock-like cardiovascular collapse, profound disturbances in alimentation, skeletomotor performance and hormonal biorhythms. Such global gustatory responses in turn produce a veritable barrage of secondary narcissistic sensations that are also codified by the old prefrontal cortices and give rise to secondary motor responses whose sensory impact is again represented by this orbital area. This process of continuous reception and abreaction is the psychoneurological basis of emotion. Further, these primitive firing patterns are diagnosed and codified with reference to the gustatory pleasure/unpleasure cortical detectors. Indeed, in the functioning adult brain, *all* the sensory modalities: touch, audition and especially vision, as well as narcissistic libidinal sensations, all project to the orbital cortex. Thus, any event associated with strong emotion is labelled here for later recall, prior to its projection to the brain's primitive memory, the hippocampus of the temporal lobe.

'Thus, the original "programming" language of the prefrontal system comprises a vocabulary of deep taste qualities. The first purpose of this system is to enact the judgement as to what may be incorporated into the body as food and what must be rejected as poisonous or tainted. However, in the human brain, this primitive system has undergone a unique expansion and transformation of function. In man the orbital gustatory palaeocortex is surrounded in front and above by the most recently evolved and advanced neocortex which is unique to man. This acme of cortical neurotechnology is driven, on the one hand, by gusto-affective data but, on the other, by highly-processed visual data projected forward from the posterior parieto-occipital areas. This serves as the neurological substrate for the human capacity of transforming inchoate feelings and sensations into internal imagery. Such synthetic *a priori* "pictures in the head" are a dominant content in the archaic mental life of infants and in adult life provide a way for the mind to identify and prioritise the libidinal demands of its psychesoma. In the terms of modern biological psychiatry, much has been made of the case to view schizophrenia as an example of a genetically-dependent brain pathology. For example, *in vivo* studies of patterns of cortical activation in schizophrenic patients show what has been termed pathological hypofrontalism, by which is meant that normal prefrontal cortical activity is much reduced by some sort of synaptic hyper-inhibition. Biological psychiatrists explain this result in terms of heritable malfunction of the brain's (chemical) arousal systems. I would argue that it is the ontological impact of certain severe infantile traumas that have succeeded in producing such patterns of long-lasting cortical suppression.'

4. The Hypothalamus: Hormones and Homeostasis

There is a time to grow, a time to love, a time to fight, a time to sleep and a time to die. These processes, among others, are controlled by the body's hormonal system in the service of its homeostatic regulation. The basic metabolic rate of the body is controlled by thyroxine produced by the thyroid glands in the neck, the metabolism of calcium and phosphorus and part of urinary excretion by the parathyroids close to the thyroids. The preparation of the body for flight or fight is largely achieved by the secretion of adrenaline by adrenal glands, which alters heart rate and blood circulation, the state of sexual preparedness by the sex hormones, testosterone, progesterone and oestrogen.

However, all these hormonal activities of the nervous system are to a large extent controlled and regulated by cortical and subcortical areas of the brain, though normally operating below the level of consciousness. For instance, breathing is controlled by the medulla in the brain stem which is connected with the cortex and its frontal regions in such a way as to make breathing capable of rapid transition between conscious (voluntary) and unconscious (reflex) control.

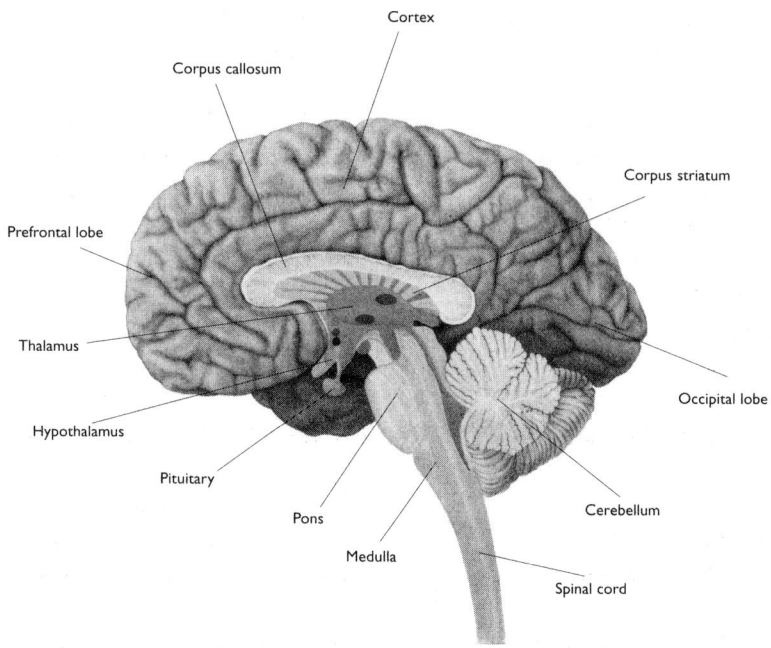

One half of the human brain, showing the subcortical areas.

Interaction between hormonal production and the brain is clearly shown by their close interaction with the pituitary gland, which is itself a part of the brain, and not, as has been assumed, independent of it and determined by genetic programming. In particular it is the discovery that the pituitary is connected and largely controlled by the hypothalamus which throws a new light upon the fundamental vegetative and homeostatic functions of the human body. The hypothalamus is a collection of several related groups of neurons lying just below and in front of the thalamus. Its connections apart from the pituitary and certain regions of the brain stem are with a group of structures known collectively as the limbic system. This is the area most extensively connected both with homeostatis as well as emotions and subconscious motivation. As one moves higher in the evolutionary process, we find that among the species closest to humans the proportion of the limbic area in relation to the cortex diminishes and the preponderance of the cortical system allows for greater modification of the limbic controls.

Since the discovery of the hypothalamus as a visceral and limbic centre, a multitude of separate functions, apart from those described above, have been ascribed to it, such as rise in blood pressure, arterial constrictions, dilation of the pupils, increase in blood sugar and circulating adrenaline, dilation of the bronchi, contraction of the bladder and uterus, inhibition of the mobility of the gastro-intestinal tract, secretion of tears and saliva, and alteration of body temperature. The cortical connections with the vegetative nervous system have been the subject of intense investigation, and there is abundant evidence of vegetative centres in the central cortex including the forebrain. The cortical influences upon the hypothalamus on the one hand inhibits its function, or stimulates them upon appropriate occasions. If this were not the case, stimuli of all sorts would evoke reflexes which would be inappropriate and harmful to the individual. The cortical information relates to the hypothalamus and via the hypothalamus to the more primitive centres of the brain, and generally speaking assure appropriate reactions to external stimuli.

This discovery enables us to arrive at an understanding of the importance of the nature of interpretations which the neocortex sends to the vegetative system. These interpretations can be realistic, i.e. correspond to the conditions of external reality, or they may be distorted, sending the wrong messages to the vegetative system: states of anxiety, apprehensions of danger or dread of persecution – imagined or real – evoke contractions of the musculature, the digestive and circulatory as well as respiratory functions – we become breathless with fear as we freeze on a sudden encounter with danger or what we perceive to be a dangerous object or situation. This is usually followed by a compensatory charge of adrenaline producing anger, aggression and the drive for violence. We can say that this can occur in 'normal' people in response to some perceived danger, or can be produced by compulsive-obsessive fantasies in neurotics or even more so in psychotics. In all such instances these misrepresentations of the cortex and in particular the neocortex of the forebrain are relayed to the hypothalamus via the thalamus, and influence the reflexes of the cerebellum, the medulla and the pons. Thus the life-promoting interaction between the cortical and the vegetative system can be defeated and turn against themselves. If these misrepresentations are collectively shared they can arouse tribal, national or religious hysterias.

The cerebellum is located at the back of the head underneath the occipital lobe of the central hemisphere. Its function is particularly connected with a control of fine movement, that degree of co-ordination which makes it possible, for instance, to reach out and pick up an object accurately. It can be said that it is connected with the efficiency of skilled movement, and monitors all those tiny muscular movements that are made in purposeful action and ensure that they are adapted to their purpose, not being too wild, too aggressive, too gentle, too far or too near for the purpose. This may be due to inexperience, lack of confidence, insecurity or some kind of inhibition. It can be seen most strikingly in the relationship between people and the way one handles them, how one approaches, holds and touches a person whom one loves or wants to be close to. A person can be too aggressive, too demanding or too gentle and indecisive in the manner in which he touches his friend or lover.

We can say that the medulla needs to receive from the cortex certain messages of commitment for its task for which it provides the necessary reflexes. If, for instance, our attention is directed to a tree which we intend to cut down, the intention may be distracted by considerations concerning whether the tree provides the correct type of wood necessary for some furniture we wish to make, or whether the cost of operation is a good or a bad investment, or whether it would damage the environment. Thus the hierarchy of choices the forebrain has to make may affirm or disturb the automatic reflex actions and blocks their performance. This can be extended to an almost endless variety of contact making. Acute anxiety states or shocks can also, as is well known, produce shaking and hand tremors.

The most ancient and primitive area of the central nervous system is the brain stem which runs up from the spinal cord into the centre of the brain. It begins to thicken as it emerges from the spine into the skull cavity, first into the medulla and then the pons. These primitive areas of the central nervous system operate in the form of reflexes which are not learned, but their functions are controlled by the cortical interpretations, its goals and purposes which it relays to these primitive areas which then enacts them by its reflexes. The neocortex says I want to do something, or have to do something, according to my values or compulsions, and the medulla and pons provide the muscular co-ordination or hormonal stimuli to carry them out. The brain stem as such is mindless, so to speak, and cannot by itself modify its reflexes. It represents an epoch of evolution when reflexes predominate and are incapable of learning. One can give endless examples of how primitive animals will repeat the same behaviour impelled by their instincts, even if its consequences are endangering the animals' survival.

The realisation of the multitude of interactive processes of the brain of higher animals and in particular humans, paves the way to a new appreciation of the significance of a wide range of not only mental but also somatic functions and disturbances. Neurophysiological studies can be supplemented by psychoneurological investigation and raise the prospect for a new integrative science of the mind.

5. Consciousness and Intelligence

That it is the forebrain, the prefrontal lobes of the cortex where consciousness and the higher mental functions are located is borne out by a comparison between other animals and humans; they represent the latest stage in the evolution of animals, and set humans apart from all other species. Even compared to our nearest relative, the chimpanzee, whose DNA differs from ours only by one per cent, the area of the prefrontal cortex is indeed several times greater in our species. It is not surprising that it is these areas of the cortex, that are the most intriguing and at the same time the hardest to understand in terms of exactly what they do and how they do it. Of all the regions of cortex the prefrontal has demonstrated the most spectacular growth: during mammalian evolution it has increased three to one in cats, seventeen to one in chimpanzees and a staggering twenty-nine to one in humans. In comparison with our nearest ancestor, the chimpanzee, our brain is not only very much bigger but, whereas much of its cortex is devoted to specific functions, the human cortex has many areas which are not allocated to definable roles.

We might compare the role of the prefrontal lobes to the ego whose task it is to co-ordinate the vast number of impulses and drives of his instincts and reflexes into a coherent whole, an entity which we can call the self, which, while not entirely dependent upon the stimuli of the world outside, has to interpret the stimuli according to the way we evaluate them. In other words the frontal areas of the cortex are associated with a tremendous number of stimuli from our own, more primitive parts of the brain as well as from the world outside and have to discriminate between those which we allow to enter into consciousness and, in turn, choose the way we act. Indeed, it has been emphasised that it is precisely the absence of any specific task of the frontal area that leaves it open to a wide range of possibilities; it is precisely the sense of uncertainty and the need to guess and to grope for answers which characterises our higher mental faculties. Jean Piaget has emphasised that intelligence is what you use when you don't know what to do. This captures 'the element of novelty, the coping and groping ability needed when there is no *right answer*', as William H. Calvin has put it (*How Brains Think*, Weidenfeld & Nicolson, 1997).

It is a widely held belief that complex behaviour is associated with intelligence. But many complex behaviours in animals are innate and no learning is needed as they are wired in from birth. Such behaviours tend to be inflexible and often difficult to perform at will, just as sneezing and blushing. These stereotype movement patterns exhibit no more insight or understanding of purpose than does a computer program. The most mindless of behaviours are often linked, the completion of one calling forth the next. Courtship behaviour may be followed by intricate nest building, followed by egg laying, then incubation, then the various stereotype parental behaviours. Indeed, the more complex the behaviour is the further it may be from intelligent behaviour, simply because natural selection has evolved a sure-fire way of accomplishing it, with little left to chance. While we often take intelligence to mean both a broad range of abilities and the efficiency with which they are done, it also implies flexibility and creativity – in the words of the ethnologists James and Carol

Gould, 'an ability to slip the bonds of instinct and generate novel solutions to problems'.

Instinctual responses have been shaped by evolution and occur automatically or, as Darwin pointed out, involuntarily. They take place before the brain has had the chance to start thinking about what to do. Thinking takes time, but responding to danger often needs to occur quickly and without much mulling over the decision. (Joseph LeDoux: *The Emotional Brain*). While many animals get through life mostly on automatic pilot, those animals that can readily switch from automatic pilot to wilful control have a tremendous extra advantage. Cognition gives us the ability to make decisions about what kind of action should occur next, given the situation in which we find ourselves now. One of the reasons that cognition is so useful a part of the mental arsenal is that it allows the shift from *reaction* to *action*. The survival advantages that come from being able to make this shift have been an important ingredient that shaped the evolutionary elaboration of cognition in mammals and the explosion of cognition in primates, especially in humans.

We don't really fully understand how the human brain sizes up a situation, comes up with a set of potential courses of action, predicts possible outcomes of different action, assigns priorities to possible action, and chooses a particular action, but these activities are unquestionably among the most sophisticated cognitive functions. They allow the crucial shift from reaction to action. From what we currently know it seems likely that regions like the prefrontal cortex may be involved. The prefrontal cortex is the part of the cerebral cortex that has expanded the most in primates, and it may not even exist in other mammals. When this region is damaged in people, they have great difficulty in planning what to do. So-called frontal lobe patients tend to do the same thing over and over again. They are glued to the present and unable to project themselves into the future.

Reports of mental disturbances due to injuries of specific areas of the brain have filled innumerable books about brain pathology, such as the patient's inability to recognise (musical) melodies, his inability to read or write, the imitation of simple geometrical designs, the failure to recognise familiar faces, to perform very simple mathematical calculations or to recognise places. But when they attempted to answer the question where our intellectual activities can be specified in the brain, the answer seems to be – nowhere: they had to acknowledge that there are certain areas of the cortex and in particular of the prefrontal lobes which do not seem to have any specific function. When any of these areas were electrically stimulated during a brain operation nothing happened. When patients suffered major injuries to the forebrain and it was severely damaged, there were no discernible impairments in their overt behaviour or even intellectual functions. People who in consequence of a severe injury to their heads suffered from a more or less complete destruction of the frontal cortex, could read, write, make mathematical calculations, and continued to carry on their profession with apparently unimpaired ability. When after their operation they returned to their jobs, sometimes as accountants or lawyers, their employers could see no deterioration in their work. All the medical tests failed to discover any obvious impediments in their performance. This apparent lack of any particular specific function of the frontal lobes appeared particularly puzzling and contradicted the fact that from an evolutionary point of view it is the most human of all human characteristics.

While the doctors who investigated these patients' performances could see no specific changes, their families and their close friends soon became aware of changes in their personalities. They noticed that, as they put it: 'He is no longer his old self, he is slower in his movements, he talks less than he used to, he is also indolent insofar as he does not take much interest in his family and his colleagues at work and his old friends.' Events which would have previously upset them and aroused powerful emotions no longer seem to concern them, they show no signs of empathy or responsibility for people who are close to them, nor do they show any interest in politics or social matters which previously would have engaged their interest. They no longer seem to care or be aware of what people think of them. They no longer care about their appearance, they dress carelessly, and occasionally show complete lack of tact, and have outbursts of obscenities and aggressiveness without apparent cause.

6. The Neurons of Morality

It is in the impairment of the mental qualities which we associate with being 'human' or with civilised behaviour caused by the damage of the forebrain that we can begin to understand it; by what it cannot do when it is severely damaged, we find a clue to what it does normally. Persons whose forebrain is severely damaged or destroyed manage to perform the tasks connected with what we call intelligence, their reading ability, their writing, mathematical calculations and the exercise of skills of their professions. In other words, they are able to pursue the activities and skills they have learned in the past, and continue their professional activities which to the astonishment of the neurologists appear to be unimpeded. But the point is that their performance is entirely based upon previously acquired skills which continue to operate as reflexes to previous conditioning. But while acquired abilities were hardly diminished, they were unable to show empathy with their families and friends and lacked a sense of responsibility for them, they were baffled when confronted with new and unfamiliar tasks, they were unable to respond to new situations and intellectual challenges. They not only became indifferent to those near to them, or indeed to what was happening in society, but lacked intellectual curiosity and interest in anything they did not already know. They lived in the present only, and their intellectual functions were performed in a robotic kind of manner. It became clear that they were unable to take initiatives or confront new situations and they showed a lack of ability to experiment in new ways of solving problems; their capacity of foresight, planning and of making choices in new and unfamiliar conditions is either severely reduced or non-existent. They lack self-criticism, moral considerations and empathy with others.

We can therefore recognise that the prefrontal lobes of our cortex provide the physiological foundation for what we consider to be the 'human mind'. Neurologists have for long recognised that the frontal areas of the cortex are far more highly developed and much larger than that of all other animals and represent a relatively new acquisition, but we can now identify the so-called spiritual dimension of mankind which gives it its special characteristics, namely the capacity of the intellect to discriminate between different situations and conditions, to make choices, to uphold certain values and purposes, both in the short run as well as the long run, to anticipate in our minds possible or probable situations and the effect of our actions upon them: what we ought to do and what is right to do, and to discriminate between good and evil; in other words, to uphold moral principles to guide our behaviour and our judgements.

In his book, *The Feeling of What Happens*, Antonio Damasio describes his researches into the functions of the prefrontal lobes, which he calls the moral centre of the brain. He gives detailed reports of many cases where patients have suffered major damage to the front of the brain through tumours or accidents which rendered them incapable of social relationships, concern for others or any sense of responsibility. They cannot learn from mistakes and appear utterly unaware that their behaviour is antisocial and irrational. But Damasio and his team of researchers are careful not to conclude that every person guilty of antisocial or immoral behaviour suffers from brain damage, and they ask what it is about people whose frontal areas of the brain are not damaged but nevertheless suffer from a malfunction of their prefrontal cortex. How then do we explain the absence of moral feelings in people who engage in criminal, destructive activities, violence and murder without any emotional awareness of the danger and the suffering they cause, without having suffered physical damage to their brains.

We may find a clue to this question if we consider psychological traumas, particularly during the early stages of a person's development; there is in every normal or healthy brain an area which registers and stores the responses of parents and the early environment which influence and stimulate the moral neurons, either by their show of love and concern or indifference and rejection.

It is no exaggeration to say that our need to be loved and cared for, and in turn to love and care for others, is represented to the mind as a concept of morality. We might say that these needs are externalised and perceived by the mind as moral principles. Not being programmed by genetic inheritance they have to be learned, so to speak, in the early stages of our life and stored in our memory, to act as a model by which we select and judge the world around us as well as our reflexes and impulses. Thus the neurological processes of our brain and in particular the activity of the frontal lobes are determined not only by physiological but also by psychological processes.

It is well known that neurons and synapses become inactive or even decay if they are not stimulated – fired for a lengthy period – and they become redundant, so to speak. We may call this the learning process which relates not only to cognition but above all to the emotions. Under stressful conditions which produce tension and fear the higher functions of the brain become short-circuited by reflex and instinctual responses which come to dominate the mind and our behaviour. I shall refer to these problems of a person's psychological evolution in a later chapter.

We have seen that the innumerable impulses from many areas of the brain send their messages to the frontal areas of the cortex, which in turn interprets or modifies them, both internally, i.e. inside the body, as well as towards the environment, and selects those which may enter consciousness and those which have to be repressed. Thus Descartes' dictum: 'I think therefore I am', has new validity. It also validates Sartre's paradoxical statement that: 'We are condemned to be free and obliged to make choices.'

The most human of all human characteristics is made possible precisely because its new brain area appears 'empty' and therefore can respond to many possible ways of thinking and acting. It is open to all kinds of aims and purposes, and its 'emptiness' provides it with an elasticity which is not confined to instinctual reactions and specialised tasks, but provides our species with the potential for a variety of responses, new adjustments and forms of behaviour.

But there's the rub: the freedom granted by nature through millions of years of evolution gives us the freedom to go mad, both individually as well as collectively. It enabled us to have moral concepts and convictions, but what is considered moral can apply to universal ideas of compassionate empathy, can also be used to justify tribal or religious obsessions: from the conception of metaphysical systems to the building of concentration camps, from the ideals of compassion and empathy with our fellow humans to the utmost indifference and cruelty. The miraculous gifts given to us by nature can be turned into their opposite: reason all too frequently is transformed into unreason, freedom into the denial of freedom; and the capacity to plan ahead can serve destructive and self-destructive goals. We can no longer speak of a *causa prima*, of a God who in his wisdom created the world and made it the way it is, including humanity with its rational capabilities but also its savagery, and we can no longer answer this question by genetic determination. One has to face the astonishing fact that human beings can immobilise their forebrain without any physical injury: they can be clever like those with severe damage to their brain, they can read, write, do mathematical calculations, use computers and deal with stocks and shares, and give their children computer games which glorify aggressiveness and find apparently rational justifications for all kinds of atrocities. We can frequently notice that very clever people who can make brilliant mathematical calculations for nuclear or biological weaponry and make them available for dictatorships, for instance, lack any moral feelings by which to evaluate their actions and are indeed very stupid. We have to confront the fateful paradox that humans can immobilise their capacities of long-term foresight as to the consequences of their action or empathy with their fellow humans, and act with unspeakable savagery, as shown throughout history, including our own times. But if we fail to analyse this paradox we neglect the task imposed upon us by our extraordinary brain. How then, we must ask, has this fateful quality of our brain, this miracle of our mind originated.

There is much work to be done to investigate how psychopaths, criminals and ruthlessly aggressive dictatorships without a sense of responsibility for the damage they cause can neutralise or inhibit the function of the moral neurons.

It is the task of the neocortex to analyse the multitude of impulses it receives from the older areas of the brain, to discriminate between them and choose those which serve its quest for survival and well-being, so we have to analyse why men choose to follow irrational and manifestly harmful pursuits. These are questions for psychoanalysis and anthropology.

Chapter 4

The Origins of Consciousness and Morality

1. A Psychoanalytic Anthropology

In the last chapter we have observed the evidence for the neurological foundations of consciousness with its capacity to 'slip the bond of instinct to generate novel solutions to problems.' But in the evolutionary view we must ask how and why this extraordinary capacity of our forebrain, which has given our species an enormous advantage over all other animals, has developed. The first thing we have to bear in mind, as Hoimar von Ditfurth has pointed out, is that the roots of consciousness must be older than our neo-cortex, that it is the instrument for thinking and not its cause (Hoimar von Ditfurth: *Der Geist fiel nicht vom Himmel*, Dtv, 1991). It stems from the need to reflect and think and to anticipate in imagination what would happen if we do this or that. If one makes the mind and the psyche of man contingent upon the anatomy of his central nervous system, one runs the danger of confusing cause with effect. The brain has not invented thinking, but rather it is the other way round, in the same way as the legs have not invented walking, nor the eyes invented light and shapes and colour. The origin of legs during the course of evolution stems from the need for fast movement on the savanna, the development of eyes was a reaction to the possibility of seeing the light of the sun for the purpose of orientation and discrimination.

If we approach the psychic life of our species from an evolutionary point of view, and follow the processes which have taken place over some twenty to thirty million years, we can recognise that it is the product of its history and may be able to trace the actual events which made man the pinnacle of evolution.

The dominant role which the frontal lobes of man's brain has acquired stems from the need to think, to anticipate the outcome of his actions, to foresee and to predict, to plan and to evaluate before he commits himself to any particular action. It is the nature of his intellect to question what he already knows, to experiment in his mind with new possibilities, and to modify his perceptions as to the nature of things and his concept of reality. In the multitude of possibilities he has also to create a sense of moral judgement which concerns not only the correct way of understanding the world around him but also what is the right and what is the wrong attitude to nature and to his fellow men, and how he should behave towards them. He has to acquire a measure of certainty about the right way of interpreting the enormous number of messages which enter his mind, and to select between those which promote his interests and needs and those which will be detrimental or even self-destructive. Lacking a guide upon which he can focus his mind he would be lost in a chaos of drives and impulses, of reflexes and instincts, which would leave him in a state of confusion and disorientation – he would be unable to act in a coherent manner. He would not know what to do, and would be overwhelmed by a state of paralysis and even with a loss of his will to live, or he would be dominated by a rage – which stems from a feeling of helplessness – and react to the world around him with a sadistic-destructive or self-destructive manner.

As I said, we can observe this in individuals as well as in cultures. We might call this a state of existential anxiety, when confronted with changed conditions for which habit or tradition or heredity no longer provide an answer. These can be considered times of crisis for a species. In such situations a species is faced with the alternative between being able to adapt to new conditions, which entails a reconstruction of its judgements and responses, or to being defeated in the battle for survival. Our hominid ancestors had to have a sufficiently large area of the brain which could transform their instinctual reflexes and habits, in order to cope with the new conditions for which the instincts had not prepared them.

2. Tool-making and Intelligence

It is always said that man is a tool-maker or that he is a moral being which sets him apart from other species. Besides being a tool-maker and moral being, he is also distinguished by his acquisition of language and intelligence. These human abilities are referred to genetic causes, including his DNA. But nobody seems to ask how and for what purpose these abilities emerged and why his genes and his DNA developed in the way they did. There are an almost endless number of studies concerning the transformation of ape-like hominids to Homo sapiens by means of anatomical, physiological as well as neurological observations, and we know a great deal about how these transformations occurred but do not ask why they occurred. If we uphold the evolutionary view, we ask why the different stages of development with their often radical transformations have taken place. We can reasonably say that they were responses to crises in the life of a species due to radical and dramatic changes in the environment which threatened the species with extinction. It had to acquire new physiological and mental capabilities in order to survive.

The old Darwinian concept of the drive for survival and survival of the fittest can serve as an explanation but not as chance events. Chance plays a role in life, but often it is a concept by which we explain something, the cause of which we do not understand. Even Einstein could not reconcile himself with the statistical chance theories of quantum mechanics, and with an intuition of genius declared that: 'While God may be crafty, he is not a dice player.' He could not dispense with the causality principle, and spent many years attempting to find a general field theory which would explain the causal interactions of the phenomena he discovered.

The idea that things are the way they are reminds one of the Judaeo-Christian cosmology where the phenomena of nature are seen as a kind of museum exhibiting God's creations. The evolutionary view considers life as we know it as a stage in the continuing process of transformation and what we perceive as reality now is but one of its temporary stages. It is of course difficult enough to find a consensus among archaeologists in the various descriptions of the time-scale and the characteristics of the fossils they have unearthed, and their interpretation as to which species or race they can be identified with. There is an often acrimonious debate whether our ancestors like Ramapithecus, Zinjanthropus, Australopithecus and Paranthropus belong to the species Homo, and whether the stone tools associated with them and found in great profusion in Olduwayan sites were the product of natural processes or of early man's labours.

These questions are of considerable importance because they concern the decisive characteristics which differentiate man as the gatherer of natural objects which he uses as tools, and whether he had developed the intelligence and the techniques of making tools according to the purpose for which they were meant to be used and had developed a standard technique and pattern in the making of implements. This needed not only the evolution of hands capable of grasping objects and of supporting him on the branches of trees, but a pronounced upright gait which made his hands free to manipulate objects.

3. Tool-making and the Origins of Culture

If we attempt to formulate a basic principle upon which the making of tools can be based then it is the principle of externalisation. It is a fundamental characteristic of man that he externalises his mental processes by reproducing them outside himself in material symbols and cultural ideas. This process of externalisation of man's psychological-mental activities is fundamental to all human cultures and commenced with the emergence of the human being as a species about one million years ago. It is a characteristic of man that he is a culture creator, and there are no human beings without a culture.

While Hegel and Marx spoke of externalisation (*Veräußerlichung*) as an aspect of alienation, I use the term to describe a fundamental human capability for work and to create his own environment, thus transforming biological evolution into cultural evolution; the mind takes over from biology as the agent of evolution.

Due to the enormous expansion of the prefrontal areas and of the visual area of the cortex, man can have an image of an experience even if it does not actually happen; he can see himself doing something even if he is not actually doing it. He can experience sensations and impulses in his mouth, in his teeth, hands and fingers, for instance, and enact those impulses in his imagination. He can visualise and conceptualise possible or potential activities and anticipate future situations, and deal with them in his imagination. (The future exists in the present as an imaginary condition, and, in turn, the present is influenced by the images of the future.) Thus he can engage in a great number of different activities in his mind, compare their usefulness, and choose the best one before he commits himself to action. The enormous value of this capability from the point of view of natural selection and adjustment to the environment is quite obvious. It has indeed allowed humans to make adjustments and modifications to their behaviour in a few minutes or even seconds, which would take other animals subject to instinctual responses many thousands of years of natural selection.

However, man can not only initiate his own natural selection by doing experiments in his mind, he can also experience his own impulses and motor sensations in objects, that is to say, he can project his peripheral and motor sensations upon external objects. As he wishes his teeth and his fingernails, for instance, which are so important for attacking, biting, as well as cutting, piercing and scratching, to be firm and powerful, he can identify certain stones as potential teeth and fingernails, visualise them as teeth and claws and see them doing their work even more powerfully and efficiently than his own. Thus certain stones will acquire the vitality of his own organs: he can externalise his sensations upon such objects and make them into tools or weapons. He will thus invest external objects with the emotional experiences of his own motor organs, he will recognise a stone as a potential claw or fist. In the stone there is hidden, as Plato would have said, the idea of the tool, the essence of the tool which the worker or sculptor has to bring out of the stone.

The ability to 'recognise' a human motor organ in a stone or a stick, moreover, implies the ability to project his sensations and impulses upon external objects. In the making of the tool man reproduces parts of his own body and enhances its powers. A spear represents flight; it represents an arm that follows its own impulses and becomes free from the limitations of the body; the spearhead represents the claw that tears at objects, the tooth that penetrates; spear and spearhead represent the satisfaction of the movement of flight and the power to penetrate the flesh of the quarry or of an enemy.

However, humans not only project their own feelings of new-found power and strength upon the weapons and tools they have made, giving them a kind of soul, but they will also introject their powers and identify with them. The better and more powerful his weaponry the more powerful and secure he will feel in his encounter with the world, as can be seen in the pride individuals, tribes and nations acquire in the weapons which they possess. We can witness this in the relentless drive to improve weapons and tools into weaponry and machines of a more and more sophisticated and complex type, and in the sense of status which they provide for nations as well as individuals.

However, these processes of projection and externalisation are not confined to the motor organs, but equally apply to the emotions and psychological processes; men can recognise their own feelings in a wide range of natural objects, in living and inanimate things.

Here I want to say a few words about symbolisation and symbols. A symbol represents both concepts as well as urges and feelings made recognisable in the form of visual images. Every emotion and every idea subjectively experienced finds its visual representation in a symbol. Man will make efforts to reproduce these symbolic images by means of drawing, painting, sculpting and building, and he will also seek to find representation of his symbolic images in external objects of nature: trees, flowers, the sky, the sun, the sea, clouds, meadows and clearings in forests symbolise states of mind which we project onto them. A tree can be seen as a powerful and proud being symbolising the confident strength of the male or the embracing and protective mother, a flower can present the delicate maiden showing her erotic sensations to the world; delighting in its delight and celebrating by its colours the excitement of yearning and desire, it can be brazen or blushing with shyness, and vulnerable and delicate by its openness, liable to be threatened by the violence of passion and insensitive possessiveness of men – as in the poems of Heinrich Heine.

A whole host of fantasies and, indeed, unconscious complexes and fears are projected upon the objects of nature. To the scientifically-orientated beholder a tree will be perceived as a phenomenon of nature, not possessed of a mind and of fantasies but composed of wood, roots and leaves, having nothing to do at all with such projected fantasies. If he happens to be a merchant he will see a tree as a source of revenue which can be statistically or economically evaluated, or, if he is a friend of the earth, as an essential provider of oxygen for living organisms, and as such to be protected from commercial exploiters. While such people consider themselves to be entirely empirical, it would be difficult to deny that they do project their own particular conceptual and emotional attitudes upon the tree. Even the strict empiricist cannot entirely obliterate the symbolic meanings of natural phenomena which will re-emerge in his dreams or preconscious fantasies.

Indeed, we can say that the animistic world-view, with its spirits and souls, fairies and monsters, no longer appears in the conscious mind of man. Even though it had been ousted by religious and scientific cultures, it continues to lead an underground existence, occasionally re-awakened by artists, poets and mystics.

Thus man is an organism which can externalise itself. He can be inside himself and outside himself (what Hegel has called the objectivity of the spirit or the God who can have a view of man, are manifestations of self-externalisation.) Man can feel himself in the things he creates, and he can, on the other hand, be alienated from the things he has created and become a stranger to them, as for instance in the strictly scientific mind-set or in the philosophy of the market economy. Externalisation thus is the basis for tool-making, and work, animism, totemism, God-worship and ideologies, or whatever name they are given.

4. The Evolution of Hominids to Humans

Self-externalisation is possibly one of the most extraordinary capacities of human beings, and one that definitely differentiates them from all other animals. It would be intriguing to ask how and when this capacity in the ape who became man, emerged and developed. Insofar as externalisation is basic to the tool-making ability of man, we can trace it back to the Middle Lower Pleistocene, to Homo pithecanthropus erectus and Homo pekinensis. These two races, who belonged to the same species, are reckoned to have lived in Java and China between one million years and seven hundred thousand years ago. They are widely considered to be the first known members of the species 'Homo' and were definitely tool-makers. Also, the volume of their skulls was far superior to that of any known previous species, ranging from 750 cc. in the earliest known pithecanthropus to 1,150 cc. in the later Homo pekinensis. Insofar as I link the tool-making capacity to the process of externalisation, I would say that these early men developed externalisation processes and, in so doing, laid the foundation for the further mental and physical development of the human species.

It can be said that humans are forest creatures to the extent that their basic structures, brains, sense-organs, limbs and reproductive systems evolved in the forest. Later developments, namely life in the open country, called for modifications and elaborations of these structures rather than totally new ones. Thus the arboreal existence of the ape ancestors of man was a necessary pre-adaptation for the emergence of human characteristics. It was the achievement of the human species to transform its basic primate characteristics when such transformation became necessary.

In the evolution from primate to man we can observe a number of stages: the transformation of the environment from huge unbroken forests into fertile open land – the savanna – and gradually over the millennia the erosion of the savanna and the need for man to hunt, not merely occasional small animals but large animals, to become a big-game hunter in order to survive.

It has been estimated that the broad subtropical forests, which extended from the West Coast of Africa to the West Indies, from South Africa to Scandinavia and from the southern tip of Australia to Siberia, began to be invaded by the savanna some twenty-five million years ago. Grass spread amongst the trees, and dry plains emerged as wide as oceans. It was the beginning of geological upheavals which started during the Miocene period of the Tertiary and culminated in the cataclysmic transformations of the ice ages during the Pleistocene. The primates and apes of the forest spent much of their time in the shade leading enclosed lives inside 'green caves' of leaves and branches. The vegetation of the forest provided both shelter, protection and sustenance, just as it continues to do so for the chimpanzees, orang-outangs and gorillas of our world. They scampered along tunnel-like trails through the underbrush, leapt and swung high in the canopies of tall trees and generally avoided the bright uneasy places where savanna grasses began to encroach upon the edges of the wood. But while our gorillas are being threatened by the still-encroaching plain, which is artificially produced by modern man in his relentless quest for agricultural produce, and cannot leave his ancient habitation, some twelve million years ago a new type of primate appeared along the irregular borders of forest and savanna. This new primate ventured out into the open spaces which was rich in grass and tender shoots, perhaps chasing and catching small animals. He probably took greater and greater chances as food supplies near to the trees became exhausted, and went further into the savanna. 'Evolution often works most intensively at the edge of things, where the two environments intersect, when something very different lies close at hand and the lure of novelty is strongest' (John E. Pfeiffer: *The Emergence of Man*, Thomas Nelson, 1970).

These creatures were primitive pre-man, pre-human apes who were certainly much smaller than the gorilla. The fact that these forest dwellers took up life on the ground indicates that they were less fully committed to life in trees than chimpanzees, for instance. They did not have, or had lost, the special limb and shoulder structures which permitted highly advanced branch-to-branch swinging. Remains of such a pre-human ape were found in India and dated about twelve million years ago. He was given the name Ramapithecus. Not many Ramapithecus specimens have been recovered so far, less than a dozen in all, but that is enough to serve as a basis for speculation about early man's evolution.

While fairly sudden ecological changes occurred during the Pleistocene and gave rise to the extreme climatic changes of the ice ages which forced the primates to face an extremely inhospitable and dangerous environment, we now know that transformations of a less catastrophic kind occurred much earlier. These transformations were of a milder and more gradual nature, the erosion of the forest was much more limited and the plain land, the open savanna, was not a frozen tundra devoid of vegetation, but open grassland, rich in shrubbery, providing plentiful nourishment to a vegetarian species ready to adapt to life in the open. However, wherever possible these earliest ancestors of man returned to the wood to sleep in the shelter of the trees. When the trees were no longer available, they chose places where predators could not follow easily, perhaps spending the nights on ledges of cliffs facing the cliff wall as some baboons do in our time. During the day they ventured into the open grassland or semiarid regions, exploiting every available ounce of food. They increasingly used digging sticks and pointed rocks to get at water-containing tubers and berried food. The rocks and digging sticks could also have served as weapons to ward off carnivores which came their way.

An apparent contradiction arises when we consider the size of their teeth, especially the canine teeth, which provide a significant clue as to how they lived. Most primate species have large canines and put them to good use. The baboon, for instance, another primate whose ancestors turned from tree-dwelling to life on the ground, will face an opponent by opening his mouth wide and flashing a set of huge and sharp canines. This elaborate show of his weapons is a symbol of warning and enables him to avoid any further trouble, and usually his opponents get out of the way. When threats and warnings fail, however, these teeth may go into action. They are a baboon's most formidable weapon and, in the last analysis, his social order in the troop depends on how well he can fight, and his canines symbolise his prowess.

But it is known that Ramapithecus was not equipped with such large canines; they were comparatively small and had shallow, small roots. Indeed, he was the first pre-human known to us who did not possess natural weapons. Since the survival of a species depends on vigorous offensive and defensive capability, there must have been some reason for this significant development.

L. E. Simmons observed: 'These hominids were not feeding and fighting in the way apes feed and fight; they certainly would not have used their teeth as effectively as apes in shredding up plants and in aggressive displays against predators. Indeed, it seems likely that their hands played a major role in food-getting and defence. Furthermore, the extensive use of the hands implies that they walked upright' (L. E. Simmons: *The Early Relatives of Man*, 'Scientific American', July 1964).

The advancement of the use of tools was no doubt enhanced by the hominid ape's ability to stand erect and to walk on two feet for a few minutes or even longer. Bipedalism increased the freedom of the hands and provided more time for acquiring new manipulative skills. It also resulted in a more continuous and panoramic view of the savanna, an increased ability to see things as they occurred and to detect and anticipate dangers. One can also speculate that the erect posture helped to discourage the most dangerous predators – the big cats. George Schaller, who has observed tigers in India and lions in Tanzania, comments on this possibility: 'Big cats hunt by lying in wait or approaching stealthily and bounding on the victim's back, and they bite at the neck. Man, being bipedal, does not furnish a good target, a horizontal plain for the cats to jump on. Perhaps that is one thing that deters them today and deterred them in the past.'

There is no doubt therefore that the ability to walk erect at least for some distance was a decisive advantage for an ape forced to live in the plain. It freed the forelimbs from the necessity of propulsion and opened up new areas of skill for the hands, for the handling and manipulating of objects and the increased use of objects for the purposes of self-display, for food-getting and for attacking animals. However, Ramapithecus, the pre-human of twelve million years ago, was still essentially a vegetarian like his cousin the ape. He gained a large proportion of his sustenance from the fruits and grains and grasses of the savanna, and only occasionally had to kill animals. The animals he killed were small prey, and he took good care to avoid the larger animals. Also, he would probably have tried to keep close enough to the forests to spend an occasional night in them, and he could still regard the forest as a refuge from the rigours of the plains. In other words he would not, at that time, be exposed to the ultimate loss of forest shelter or edible vegetation. But Ramapithecus laid the foundations which made the emergence of Homo erectus possible, for the emergence of a species which could meet the challenge of an ecological catastrophe and become human.

The Australopithecines, with their relatively small front teeth and fairly erect posture, developed a high capacity to manipulate objects with their hands. Their hands had a far greater range of movement than that of our ape ancestors, and this means a far greater range and facility for experimentation than is possible for the apes, whose lips and teeth are more highly skilled in the manipulation of objects. With the addition of a pair of stereoscopic eyes watching and taking note of what the hands are doing, and the discovery and invention of new skills, thus developing manual behaviour patterns in the cerebral cortex, we can see that a much faster increase in the size of the brain was now possible. The increase in the cortical areas, which we can observe in Pithecanthropus, means a large increase in memory and above all in internal imagery of possible actions and situations, an enormously enhanced capacity of internal perception and presentation.

The first man, probably Pithecanthropus, could imagine events, and would react emotionally to these internal presentations more or less as much as he would to external stimuli. (In our own time, our mental interpretations of the world around us, our images and fantasies, have a powerful impact upon our psychological as well as our bodily functions: bad thoughts can make us ill, as they say.) He could have wish-fulfilment fantasies, he could imagine dangerous animals being hunted by him in all sorts of possible ways, he could master emotional pressure such as fear and hunger by enacting in his fantasies the conquest of the prey or threatening beast. And under the pressure of hunger and anxiety, he would imagine himself with powerful weapons, and he would associate these images with stones and other objects around him and shape them accordingly. He would therefore transfer his image outside himself and make it real by means of work.

5. Totems, Ghosts and Spirits

But the externalisation of urges and their symbolic images through work is only one of the many aspects of externalisation. Once the externalisation of the emotions of aggression and defence had been achieved by means of tools and weapons, the gates were open for the externalisation of a variety of fantasies and emotions. These psychic experiences could be seen to exist in the world outside; 'exists' = 'is outside'. Emotions of love and hate, security and anxiety, destruction and restitution, guilt and sacrifice, would find symbolic presentation in fantasy images, and these symbolic images would be thought to exist outside man – out there in the world. The drama of his conflicting emotions, presented in symbolic imagery, would be experienced as if they took place in the world outside, the battle of emotions would appear to be enacted by the spirits, ghosts and monsters. Man would no longer be alone. He would not face the unknown universe by himself; the ghosts and spirits would both protect him and threaten him, fighting his battles and teaching him how to act. He would recognise himself in the spirits which he projected into the world, and would acquire a sense of identity and security in relating to them.

Once man had learned tool making and created language, the spirits could be represented in signs and symbols, in drawings and sculptures, as well as verbally; a new world of meaning and drama would emerge, and culture as we know it would be born. Culture signifies the capacity to populate the world with ghosts, spirits, divinities and myths, to communicate them to members of a community and relate to them collectively through common worship and ritual. By means of cultural symbols members of a community share their emotional experiences and find communion with each other.

Ghosts and spirits also represent people whom we have known and of whom we think. Just as our parents appear to us as living people in our dreams after they have died, primitive people ascribe a continued existence to the apparitions of their dreams and fantasies. They would imagine the deceased to exist in another realm and find ways of communicating with them by means of sacred evocations, signs and incantations. So ghost worship would begin, facilitated by words and names, by appropriate signs and graphic symbols. Eventually, the name pronounced would be an invocation of the ghost, a ritual, a magic act. In fact, the ghost would be in the word which pronounced his name ('In the beginning was the word, and the word was with God, and the word was God', *The Gospel according to John*).

Primitive man would have learned to appreciate the importance of his mind. His mind would become highly libidinised and would be the most important organ in his battle for survival. He may have realised that the ghost resides both in his mind as well as in the world outside, and in order to communicate with or possess the ghost of an ancestor, he would eat his brain. We 'devour the brains of our teachers'; we 'pick their brains' and 'digest' them. But what we as Homo sapiens express symbolically, early man enacted. He made a hole in the skull of his ancestor, took out the brain and ceremonially devoured it. By doing so, he absorbed the strength and skills of his ancestral ghosts and reassured himself of their assistance and love. He introjected the loved ancestor.

The first remains showing signs of culture and ritual were discovered in the caves of Choukoutien, the habitation of Homo pekinensis. Great numbers of the skulls of Homo pekinensis were found there with holes made in exactly the same place. Many skulls were laid out in circular patterns, and there is little doubt that these holes enabled them to remove the brains from the skulls and devour the ghost who dwelled in it. This was probably a communal feast, a primitive version of the Christian Mass, a partaking of the Host and the Wine, i.e. the symbolic eating of the body and the drinking of the blood of Christ. It represents the same mechanism which operated in the totem feast, namely identification of the members of a culture with the totem by ceremoniously eating its body and thereby absorbing its powers, its skills and its wisdom.

Thus early man regained the security which he had lost when he had to step beyond his instinctive orientations and entered into a world dominated by mental images and symbols and produced his own organs for survival. His mind replaced natural selection, his imagination and his skill replaced, or rather supplanted, his instincts as the agents of his evolution. Having lost the security of his instincts, he entered into a universe dominated and directed by his mind, the world of images, symbols and artifices of his own making.

6. Big Game Hunters and Homemakers

With the development of cortical activity and the general increase in brain size, the process of maturation becomes delayed. Humans remain infants and depend on their parents, particularly the mother, for increasingly long periods in proportion to the complexity of their brain structure and the need for learning to co-ordinate reflexes and to acquire the skills accumulated by their culture. With the prolonged helplessness of the infant and its need to be protected by the mother, the home base has to become more permanent and protective and provide more secure shelter from predators. An added and very important incentive for this would be the increasingly cold climate which emerged during the Pleistocene. Not only mothers and children, but also the grown Homo erectus needed shelter from the climate and had to be able to return to it from his hunting expeditions.

Early hominids, like their fellow primates, lived mainly exposed to the elements. Sometimes on cold or stormy nights they may have been driven to seek cover under overhanging cliffs where they huddled together in a world still dominated by other animals. But if they huddled under rock shelter or even entered caves for short periods, then it was to avoid momentary inconvenience of weather, knowing that it would not last long and that they would return to their normal habitation in the open plains. But Middle Pleistocene man had no such expectation of an imminent improvement of the weather – it remained freezing cold for generation after generation, and the shelter of a cave became a necessity.

More than any other element of nature, it was fire which provided early man with warmth and with a sense of security from dangerous predators. He brought fire to the places where he established his home bases, he created zones of warmth and light in his caves and achieved a way of keeping the harsh elements, the night and the prowlers at bay. Man's ancestors first put fire to work on a regular basis to keep themselves warm in the Arctic and subarctic zones of Europe and Asia. No hearths have yet been found in Africa.

Among the earliest known fireplaces are those discovered in the Escale caves in France dating to some 750,000 years ago, being largely contemporary with the fire-bearing hearths found in the caves of Peking man.

The caves were originally occupied by powerful and long-established carnivores like bears and hyenas, wolves and probably tigers, and these animals had to be chased from the caves before man could come to occupy them; and he had to make sure of keeping them out by having a fire burning near the entrance. Apart from providing warmth and defence against large predators and the security of a permanent home, fire also provided light. It increased the length of the day; the hours of the dark became hours of leisure in which man could plan more and more complex activities. The fireside became an institution, a cohesive force bringing members of the band closely together, old and young. Individuals too old to hunt became important because they remembered things beyond the memory of the others, they increased the memory store of the group by telling of things long past; the old man could relate to them old adventures and skills, and he provided a sense of continuum between past and present. His stories would become the core of mythology, a system of sentiments which gave a deeper dimension to the psychological cohesion of the group. He reinforced the imagination by which the concrete experiences of daily life were integrated with things of the spirit. He became the link, between men and their ancestors, and he made their life and their experiences real to the present generation. And when the old man died, they ceremoniously consumed his brain and assured themselves that his store of memories would live on and his myths would be perpetuated.

The internal mental life which prevents the past from disappearing and preserves it in the present thus became enormously enhanced, and so did the mental representation of a wide range of feelings. Fire, for instance, became not only a natural object but the symbol of security and salvation in times of freezing despair. Men imagined it in their minds as the symbol of warmth and light, transforming the cave into a welcoming shelter one could return to after the hunt. It represented the image of a home, the mother's protection, the woman's embrace and her welcome.

With the increased differentiation between the sexes, the woman, staying for longer periods in the cave as the period of dependency and helplessness increased among the offspring, became more and more associated with home, with the image of protectress and with love.

But here we come across the problem of the dominant male. When we speak of the psychological element in sexual relationships, of the male desiring the female and vice versa, making a powerful bond between them, we introduce the elements of possessiveness and jealousy. This does not mean that the powerful male who feels himself responsible for the protection of the troop could only establish one-to-one relationships with a female; he would be attracted to a number of women in the tribe and, being their protector, would consider himself their possessor. He would be jealous of other males, and the young males would threaten his harem and challenge his power. We can observe harem groups or one-male breeding groups among gibbons of the plains, and many students of early man have referred to them as showing many similarities to early human societies.

According to the anthropologist Clifford Jolly, there is an important resemblance between Gelada baboons who live on the plains and humans, namely the common characteristic of a one-male breeding unit. The Gelada baboon's social structure is described by J. H. Crook as follows: 'The "one-male group" is the reproductive unit of a Gelada population. It consists of a large adult male, a group of females including both mothers and non-maternal animals in all stages of the oestrus cycle, variable numbers of juvenile animals, infants and babies, and an occasional sub-adult male often almost totally grown but not sexually mature. In areas where the population is widely dispersed, such social units are the commonest observed, associating inconstantly with small groups consisting wholly of large sub-adult males and mature males not possessing "harems". These "all-male" groups likewise move independently from other units and show considerable cohesion over several weeks' (J. H. Crook, *Gelada Baboon Herd Structure and Movement*, Symposium Zoological Society London, 18, pp. 237–258, 1966).

Such a social structure is precisely that which Freud termed 'the primal horde' and which he considered to be the original condition of human society. We have here the same despotic adult male who monopolises a group of females to the exclusion of the younger but sexually mature males; these are chased out of the family circle and form a group of brothers (the all-male group), who form a close association of predators or hunters, while the adult, dominant male stays at home guarding his women.

In the baboon society, as well as in the society of the primal horde as envisaged by Freud, we find a dual structure in the social organisation, namely the one-male breeding unit of the dominant male exercising his despotic powers, guarding his females and keeping the young males, his sons, out of his 'bedroom', his empire, and making it necessary for them to roam outside forming close associations of co-operative hunting and foraging units. This dual structure would lay the foundations for the father-murder by the band of brothers when their sexual needs for women became irresistible and the elimination of the tyrant the only means of gaining access to them.

7. The Primal Community

The harem society of the Gelada baboons shows psychological traits among its members which are in many ways comparable to those manifested among human beings dominated by the Oedipus complex. It shows a remarkable degree of mistrust and anxiety, with considerable aggressiveness erupting frequently in fights and much jealous irritability. The dominant male repeatedly has to assert his authority in an aggressive manner, is often engaged in fights with younger males and, although no one has yet reported an act of father murder, he does have to relinquish his dominant role when he grows old and is unable to match the aggression of the younger males. Ritualised rivalry among the young determines the emergence of the new leader. While there is little doubt that modern man shares many emotional characteristics with the baboon, even though they are largely repressed from civilised consciousness, this does not necessarily mean that man's human ancestors of the Pleistocene lived in societies similar to those of baboons and governed by the Oedipus complex. Indeed, there were many reasons why this type of group structure would have been most unlikely.

The exclusion of the young males from the father-dominated group, involving their expulsion from the protective security of the cave and hearth around which life revolved, would have been impossible, for they would not have survived the rigours of climate and the danger presented by powerful carnivorous predators. Hostility of the dominant male and a rejective attitude of the females would have transformed the cave from being a symbol of libidinous pleasure and warmth into a symbol of rejection and anxiety. If the young male were deprived of the assurance of a warm and affectionate welcome home from his sojourns in the hostile world outside, he would have perished from cold and anxiety. It would have been essential for him to carry in his mind a sense of belonging to his community, a feeling of cohesion and mutual affection to sustain him in his activities of big-game hunter during the ice ages.

Furthermore, the role of the dominant male as the leader of the hunt would have made it necessary for him to participate in the hunting expeditions and to act as teacher and inspirer to the younger members of the troop. He would be a member of the all-male group of hunters, form a close emotional tie with them as their leader, and encourage them to establish a sense of identification with him. He would therefore have had to avoid the conflict between the all-male group and the one-male group; the sons would have to identify with the dominant male without suffering anxieties about his enmity and jealousy and without fear of rejection by the females in the troop. This means that, not unlike the gorilla troop of our time, the dominant male would have taken a very tolerant attitude towards the sexual needs of the young males, and allowed them to share in the erotic attractions exercised by the females, thus reinforcing the warmth and unity of the home and of the group.

There is another important factor which would considerably reduced the motivations for an Oedipus complex, and that is the short period of sexual delay and relative absence of a latency period in primitive man. The gap in modern man between the first puberty at the age of five or six years and the second puberty at thirteen or fourteen is largely due to a delay in cultural maturation. Psychoanalytic investigations have shown the latency period to be a period of sexual repression during which the young male has to acquire the skills and knowledge of his culture before he can fend for himself and be accepted as a mature member of the male community and ready to procreate and be responsible for a family. He has to wait eight years or so during which he has to recapitulate by training and learning the cultural attainments of his race. Those eight years represent a condensed acquisition of the hundreds of thousands of years during which man learned to read, write, think in numbers, acquire the skills of work, know about the properties and behaviour of material objects, about the history of his people and the geography of his environment, and master the rituals and ceremonies of his culture.

During this period, the boy has to submit to and identify with the males, the teachers, in order to learn from them, to become one of them and be accepted by them. In this purpose of identification with the males, his heterosexual needs become repressed and homosexual patterns of male relationships occur in the form of identification with and introjection of current patterns of maleness.

In Homo erectus, the amount of new skills and knowledge to be acquired was relatively small (we must emphasise however the word 'relatively', because already for the young Homo erectus the efforts needed for the acquisition of current skills and knowledge must have appeared formidable), making the cultural maturation lag fairly short. In fact, we can measure the complexity and advances of a culture by the length of the latency period. The higher and more complex a culture, the longer the latency period and the more prolonged and intense, sexual repression. In Homo erectus, the element of sexual repression would hardly occur, first of all because the infantile eroticism would have been encouraged or accepted for the sake of libidinous bonding within the group, and secondly because maturation delay would not be a major factor in their development. The process of skill acquisition and identification with the grown-up males would not have entailed sexual repression. In other words, a young male did not have to leave the bedroom – the home (bedroom and home being the same) – upon reaching sexual maturity, and he would not have had to repress his sexual desires while he acquired the skills of his culture.

8. Myths, Gods and Morality

It would be tempting to say that morality first appeared when God revealed himself to mankind and it became aware of his existence.

We have spoken of the ancestor's ghost and the spirit of the leader and teacher engaging and encouraging the higher faculties of the mind to acquire new skills and acting as an example of good behaviour. While thus their presence in the mind of the community would be immortal, they did not present the image of a being that has caused the world to be the way it is. They were not seen as the creators of the universe. God, on the other hand, is both teacher and omnipotent creator. He is a person even while his wisdom and his powers are beyond our understanding, impossible to encompass the range of his mind. Nevertheless, there is a constant attempt in man's history to ascribe a visual image to him, and the many myths and religions depict him in recognisable human-like forms, as in Mesopotamia, Babylon, Egypt and Greece, and other cultures. The various divine images each have a character, a personality, an ego upon whom we project our own desires, aspirations, hopes and fears, of love or hate, of war and peace.

The gods can be considered to be an externalisation not so much of the motor senses but of the ego in its various moods and characteristics, the mind of man projected into an external being with an existence which is outside us in a different realm but controls, teaches and punishes. Just as the ego has to interpret and judge the manifold instinctual drives and impulses from the older areas of the mind, so the god or gods represent the unity of our internal world as well as of the world around and gives them meaning according to their purpose and plan. It may be presumptuous to say this, but we might call God a mind tool which creates a universe which is comprehensible and explains the connections between the manifold phenomena we perceive and encounter. He will be angry if we do not obey and worship him, and will impose rituals which have to be meticulously observed or make us guilty and afraid. While it is very comforting to be protected by a being which knows all the answers and has the power over life and death, sickness and health, poverty or plenitude, our relationship with him is full of ambiguities.

He makes us suspicious of our sinful nature, and we are suspicious of those who do not worship him – 'the others' who represent our own disobedience – and will regard them as our enemies; we have to repress and fight the sinful urges in ourselves.

This then is a problem which has bedevilled mankind's existence and has torn humans apart and made them both angels and devils. But rather than ask God and the heavenly realm for an explanation for this fateful split in man's mind, we shall return to the more earthbound processes of man's evolution.

9. Worship and Rituals of Propitiation

The first 'symptoms' of guilt with a need to propitiate the dead ancestor and the slain animal can be traced to Neanderthal man who made his appearance about 110,000 years ago. Most of his tools were flakes of flint struck from a core and trimmed into projectile points, knives and scrapers. With his new method of flake striking and edge chipping, Neanderthal man initiated a revolution in the art of tool-making. He became a most efficient hunter, well adapted both in his physique as well as in his technology to the Arctic conditions of the last glaciation, and he spread in large numbers over many parts of the globe.

By the onset of the 4th, or Würm, glaciation about 90,000 years ago, the Neanderthals had established themselves as the dominant human species, extending across Europe into the near East, Central Asia and China. The record of this era demonstrates man's extraordinary ability to adapt, to live practically anywhere and under any conditions. Indeed, the last glaciation probably presented the most severe climatic conditions of the whole Pleistocene era. Ice descended upon the British Isles and upon Europe, and came down over the Alps and beyond into the regions south of the Alpine mountains. This turned Central Europe into an Arctic province.

However, these extremely cold conditions brought about a considerable lowering of the levels of the sea and rivers, due to the absorption of the waters by the ice, exposing large numbers of caves, and Neanderthal man made good use of them. With his ability to make fire easily and his efficient weaponry, he took possession of the caves, protected them from ferocious animals and managed to achieve a reasonable degree of comfort and security. The exposed cliffs and caves provided abundant raw material for his tools as well as shelter. His tools also enabled him to make clothing out of the furs and hides of animals. But survival would have been impossible without reserves of food and fuel. And, as we shall see, the need to save and to accumulate possessions had a major impact upon the development of man's culture. While we can say that Homo erectus was almost certainly our true ancestor, who laid the foundations for our human characteristics because he existed for a very long time, probably over a period of some 600,000 years, and we are bound to have many of his traits ingrained in our psycho-biological system, it was Neanderthal man who laid the foundations for religious worship.

Apart from the astonishing wealth of implements discovered in Neanderthal caves, the arrangement of the caves and their 'furniture' can be considered even more significant as they indicate the importance of cultural and religious rituals: flagstone floors, work tables, benches as well as altars and burial places with their own ritualistic implements. Man had begun to face the mystery of death, both of the animals killed in the hunt as well as of his deceased ancestors. He conducted funeral rites and entertained ideas about the continuation of existence after an individual's death, and he wanted to ensure that the deceased would enter his new existence well provided for. Instead of identifying with the ghost of the ancestor by eating his brain, he identified with him in his imagination; the dead were given tools and weapons and other possessions as well as food supplies to take on their journeyings into the land beyond, the eternal land of the spirit.

The many burial sites discovered in caves inhabited by Neanderthal man provide ample evidence for his concern with life after death. At Le Moustier a boy of about fifteen or sixteen years old had been buried in a cave. A pile of flints lay under his head to form a sort of stone pillow, and near his hand was a beautifully worked stone-axe. Among the remains were wild cattle bones, many of them charred, the remains of roasted meat which may have been provided to serve as sustenance in the world beyond. One spring day about 60,000 years ago, members of his family went out into the hills, picked masses of wild flowers and made a bed of them on the ground, a resting-place for the deceased. Other flowers were probably laid on top of his grave, still others seem to have been woven together with the branches of a pine-like shrub to form a wreath.

These concerns for the dead show a great leap forward in the mind of Neanderthal man. He had developed a spiritual capacity made possible by his astonishingly large brain – between 1,200 cc. and 1,600 cc., with a particular increase of the parietal and occipital lobes devoted to imagination.

In southern France, in a cave at La Ferrassie in the Dordogne, the remains were unearthed of two Neanderthal adults and two children who had been ceremonially buried. One of the elders, probably a woman, had been placed in a crouched or flexed position in a cavity dug into the floor, legs pressed against her body and arms folded upon her breasts, an attitude that can only have been brought about by binding tightly with thongs before the corpse stiffened. The other adult had his head and shoulders protected by slabs of stone. The two children, lying supine, were in shallow graves, and close by were holes with the bones and ashes of a wild ox, the remains of an offering to sustain them on their journey.

There is an ambiguity in the burial rituals which we should not overlook. The flexing of the lower limbs in the cave of La Ferrassie which would have been brought about by binding the lower limbs with thongs seems to have been widespread Neanderthal practice, since it has been noted as far afield as Kiik-Koba in the Crimea and Mount Carmel in Palestine. There has been speculation whether this practice indicates a desire to symbolise the foetal position or whether it was intended to prevent the dead person from coming back in order to haunt the living. However, we can assume that the tight binding with thongs of the lower limbs shows a defence mechanism – a need to inhibit the dead. The concern for a dead person's future journey and his continued safety in the other world is accompanied by apprehension that his ghost may return. The burial ceremony of the Ainus ends in the following manner: 'After the celebrant has finished his instructions and assurances to the deceased, the coffin is not carried out through the door, but a part of the side of the house is taken away and repaired before the mourners return. The ghost will then not know how to get back in. And when the burial has been completed, the mourners leave the grave walking backwards, lest turning, they should be possessed of the ghost of the deceased; and they are holding weapons in their hands – the women sticks, the men their swords – which they wave back and forth for their defence.' (Joseph Campbell, *The Masks of God: Primitive Mythology*, 1973).

This ambivalence between concern for the dead man's safety in his journeys to the other world and the fear that he may return to haunt the living indicates not only the notion of eternity but also of guilt. It means that the ritualistic assurances and prayers for his safety serve to ensure his goodwill towards the living, so that he should be grateful and think well of them and not harbour any resentment and come back and punish them.

In the ceremonial assurances of the dead ancestor's future life, the mourners partake in his continued existence by the collective identification with his spirit, and thus ensure the group's sense of immortality. The group, the community who worship the dead, acquire his immortality, and by showing their concern and their love for him they are assured of his goodwill and his love. The spirit of the ancestor will be well-disposed towards us and not angry, for by his anger he would make the community feel bad and produce a sense of collective anxiety, tension, fear and apprehension. So we worship him and make him feel our love, in order to be worthy of his love and feel good.

These early burial rites show both man's concern for his fellows as well as propitiation of guilt feelings. In the ceremonial assurances of his future life the mourners partake in his continued existence, thereby alleviating the shock experienced by his loss, and at the same time overcome the fear that he might return and punish the community for any death-wishes which it may have harboured against him.

The ambivalence between the bad ghost and the good ghost, the processes of propitiation and restitution find further expression in the widespread rituals of animal sacrifice and primitive totemism which played a large part in the culture of Neanderthal man. The records provide rich evidence for these cults. More than any other animal it was the cave-bear who figured in his totem worship. These animals had to be driven out of the caves before man could move into them, and they were killed by the hundred and eaten. Indeed they were a major supply of nourishment. They were most probably considered as the original inhabitants of the caves, their original owners, so to speak, and the caves would have retained some of the bear's spirit. A mountain cave in eastern Austria contained a rectangular vault holding seven bear skulls all facing the cave entrance, while a site in Regoudon in southern France represents perhaps the most elaborate bear cult burial known. It included a skeleton, stone drains, a rectangular pit covered by a flat stone weighing nearly a ton, and the remains of nearly twenty bears. A cave in Germany, Petershöhle near Velden, which was excavated from 1916 to 1922, had closet-like niches in the wall which contained five bear skulls as well as their leg bones. We see here altar-like edifices upon which the remains of cave-bears were laid to be worshipped, or at least kept as monuments of their continued existence. The animal of the hunt which was killed and eaten had to be propitiated so that its anger would not enter into the hunter. While the bear was killed and eaten, his good spirit would remain and continue to populate the hunting grounds and the caves. He would be offered back his home and given sanctuary, and his spirit would pervade the cave and reassure its inhabitants.

Man depended on the animal of the hunt, and it played a large role in his imagination. The animal was important, desired and even loved as the provider of man's sustenance. The slaying of the animal was necessary in order to provide food, but this food had to be freed of the animal's anger and its suffering, and its good libido had to be assured. It had to be good food, not angry food. The spirit of the slain animal had to be propitiated so that it would love the hunter and enter into him as a good spirit. Man had to be sure that the devoured-internal object was good and not angry, accepted and accepting. We eat not only the flesh of the animal but also its spirit, its state of mind, and if we introject an angry animal – bad food – we might become guilty and get stomach ulcers, or become tense and anxious. (Psychoanalysis provides many examples of the child feeding from an unhappy or rejective mother, and the unhappiness and the conflicts which result.) Furthermore, man had to be assured that by eating the dead animal it would not disappear but that its existence would be perpetuated. By ritualised presentations of the spirit of the dead animal it would remain forever and continue to provide security. The animal would be inside the man and outside him, and by being assured of its special status it would be restored and become a good and protective spirit.

Neanderthal man has left us no man-made relics of his worship, but we must assume that ceremonial dancing and singing would have accompanied the rituals of propitiation. Being unable to carve images or paint, Neanderthal man would have laid out the skulls and the bones of the bear in a ceremonial manner and danced around them, probably accompanied by ritualistic chanting, thus assuring himself of the animal's goodwill and eternal existence.

However, the worship of the deceased ancestor and of the slain animal does not indicate a concept of a God who is the creator of all things, who by his will and his omnipotence has made the world in his own image. Neanderthal man, although a well-equipped and efficient hunter, was not an innovator or creator.

He would have been capable of animistic thinking, whereby objects of nature acquire a soul and a sensation of being alive. On the other hand, however, he would not have been capable of performing the tasks of shaping inanimate objects, he would not have been able to sculpt or paint. He would only to a very limited extent have been able to experiment with new possibilities.

If we look at the skull of a typical Neanderthal man we find that the frontal areas of his brain are much smaller than those of Homo sapiens, while the parietal and occipital lobes are very large, indeed, as large, if not larger, than those of Homo sapiens. While the frontal and prefrontal lobes of the cortex are, as we have observed, the areas responsible for intelligence, the capacity of foresight, planning, anticipation, purpose direction, experimentation and the concept of rules related to abstract ideas, the parietal and occipital regions determine the co-ordination and control of sensory input and output, visual imagination, body sense and body awareness.

We must assume that Neanderthal man's capacity to entertain abstract ideas, his ability to plan ahead and to experiment was limited. Thus his skills would rely on his actual experience with objects, and he would not be inspired by concepts of general laws or by abstract ideas governing the behaviour of things. François Bodes, an archaeologist who has done more detailed work in the classification of Neanderthal tools than possibly any other investigator, was impressed not only with their craftsmanship but also with the fact that the Neanderthal craftsmen were working in an almost automatic fashion, as if they had perfected their technique and then stopped inventing.

For the emergence of an image of God and of metaphysics and, in particular, the concept of a universal morality, we must look to Homo sapiens and the invention of agriculture.

It is interesting to note that foraging and hunting cultures do not have an image of a god who has created the universe but have a wide range of deities and spirits symbolising aspects of nature which play an important part in the life of men and evoke powerful emotions. These objects acquire a soul and have magic powers for good or for evil, and have to be influenced to benefit the group who identify with them by means of mourning ceremonials, the incantation of words and phrases, chanting and dancing. These ceremonial activities themselves acquire a sense of magic. He who can influence the deities and invoke their good will or avert their anger acquires magic powers.

With the emergence of Homo sapiens the power of magic is presented in sculptures and painting, and the images are reproduced in visual form, as we can observe in the marvellous and awe-inspiring cult of the cave paintings. For further details of the culture of early Homo sapiens, see my *Archaeology of the Mind* (Open Gate Press).

The generic term given to the first representatives of Homo sapiens in Europe is Cro-Magnon man, after the cave of Cro-Magnon near Les Eyzies, where his remains were discovered in 1875. Subsequently many other sites were discovered belonging to the early representatives of this species, particularly in Combe-Chapelle, Les Eyzies, and many others in the Dordogne valley. Les Eyzies has been called the prehistoric capital of Europe because it was the centre of a region especially rich in sites and artefacts relating both to Neanderthal as well as to Cro-Magnon man. During the warm spell of the Würm glaciation, the valley of the River Vézère as well as the Dordogne were a concentration point for game. Forests of spruce, oak and ash blossomed with strips of vegetation which attracted reindeer, bison, great numbers of rodents and later, flocks of sheep. There was ample supply of game, and water was plentiful and the forests provided wood for the new man who knew how to fell them with his polished axes.

Cro-Magnon man has been described as tall, handsome, with regular features, high forehead, a prominent chin, small teeth and delicate face bones, without the huge brow ridges that characterised Neanderthal man and all his predecessors. There is no doubt that he was of a Caucasian racial stock. If one looks at the only painting known so far of this man – a small bas-relief at Angles-sur-l'Anglin – one is astonished at the break with all earlier types of man. The straight and high forehead, absence of pronounced brows, straight and narrow nose, and white skin with black hair and black beard, give us the modern white man. His tools and implements represent a revolution in technology; they show that the makers of these tools could strike off a flake from a core in such a way as to get a knife-like blade; these blades were marvellously delicate, their knives thin and sharp, their spearheads follow a precise pattern expressing a symmetrical concept which we still regard as perfect for spearheads and arrowheads. They made spears, blades, knives, scrapers and polished axe-heads in stone compressed and beaten to an exquisite sharpness and thinness which is unrivalled in any palaeolithic culture. Furthermore, they used bones from horses and stags, and ivory from mammoths from which they made pointing drills, arrowheads and needles. The new culture of tool-making is called Aurignacian and it is not only an improvement on the old, it is an evolutionary jump in the quality of tools. Aurignacian man could tie thongs to his spearhead by boring holes in it and fasten it to the shaft. He could carry a supply of these spearheads with him, and thus be able to kill a great many animals before having to return home for new weapons.

Perhaps their most important technological invention was a tool called the burin, a special kind of chisel or graving tool which made it possible to manufacture tools of bone, amber and ivory of a precision and efficiency that surpassed by far anything man could do before. It is a tool-making tool and its basic shape and principle is still used in our time as the cutting knife for machine tools. It made it possible to develop a whole host of household utensils out of bone and stone; but the manufacture of needles and pointing drills facilitated the art of clothes making and hut making from animal skin and enabled man for the first time in his history to create permanent artificial homes which could provide warmth and protection, and replace the caves.

10. Matriarchy: The Original Culture of Homo Sapiens

Besides the technical advances of his Aurignacian culture, Cro-Magnon man introduced a completely new dimension into human civilisation. Out of ivory and stone he created statues in great numbers, mostly female figures, and he carved abstract as well as realistic patterns. A new ability to concretise symbolic concepts emerged here – art, as we know it. This new dimension of symbol presentation was motivated by a new type of psychological preoccupation and facilitated by the new technology. The burin enabled man not only to enhance greatly the precision and the efficiency of his tools but also to make precise and delicate engravings and sculptures.

The sculptures mostly depict females, often with grossly exaggerated sexual features, and there is no doubt that they were cult statues. It is interesting that they usually have no feet and that their legs end in a point. This indicates that they were stuck in the ground to preside over some household shrine. They do not represent individual women, for their faces are mostly left blank, but can be taken to represent symbolised concepts of fertility, security and plenitude. From the great number of almost exclusively female statuary, as well as from the structures of the compounds, which resemble quite closely those of recent matriarchal civilisations, we can confidently assume that we here deal with a matriarchal culture. Thus Homo sapiens introduced not only a revolution in technology and the invention of man-made habitations but also the social and psychological structure of matriarchy.

In the new habitations, women had begun to play a much more important role as they became productive in their own right. The higher levels of technology provided women with a much wider range of activities, and they would take over a larger area of socially necessary work than ever before, including the growing of fruit and vegetables – they were the initiators of horticulture. With the refinement of hunting tools, men would venture out further afield and remain away for longer periods, and women would stay behind in the compounds, no longer merely tending to the children and waiting for the men to return, but making utensils of all kinds. With the invention of the needle, they would sew clothes and make roofs for the huts out of animal skins. These activities would emphasise the importance of females in productive activities.

With the expansion of the settlements consisting of a fairly large number of huts encircling an open courtyard, women would take over a wide area of responsibility and engage in various activities, so that children would no longer find their mother's attention undividedly centred upon them. The new woman of Homo sapiens communities became an individual in her own right, a separate person, so to speak; she was no longer wholly a mother as she was in the cave, but a person with responsibility to her society as she was absorbed in the larger responsibilities of the village society, and the child as well as the man had to share her with other members who were instinctively strangers to them. The very successes Homo sapiens had achieved with his new technology – his 'means of production' – had created a different environment and with it a crisis in his emotional expectations. He had to face new conditions of his own making. The child's narcissistic need to be surrounded and embraced by the mother's libido and her attention would be subjected to a trauma of separation and of insecurity. Memories of these traumas of separation would remain in the mind of the grown Homo sapiens. On his return from the hunt he would no longer receive the undivided welcome of the cave home pervaded by the woman's libido and symbolising her embrace, but instead would have found women active and busy organising the life of the village compound, working at a variety of tasks, and absorbed to a large extent in the community of women who organised the village in the absence of men.

So both child and man, the child in the man, would be overtaken by the urge to recreate the lost magic of her love and her presence, and he would shape images of her and surround himself with the libido which they represented. In this way the spirit of the mother would be omnipresent again and cast its protection upon the home. The intimate union of the cave community was lost in the larger and complex world of the compounds and villages, and had to be recreated by symbolic representations. And Homo sapiens made images of the woman emphasising her sexual characteristics to assure himself of the permanence of her libido. And also, having lost the intimate distinctive sense of his own identity of which he was assured in the close circle of the cave and the spontaneous and unquestioned recognition by the mother, he reassured his narcissistic needs by creating ego symbols; he painted his body in various colours in abstract designs, in order to affirm his individuality as well as his belonging to the new community. He adorned himself and made himself a new skin in order to compensate for the deprivation of his narcissistic libido. Cro-Magnon people used cosmetics and made the earliest known jewellery. They wore clothes decorated with rows of coloured beads, ivory bracelets and necklaces of pierced teeth and fish vertebrae. These elaborate decorations compensated for the general increase in the complexity of society and to the rise of mass hunting methods. Jewellery, as John E. Pfeiffer has observed, may have done more than beautify. It may have helped to identify the clan or the status of people associating in groups too large for individuals to know one another by sight or by name.

The village group consisting of a number of families took on the characteristics of a tribe which, to some extent, attempted to regain the embracing circle of the cave. Having lost the enveloping security of the maternal cave, man reproduces it in his imagination. He draws its circle around him to encompass not only the new habitation, which thus becomes a new mother-protected community, but also the world of the hunter outside. Thus, the whole of perceived nature, the sky and the horizon as well as the earth and all the things that grow and live on it are surrounded by her libido and her presence. The plants and trees, flowers and rivers that spring from the earth are a new extended family, they are her children manifesting her vitality and her libido. The world will be populated by fairies, sprites, spirits and gnomes. The sunshine, the verdure of spring and summer will be perceived as an expression of mother's joy, while the cold and the snow will, no doubt, express the mystery and maybe the fear of her withdrawal.

While the Aurignacian mural paintings were linear and somewhat stiff, though by no means crude or incompetent, most of the bone, ivory and stone figurines were of consummate elegance. These figures have been found in immense numbers, from the Pyrenees right across Europe and Russia to Lake Baikal in Siberia, indicating a common culture of the mother goddess and showing astounding similarity in technique. Among the most famous of them is the Venus of Willendorf – a statue made of stone and found in a Gravettian site in Austria. Traces of paint suggest she was covered in red ochre. The precise depiction of the hair contrasts with the absence of a face.

Most palaeontologists have divided prehistoric art into home art and cave or parietal art, that is, sculptures, carvings or paintings which were kept in the home, and such paintings and sculptures which by their very nature were part of a cave. The sculptures and engravings mentioned above would be designated as home art, as they were part of the life in the village compound.

In this way the primal communities of the cave founded on the family or enlarged family gave way to complex social organisations held together by the new cultural symbols. Man developed graven images, a wide variety of sculptures and paintings which had a sacred symbolic meaning and were objects of worship. His culture was of a matriarchal order and his communal organisations were based upon the authority of women.

The chief classification of early Homo sapiens is derived from their tool-making technology representing major cultures, with the following approximate durations in Europe:

Perigordian – named after the region which includes Les Eyzies, more than 35,000–c.22,000 years ago.

Aurignacian – named after the Aurignac site in the Pyrenees, about 35,000–20,000 years ago.

Solutrean – named after the extensive open-air site near the village of Solutre in east-central France, 20,000–17,000 years ago.

Magdalenian – named after the La Madeleine shelter, about three miles from Les Eyzies, 17,000–12,000 years ago.

11. The Art and the Culture of the Cave Temples

The transformation from home art – statues, relief carvings and paintings placed on the surface or engraved on rock walls as visible representations of the deity – to cave art occurred some 18,000 years ago with the re-emergence of the cold climate of the Würm glaciation. Caves once again became centres of security, but with the difference that while he had acquired the ability to live in hut compounds, Homo sapiens placed his goddess inside the caves and they became her sanctuary.

Homo sapiens had made enormous advances both in technology and culture and in his method of the large-scale hunt. Although some used caves once more for occasional habitation, they mostly lived in man-made compounds with well-constructed huts similar to those still used today by Siberian hunters and North American Eskimos. Indeed, Cro-Magnon man's compounds, his huts and clothes would have been similar to those of his contemporary cousins, who are still Arctic hunters. The large caves in whose recesses he painted the scenes and animals of the hunt, those marvellous temples of his art and religion, may have been inhabited at times, but the main sanctuaries containing his masterpieces were largely inaccessible sacred chambers which remained separate from the profane occupations of daily life.

The artists who produced the paintings and engravings in the caves displayed very considerable versatility, and, considering the means at their disposal, the results they achieved were of an extraordinarily high order. Painting was carried out by means of the finger being dipped in pigment, by the use of some kind of brush, by means of a pad of feathers or fur, or by blowing through a pipe. The only pigments to survive are minerals, including ochres for reds, browns and yellows, and manganese for black.

Here we come to a phenomenon which has mystified generations of archaeologists and anthropologists. The great majority of cave paintings and engravings of the European Magdalenian culture are not only located in deep chambers of the caves, but often have very difficult and tortuous access routes. What could have motivated this practice, what were the psycho-cultural developments which drove Magdalenian artists to paint their masterpieces in deep and almost inaccessible places?

We might approach a clarification of this problem if we consider that the mystery ritual of Magdalenian culture was an expression of a process of reparation, of providing the mother with the most desired objects so that she would be satisfied and loving and ready to protect man. This implies that the Magdalenians began to experience a sense of guilt as well as anxiety in their relationship with the mother goddess, a sense of separation and estrangement far exceeding that of the earlier cultures. The beginnings of tension between mother and child, men and women, must have occurred to an ever-increasing degree – possibly some 18,000 years ago – inspiring Magdalenian man to create his great works of art as a sign of devotion to her, an act of restitution towards the maternal superego.

The first traces of cave art discovered at Niaux in France were located over 500 yards from the entrance. Other examples of cave art in this region were found up to 1,120 yards from the light of day.

At Arcy-sur-Cure, a relatively small cave can only be entered through a tube-like tunnel about 100 yards long and only just big enough for a man to squeeze into. One has to go in head first, wriggling about salamander fashion over the muddy floor. This is very hard work with solid rock all round and one's face an inch or so above the mud, and sometimes in it. (The archaeologist Henry Breuil, one of the great explorers of prehistoric art, became stuck in this cave and had to be pulled and shoved through it; it was one of the last caves he ever explored.) Imagine the difficulties under which the Magdalenian artist had to work in such conditions. He frequently painted his masterpieces in areas which were not only difficult to get into, but were cramped and forced him to work in awkward positions, tight and cramped corners, or on the edges of narrow platforms above a deep pit, or at the bottom of a pit from which he had to scramble up again to find his way out.

There are many such places, and it is significant that in almost all of them, entry can only be made by a long and often tortuous route. While this has rightly been regarded as one of the most baffling aspects of prehistory, it may also provide a key to an understanding of the symbolic meaning of the cave sanctuaries. Their deep secrecy as well as the narrow passage which leads to them combine to create an image of the maternal womb and the passage of the vagina that leads to it. The male has to wind his way through the vaginal passage of the goddess in order to reach her sacred chamber and offer his seed; he has to offer her his passion and the fruit of his passion so that she would transform it into new life.

We know from the analysis of individuals that the fantasy of entering bodily into the mother's body through the vagina plays an important role in the unconscious mind of many men, particularly if their masculinity has not been readily acknowledged by the mother, and have been made to feel a sense of genital inadequacy. If the mother appeared to the boy as huge, forbidding and distant, and his malehood as not accepted by her, then the whole body is transformed into a penis symbol: it becomes a body penis. The fantasy of the penis entering the vagina is transformed into a fantasy of the whole body penetrating the mother to gain complete acceptance by her as well as orgastic gratification. We find here a combination of narcissistic and genital eroticism.

The caves of Altamira, Lascaux, Niaux, Pech Merle, Teyjat, Font de Gaume, and many others, are resplendent with animals of the hunt: red deer, bison, woolly rhinoceros, hind, mammoths, reindeer and ibex. These animal paintings are obviously magic representations of the hunter's most desired possessions. The omnipotence of our imagination makes them real, their soul is in our power and subject to our will. Thus art and magic combine to bring about the realisation of our desires or to ward off our fears. But the magic act finds its apotheosis in the approval of the god, for the power of the ego can be destroyed and its wishes brought to nought unless the superego, the god or goddess give their blessing. So the magic act has to be accepted by the omnipotent being, it has to be offered to him or her, for the power of creation and of fulfilment resides in the divinity.

We are obliged to ask how the masterpieces and their symbolic gift offerings, placed as they were in the secluded and hidden sanctuaries, would be known to the community; for what would be the point of carrying out such elaborate magic on behalf of the community if, apart from the artist-magician, no one would be able to see those masterpieces and experience their powers?

It is likely, as has been suggested by a number of writers, that the caves were used for initiation rites. When we consider that the artist discloses his wishes to the Goddess, bares his soul to her, so to speak, on behalf of the community, then every member in some way partakes in his effort. Even while men might regard the sanctuaries as sacred and secret, they would know about them, and it is likely that they would enter into the temple at crucial times in their lives, particularly during initiation ceremonies. It is, therefore, highly probable that at the moment of initiation the young man would experience the artist's courage to penetrate into the secret abode of the goddess and his ecstasy of communion with her, and prove himself to be worthy of being a man, to receive her blessing and to re-emerge into the compound as a fully-fledged member.

12. The Crisis of Matriarchy: The Goddess becomes a Witch

Towards the end of the Magdalenian period, changes take place in the nature of the paintings and engravings. They become more angular and stylised, the rounded outlines of the paintings and circular wave-like shapes of abstract engravings, which are plentiful in Middle Magdalenian times, give way to harsher forms: lines symbolising spears and arrows, and javelins piercing animals, straight lines, squares and triangles replace the much more harmonious symbols of earlier times. The feel of the artistic imagery becomes altogether more tense, aggressive and restless. The animals are shown with spears stuck into them, wounds gaping and dripping blood. The hunters are shown as pin men without flesh and colour. Aggressive-sadistic images replace the serene symbiosis between man and animal. (The similarity with contemporary art is unmistakable.)

There is little doubt that these images represent a transformation of the protective and loving maternal image into an angry mother-goddess; she becomes mean and resentful, evoking anxiety, tension and phallic-aggressive drives among men.

The great Magdalenian culture soon disappeared from the world, but the angry mother-goddess gained ground and her reign spread to other cultures and other races. The conditions which transformed the idealised protective and life-giving mother into a witch-like divinity continued to prevail in the societies of Homo sapiens and brought about cultures dominated by the rituals of blood sacrifice.

We could be justified in assuming that this dramatic transformation of the image of the goddess had as its basis a change in the attitudes of the actual mothers.

The combined effect of greatly enlarged compounds, the growing power of women in them and their new-found activities and responsibilities, the greatly enhanced efficiency of the weapons of the hunt and the longer lasting sojourns of the men in the hunting grounds away from the village settlements combined to produce not merely a sense of separation between men and women but also an estrangement between them. Mutual affection between man and woman ceased to act as a cohesive force, a bond that held the community together; indeed, the structure of the community disrupted these affectionate bonds, with the result that women became on the one hand more powerful in the villages and on the other hand more frustrated and resentful. The men, sensing their women's preconscious anger, would have made themselves more independent of them and founded homosexual bonds in the male groups of the hunt, and these communities of males became more self-contained. This in turn would have made women even more angry and envious, until they assumed an image of the witch, the hating and vengeful goddess, in the imagination of the men. She acquired the image of the angry maternal superego. However, while the matriarchal sentiments, the concept of the spiritual power of the woman, still retained dominance in the mind of men, they would have become frightened of her anger, and her powers over life and death would have become dangerous and threatening.

There are many stories and myths of the transformation from the benevolent mother-goddess into a dangerous witch amongst ancient people in many parts of the world; they are too frequent and widespread to ignore, and obviously reflect a psycho-cultural event, a major transformation, during prehistoric times. Lucas Bridges describes this psycho-cultural transformation among the Ona people of Tierra del Fuego in the following way:

'The men lived in abject fear and subjection. Certainly they had asked what use were their weapons against witchcraft and sickness. The women had kept their own particular lodge, which no man dared approach. The girls, as they neared womanhood, were instructed in the magic arts, learning how to bring sickness and even death to all who displeased them. This tyranny of the women grew from bad to worse until it occurred to the men that a dead witch was less dangerous than a live one. The legend tells how the men conspired together to kill all the women, and there ensued a great massacre from which not one woman escaped in human form. Even the young girls only just beginning their studies in witchcraft were killed with the rest.'

Among the Yahgans also, the southern neighbours of the Ona but a very different people, there was the legend that formerly their women had ruled by witchcraft and cunning. 'According to their story,' states Mr Bridges, 'it was not so very long ago that the men assumed control.' (Joseph Campbell *The Masks of God: Primitive Mythology*, 1973)

Writing of an ancient reign of goddesses, Jane Ellen Harrison observed that 'in the field festivals and mystery cults of Greece numerous vestiges survived of a pre-Homeric mythology in which the place of honour was held not by the male gods of the sunny Olympic pantheon, but by a goddess, darkly ominous, who might appear as one, two, three or many, and was the mother of both the living and the dead. Her consort was typically in serpent form, and her rites were not characterised by the blithe spirit of manly athletic games, humanistic art, social enjoyment, feasting and theatre that the modern mind associates with Classical Greece, but were in spirit dark and full of dread. The offerings were not of cattle gracefully garlanded, but of pigs and human beings directed downward not upward to the light, and rendered not in polished marble temples, radiant at the hour of rosy-fingered dawn, but in twilight groves and fields over trenches through which the fresh blood poured into the bottomless abyss. The beings worshipped were not rational, human, law-abiding gods, but vague, irrational, mainly malevolent spirit things, ghosts and bogeys and the like, not yet formulated and enclosed into a godhead' (J.E. Harrison: *Prolegomena to the Study of Greek Religion*, Princeton, 1991).

Chapter 5

... *and God was born in the Minds of Men*

1. The Revolt against Matriarchy and the Beginnings of Agriculture

At the end of the last glaciation, Magdalenian man followed the retreating glaciers and the animals of the hunt to the Low Countries, the British Isles (which were at that time still connected to the continent), northern Germany, Scandinavia and that great sweep of subarctic Russia, to the Urals and beyond. At the same time, some moved southwards and mixed with the people who had for millennia lived in northern Africa. These two migrations, the northern and the southern, came to produce the chief cultures of Western civilisation during subsequent millennia.

Out of the northern migration developed that great complex of Scandinavian cultures with their rock engravings and their megaliths culminating in the Teutonic and Slavic myths. We have spoken of the pin men, human figures depicted in thin and usually straight lines during the Late Magdalenian culture. We find such engravings of human figures in rock carvings in Scandinavia, and especially male figures with long thin legs, the body drawn as a circle often with four spokes which hold the circle together much like a wheel, the head of a goat, genitals with an erection, and wielding a hammer with a very long handle. These are obviously fighting men and precursors of the Nordic legendary myth of the Edda with its great god Thor wielding his hammer and a wheel-like body. The phallic characteristics are highly emphasised in these pictures and reinforced by the long handle of the hammer or axe as phallic weapons.

A whole assembly of men pursuing a wide range of activities – wielding hammers, throwing spears, unleashing arrows from their bows, blowing trumpets and all endowed with erect phalluses, as well as fighting ships and sun symbols – are depicted in rock carvings in Fassum, Sweden. These and similar works of art covering a long span of time obviously show the male triumphant.

On the southern stage of man's post-glacial habitations and migrations, we find a large number of somewhat similar representations of the human figure, although the art of this region represents a mixture of earlier North African cultures with an indigenous south-west European culture. They all have thin elongated bodies, while their legs are strongly emphasised and thicker than those of their northern compatriots. It is an art of rock painting and engraving alive with vivid little figures, bowmen hunting and fishing, ritual and sacrificial scenes, dancers and groups of women intent on some activity, lively scenes of human figures developed with a fine sense for the rendition of active and intense movement.

Whereas the Magdalenian art of the caves represented the timeless atmosphere of the divine animals, the embodiment of the eternal mother goddess who in her deep chambers performs the mysteries of creation, here we have an atmosphere of life on earth and the ritual acts of living communities. The emphasis is upon the intensity of human pursuits: the hunters strain their bodies with the bow and follow the arrow and the spear as if it were an extension of themselves. They represent an emancipation from dependency upon the eternal mother and the transfer of libido towards the narcissistic affirmation of man's powers and his exercise of mastery over the environment.

The heartland of this new style was the grassy land of North Africa where today is only desert but which of old was a great pasture full of game. The type station is Capsia (Tunisia) – hence the name of Capsians for these people. Besides rock paintings of elephants, giraffes, rhinos and running ostriches, and giant human forms with heads of jackals or asses, we find already the symbols of lions on cliffs lit up by the sun, and men standing in postures of adoration with uplifted arms before great bulls or before a ram with a sign of a sun-disc between its horns. (This some 5,000 years before they appeared in Egyptian mythology.)

... AND GOD WAS BORN IN THE MINDS OF MEN

While most archaeologists state that nothing is known of the early history of this culture, it is likely that the Capsian people were descendants of early Homo sapiens races who evolved in the Middle Eastern region between 80,000 and 50,000 years ago. Some of them had migrated into the rich pasture lands of northern Africa, while others came to settle in Europe 40,000 years ago. When, at the end of the ice ages, many of the European Homo sapiens migrated north and created the wide sweep of Teutonic and Slavic cultures, others moved southwards to the shores of Africa, joined the southern branch of Homo sapiens and became part of the Capsian culture. There is some evidence that Capsians gradually moved eastward and created the neolithic cultures which came to flourish in Palestine, Sumer, Assyria, Mesopotamia and Southern Turkey – the Fertile Crescent where wheat grew wild – and became known as Natufians.

Soon they were to use the wild grains they found for farming plantations and began the agricultural civilisation.

But before organised agriculture became possible, the men had to take over organisation of the communities and wrest its leadership from the women. There can be no doubt that organised farming as it began in the Middle East some ten or eleven thousand years ago, agriculture in our sense, was an activity organised and carried out by the men, as distinct from vegetable plantations and smallholdings on the fringes of villages which had been cultivated by women for millennia past. The agriculturalists established new myths and sciences based on observation of the rhythms and laws of nature, and as agriculture emerged as the chief source of sustenance, the centre of the economy and of culture, men gained a dominant role in the life of society. But this ascendancy of men cannot be simply explained by the advent of agriculture. The psychological foundations for the emergence of agriculture can be found in men's phallic-assertive drive to gain supremacy over the woman and mother nature, to penetrate her, to make her yield and submit to him and receive his seed.

2. Patriarchy emerges

In agriculture it is the seed, man's particular contribution to life, which assumes central significance and becomes the active and causative principle; it is the man who inspires and fecundates the Earth Mother; he makes her dependent upon him for the realisation of her life-giving potentials. It is not so much the worship of the earth which dominates the imagination and rituals of agricultural people, but the dominance of the man who enables the earth to bring forth the life which he plants into her. It is he who arouses her passion and her reproductive powers, and she depends on him for her fulfilment.

It is widely assumed that in matriarchal cultures people were ignorant of the connection between sexual intercourse and reproduction, and that this shrouded man's consciousness of his paternity and made the role of the father towards his children relatively unimportant. It was the uncle, the mother's brother, who assumed the role of guide and protector of the children. In patriarchy the father's role becomes at last quite clear and is strongly emphasised.

With the onset of agriculture, men challenge the mother's right of succession, they demand the right of self-perpetuation through their offspring; they assert their primacy as the productive and reproductive agents of life. J. J. Bachofen has called this the Dionysian stage of human development: 'Its mythologies are of the Sun-god at the zenith, represented by the sun-disk between the horns of the bull or as the halo which surrounds the head of the god and his saints. The Dionysian father forever seeks receptive matter in order to arouse it to life.' (J. J. Bachofen: *Myth, Religion and Mother Right*, Routledge, 1968)

One of the most important aspects of the emergent patriarchal culture, one that had the most profound effect upon its social structures, is the concept of property and the emergence of authoritarian hierarchical systems far beyond anything experienced in matriarchal societies. By their fertilising labours men claimed to possess the earth, make it their own – it became their property. While in matriarchal societies the hunter provided nourishment and sustenance, the women were in possession of the villages, of the huts and of the utensils available to them. By providing for his families and for the village, the hunter received welcome and warmth, security and sexual gratification, but he did not have ownership either of his wife and children or of his home and the ground which it occupied. Neither did he have authority over the village, nor was his name perpetuated by his offspring. It was only when the earth had to be penetrated and fertilised in order to yield sustenance, and became dependent upon the activities of the farmer, that men became owners of the land they dominated, and thus also obtained power and authority over the family and the village. They became law-makers and law enforcers, and the earth as well as the women depended on them. In this way the patriarchal family represents man's ownership over the territory which he masters and plants, it means ownership of his wife and all the offspring which she brings forth – his property – bearing the seal of his name. It is the man who now embraces the woman, encircles her with his arms and protects her.

It is one of the most startling discoveries of modern archaeology that almost as soon as agricultural settlements were built, they were fortified and turned into citadels. The most important finds of early neolithic man were settlements that had not been villages but cities. At Jericho a city was established some 8,000 years BC, which had the civic organisation to construct a massive defence wall and had developed techniques for the cultivation of wheat and barley. Agriculture, and not just the collection of cereal food, was the basis for its urban economy and its social structure.

The Natufian culture arrived in the Middle East, and particularly in Palestine, about 9,000 years BC. It is interesting that no direct genetic links have been established between its people and the people of the indigenous Kebaran culture which preceded it. Could this not be a sign that the Natufians were in fact the same people as the Magdalenians from South-west Europe and the Capsians who migrated from northern Africa to the Middle East? The Natufians established a large number of settlements on open ground overlooking lakes and marshes or near powerful springs as at Jericho. Sickles and sickle blades, querns and mortars and pestles give evidence of reaping, preparation and storage of cereals. Clay-lined storage pits imply the conservation of surplus food. This culture has been called Proto-Neolithic as it was most probably dependent on the reaping and collecting of wild wheat and barley; it is also clear from the tools and weapons found that hunting and fishing still provided an important part of their nourishment.

There is no break between the earliest Natufian settlements at the site of Jericho and the new town which arose about 8,000 years BC. It can be assumed without a doubt that the almost explosive growth of Jericho within a period of probably less than one thousand years into a walled city was due to the development of agriculture and the capacity to produce and store surplus food. The new town consisted of round houses built of mud-brick on stone foundations; the floors were well below the level of the ground outside and entry was through a door (with wooden jambs) and down several steps. (J. Mellaart: *Earliest Civilisations of the Near East*, Thames & Hudson 1978, and *The Neolithic of the Near East*, Thames & Hudson 1975.)

The wall around Jericho was a solid free-standing structure, built of boulders brought from a river bed half a mile away. It is six foot six inches thick at the base and its foundations rested firmly on bedrock. Outside the wall, the prehistoric builders had carved out of solid rock an enormous ditch, twenty-seven feet wide and nine feet deep. How they could have made this excavation in Jericho's withering heat remains a puzzle. There would hardly have been more than 2,000 or 3,000 inhabitants on the ten acres that made up Jericho 10,000 years ago. But perhaps an even more remarkable discovery than the wall and the ditch was a solid stone structure, tall enough and massive enough to have graced some of the great medieval castles of France.

This tower is more than thirty feet in diameter at the base, and even today its ruins stand more than thirty feet high. Carefully built into the centre is a flight of steps going down to a horizontal passage at near bedrock level. The passage leads to a door at the eastern end of the tower. A water channel from the top of the tower drains into a series of curvilinear enclosures. A similar enclosure has most probably been used for the storage of grain. The tower, then, combines the functions of pumping water from the well to feed the town and fields around it, of storing grain, and of look-out tower and battlement – a central part of the storage system.

Besides being the centre of an agricultural area, there were other sources which contributed to the wealth of this city. Trade must have played a large role in its economy as it commanded the resources of the Dead Sea: salt, bitumen and sulphur – all useful products in early societies. Obsidian, nephrite and other green stones from Anatolia, turquoise from Sinai and other metals were found in the remains of the tower. No doubt there were many workshops where these metals were used for implements of all kinds, and warehouses where they were stored and traded.

The city encouraged the development of a large variety of skills, and its human composition became more complex. In addition to the farmer, shepherd and fisherman, many other craftsmen entered the city and made their contribution to its existence: the miner, the metal worker, the painter and sculptor, the woodsman and weaver. From these types, which originated in the villages, still other new occupation groups developed: the soldier, the merchant, the banker, the courier and the clerk. Thus the new urban existence co-ordinated a large number of skills and produced an enormous expansion of human capabilities in all directions. However, the foundation for these wide-ranging activities was the development of agriculture and the accumulation of surplus products beyond people's immediate requirements, the concept of property and the deliberate production of surplus commodities for the purpose of trade and exchange. In order to make these activities possible, a set of values had to be assigned to each commodity beyond its immediate use; rules to govern trade and exchange had to be enforced. Such enforcement of rules depended upon the existence of authorities whose decisions were commonly accepted.

The prodigious labours involved in the erection of massive fortifications and other public activities imply a central authority to plan, organise and direct the work of a large part of the population, and an economic surplus to pay for it.

The city not only brought more people, more strangers together in one place and varied their activities, their skills and responsibilities, but also created a new concept of authority and new institutions to represent it. The ruler or king could command the services of large numbers of men and organise them for collective labours on an unprecedented scale. Man-made mountains of stones or bricks, pyramids and ziggurats arose in response to royal command; whole landscapes were transformed and bore in their strict boundaries and geometric shapes the impress of an inflexible human will. There is no doubt that without this new dimension of obedience to their king and men's readiness to offer their labours and even their life to him, our civilisation could not have evolved.

The invention of the city brought with it the invention of large-scale warfare quite different in nature and scale from anything known before. From the very first days of the cities of the plain in Mesopotamia, Ur and Uruk, Eridu and Lagash fought each other for territory, for leadership, for control of trade routes. The earliest imperial adventure of which we have the full record – that of Sargon of Akkad – added a new dimension to military power and armed conflict.

We are entering here upon known territory; history is beginning to emerge in terms which are familiar to us. We must, however, ask what it is that makes man submit to a central authority, to the ruler, the priest and the king, what it is in the nature of our own psyche that makes us respond to the call of warfare, discipline and self-sacrifice.

3. The Divinity of Kings

We can sum up the factors which led to the formation of patriarchy and the emergence of the paternal superego in this way: men had fled from the threat of the mothers to the love of the father, and developed a superego on the basis of a de-sexualised, sublimated homosexuality, an identification with the powerful father-image.

We could simply answer the above question by saying that men of great power symbolise every patriarchal man's fantasies of omnipotence, and give it full expression. Men project their desire for power and possessions upon certain individuals, glorify them as kings, serve them, and identify with them in order to partake in their glory. This represents a process of projection and identification for, on the one hand, each man sees himself as a man of power and of property, and, on the other hand, he is prepared to sacrifice and enslave himself to the image of omnipotence vested in the king. The labourers who toiled at the fortifications and the soldiers who sacrificed their health and their lives in the battle of their king, split off their fantasy of glory and projected it upon the 'great authority' whose glory, in turn, is reflected upon the citizen who serves him.

There is a dual aspect of the father's authority, namely, his authority in the family and his submission to his king and his God. By his submission to a kingly and divine authority, the father identifies with them and represents their powers. Similarly, we find that the ruler of patriarchal communities exercises his power not merely by means of his personal influence or capability, but by the charisma that is bestowed upon him by his special relationship with God. He is himself the subject of the divinity, he serves it, and by doing so he acquires its power and introjects it. This relationship of the father figure with the superior power can thus be seen to operate on three levels at the same time:-

1) every male is a father of his offspring, an authority to his family;
2) he submits to his king, and in doing so, partakes of his power;
3) the king, in turn, stands in a special relationship to the divinity, that magic spirit which ultimately represents the image of omnipotence. In this way, every male partakes in the powers of the omnipotent spirit, identifies with it and gains fulfilment for his manic phallic-narcissistic fantasies.

Apart from his fertilising powers, the manic-narcissistic element is manifest in his God's universality: he populates the heavens and covers the earth from 'one end to the other', his powers are without limits, free from restraints and inhibitions to which ordinary mortals are subject.

It is precisely this freedom from inhibitions which is the chief characteristic of the new god and his king. But of course not every member of the community can be thus chosen: sibling rivalry demands a favourite, and every man's wish to be the favourite of god is projected upon one particular individual who then becomes the embodiment of men's preconscious fantasies of erotic and narcissistic wish-fulfilment. His very glorification gives him power not only over the mothers and the home but also over the men of the community. Obedience to his orders and submission to his will became the supreme virtue of patriarchal morality.

4. The Culture of the Oedipus Complex: Patriarchal Paranoia

We see here a new type of ruler emerging, who is much closer to the dominant male of baboon communities who tyrannises the young males, frightens them into submission and demands the sole right of possession over the females. The king in his castle with his privileges, his wealth and divinely ordained powers, glorified by men as the embodiment of their collective fantasies, aroused at the same time their envy and their hatred. They envied him for his presumption and his wealth, and they hated him for his power over them. The ambiguity between adoration of the ruler and aggressive feelings towards him produced not only the profound conflicts of the Oedipus complex but also the structure of class division in society.

They want to kill him in order to regain for themselves that sense of power and dignity which they had vested in him, but at the same time they have to protect him from these urges of regicide; they develop elaborate rituals to restore and glorify the king, and ascribe to him the right to punish them and to demand their sacrifice. Service to king and country and self-sacrifice in peace and war become redeeming acts, and they liberate men from their bad consciences and reassure their ruler that not only do they not want to kill him but that they love him. For he represents them and speaks for them, he builds palaces, temples and tombs for himself on their behalf, and fights battles to enlarge his kingdoms for the greater honour of his subjects.

One of the most important psychic and political defences of the king and the superego is the process of displacement whereby the aggressive urges which are directed towards them are deflected onto alien kings and gods, the rulers of other communities who then come to represent a permitted object of aggression. The own superego encourages citizens to discharge their aggressive and hostile urges upon the 'other', the 'alien' superego, and by so doing ensures the continuation of its own powers. To kill enemies becomes an approved outlet for the forbidden murder of the own father or ruler and therefore a virtue; every enemy killed is an act of loyalty, an affirmation of love towards one's ruler or king – 'My king, my country'. Thus the conflict between love and hate is transformed into a conflict between our own and the other tribe or nation. But in the same way as the repressed sexual and aggressive drives constantly press for entry into consciousness, and thus become a threat to the ego and a source of anxiety, so the alien tribes and their gods, upon whom we have projected our own repressed urges, represent a constant threat to our own tribe and to our god. The superego – God and his representatives on earth, the kings and the rulers – has to be protected from the attacks of 'the others'; they have to be glorified, made more and more powerful and defended against the enemy. And all the spiritual powers, the powers of the will and of faith, as well as the material powers available to the tribe or the nation, all the weapons and arms provided by technology must be devoted to this task, no matter whether a civilisation calls itself democratic or theocratic or anything else. For in the same way as the repressed id impulses operating in the individual attempt to gain access to the ego and threaten to break through its defences, so the enemy superego representing those id impulses will constantly strive to penetrate the defences of our tribe or nation and attempt to take possession of its soul and its territory. The tribe will, therefore, constantly feel threatened by the 'enemy' and will inevitably become paranoid. Thus 'tribal or national paranoia' is a universal condition of patriarchy.

Just as the men have to defend their father-god and his representatives on earth, the king, the ruler or the party against the enemy outside, so they have to defend God the Father against his enemies within, the sinful thoughts and the evil that reside in the soul: 'I acknowledge my transgressions and my sin is ever before me.' (*Psalm* 51: 3). We appeal to the omnipotent being to release us from our guilt and our wickedness and we glorify him and sacrifice ourselves to him that he should be pleased and convinced of our repentance: 'Hide thy face from my sins and blot out all my iniquities'(*Ps.*51: 9). 'To the Lord our God belong mercies and forgiveness, though we have rebelled against him' (*Daniel* 9: 9). 'Oh Lord, correct me, but with judgement; not in thine anger, lest thou bring me to nothing' (*Jer.*10: 24). 'Our Father which art in heaven, hallowed be thy name. Thy kingdom come. Thy will be done in earth as it is in heaven. Give us this day our daily bread. And forgive us our trespasses, as we forgive them that trespass against us. And lead us not into temptation; but deliver us from evil: for thine is the Kingdom, the power, and the glory, for ever and ever. Amen' (*The Lord's Prayer*).

But it is not enough for us patriarchal sinners to beg God's forgiveness in prayer: we have to defend him from the external enemy and take up arms against the heathen, the non-believers who are eternally determined to destroy him and our nation. The unity of the Cross and the sword, submission to God and unbending strength in face of an enemy are the dual characteristics to which patriarchal man aspires as the highest virtue and undeniable duty.

We are now in a position to define a number of important stages in the evolution of patriarchal cultures and their moral concepts:

1. The rule of the mother-goddess and of gynocracy which unites the mother's offspring into a community and gives it a distinct identity. Her transformation into an angry witch.
2. The emphasis on phallic-aggressive primacies which serve to dominate the witch and make her once again give forth life and love.
3. The emergence of agriculture, the glorification and deification of the king and an omnipotent God who is the creator of life – the embodiment of male power.
4. The emergence of fortified towns, property and the class structure of society.
5. The conflict between love and hate towards the father-god, and the development of the Oedipus complex with its myths, religions and politics of patriarchal paranoia.

5. The Emergence of Monotheism

Between 10,000 and 2,000 years ago a very great number of different patriarchal cultures emerged across Europe and the Middle East, from Çatal Hüyük in Southern Turkey to Egypt. However, about 1,800 BC the first idea of a truly universal God, the Creator of the universe and of humanity, expressing his purpose and his aim for mankind, became manifest in the religion of Judaism initiated by Abraham, codified by Moses and elaborated by the prophets. Monotheism was a decisive step forward in theological as well as political thought, while the Greek idealisation of the human being, largely freed from the need to identify with the deity, made philosophy as we know it possible. Judaic monotheism and Greek philosophy represent the consolidation and high culture of patriarchy, and Western civilisation has inherited their aspirations as well as their conflicts.

The Jewish concept of God represents a remarkably high level of abstract thought. While the Hebrews invented the idea of monotheism, their God does not appear in terms of an anthropomorphic image. He is not presented in a perceptual bodily form, but as a cosmic spirit, endowed with will, purpose and intelligence, and revealed to man by His words and His commandments, transmitted by his prophets. His eternity and omnipotence transcend the limitations of time and space to which human perception and understanding are bound. In Kantian terms we could say that He is unaffected by the human categories of the understanding and of perception, i.e., time, space, substance and causality. He is the cause of all things, but He is not caused by anything, and thus not subject to causality. He is the beginning of time but not limited to time because He is eternal. He is both existence and essence, He is the One and the Many, for all that exists is His emanation. The world of existence is a manifestation of His will and His thought. He is not a phenomenon but a noumenon, and all phenomena, all things which exist and are perceptible, including man, are the expression, the embodiment of His mind. His will and his purpose give meaning to all that exists, and the lives of men reflect His intentions. Human history emerges as a movement towards the goal that God has set before them, and the soul of man would not be confined to an individual, with an isolated and limited existence, but become unified with eternal life through Him; by accepting His laws, men would be free from guilt and assured of His protection and His love. The Jews' image of themselves is fundamentally interwoven with the image of their God; they see themselves entirely as His children, and their historic chronicle is really a reflection of God's view of them. It is how God sees them, His experience of them that is revealed in their great writings, and their relationship to Him, and their shortcomings, their agonies, trials and triumphs before His gaze. While His mind is beyond human understanding, He reveals Himself to His highest and latest creation, mankind, by His laws written down on tablets of stone.

The God conceived by the Jews is the first truly universal God, the omnipotent creator, the father who gives birth to all life, who creates and destroys universes at His will. All human beings are his children, brothers and sisters under His divinity. His purposes and His laws permeate the universe, but humanity is endowed by Him with intelligence enabling it to understand and make choices, to learn and to perfect itself. The history of mankind is the period of struggle to fulfil God's expectations, and while men cannot, as yet, perceive His true nature, God has given them texts to guide them and prophets to inspire them. And at the end of history, when mankind has achieved a measure of perfection which satisfies God, He will reveal Himself and the Messianic Age will be initiated. It will be the time when man has achieved his maturity – the capacity to unfold his true potential. It will also herald the resolution of the Oedipus conflict, when 'Elijah will turn the hearts of the fathers to their children, and the hearts of children to their fathers.'

The people who conceived this vision of God have regarded themselves as His first-born, chosen by Him to proclaim His existence and His glory, and to reveal His purpose to humanity. They have considered themselves as a nation of priests and teachers charged with the awesome responsibility of setting an example to the nations in righteousness, to guide and educate them in the ways of God.

But they were fully aware of the difficulties of their task and the burdens imposed upon them. They had experienced in their souls the fateful ambivalence towards the father, and they knew that others would resent their efforts to teach them. They repeatedly found the task laid upon them too burdensome, but when they wanted to escape their God-given responsibility, their divine superego, the voice of God within would not release them. Their ambiguity towards God, their love for Him as well as their rebelliousness, their aspirations for greatness as well as their obstinacy are recorded in their Bible.

But God, for some reason which we can only guess at, has decided to give his special creation, namely humanity, the freedom to choose between good and evil, between submission to God's purpose or to rebel against it. He did not program them with a predetermined system of instincts which control man's activities as well as his thoughts, as He did for all other creatures, but He wanted to give them the opportunity to reach perfection by their own efforts. He gave man the potentials of reason and wisdom and moral perfection, but man had to learn ways to achieve them. He did not create a humanity which is bound by ignorance or sin but one which is perfectible and has to find ways of transcending its limitations and to fulfil God's expectations. It is a difficult task to love all of humanity as the children of God, unlike one's concern for the members of a family who are united in a common pursuit. The injunction, 'Love your neighbour as yourself', responds to one's feeling for one's family, for one's actual brothers and sisters or even members of one's tribe, but is extremely difficult to follow as a moral injunction if it extends to all mankind. But it remains the ultimate imperative set before humanity by the God of the universe.

6. The Birth of Philosophy

The quest for a universal moral concept that applies equally to all men has found another way which was to be independent of the belief in a supreme deity. While the Jewish concept of monotheism presented a stupendous step forward in theological and moral thought, the Greeks came to advocate the employment of reason in the search for a universal morality, and made philosophy as we know it possible.

The Greeks of the classical age had long forgotten their matriarchal ancestry of Cretan civilisation, but their battles for supremacy continued to be fought in their myths, long after they had in fact conquered Crete. These battles were remembered, not in terms of actual military and political events, but chiefly in the myths depicting the psychological conflicts of patriarchy. The great poets, Hesiod, Homer and Theognis, laid the foundations for the flowering of Greek culture, and they celebrated its emergence in their epics which traced the trials and victories of their gods. Hesiod's epic, above all others, attempted to provide a cohesive chronicle of the birth and development of the gods, and became an 'official' version for the Greek self-image and their pantheon – the bible of Greek religion. In the *Theogony* Hesiod traces the history of the world from primeval chaos to the establishment of Zeus as the supreme king of the gods. This epic is of particular interest to us, as it projects upon the universe stages in the psychic development of the individual: the primal polymorphous libido of the infant, the emergence of object-related libido and love, as well as oral-sadistic and aggressive drives not yet co-ordinated by the ego, the child's dependency on the mother and the demonic battles of the Oedipus complex, until the personality of the dominant male emerges, bringing law and order into the world and expressing as well as taming the passions of sexuality. Zeus himself is depicted as being at first subjected to the wild passions of what we call the unconscious, and only gradually and often painfully emerging to his status of the fully-grown male when he has to confront and defeat once more the old goddesses and the Oedipal compulsions of his sons.

The *Theogony* of Hesiod was composed at about the same time as the epic poems of Homer, during the eighth century BC, at the beginning of the classical period. They were created during the periods of aristocratic rule, and can be said to some extent to reflect it. But when these regimes gave way to the rule of the *polis*, and individuals decided to take full responsibility for the running of their society, the gods lost their power. Men took it upon themselves to be the originators of social events. But the intelligence that went into political decision-making also had to apply itself to an understanding of the world which was no longer symbolised and determined by the gods. While even during the high period of Athenian culture the Olympian myths were kept alive, the intellectuals considered worship of the gods as a kind of religious tradition which did not influence their rational judgement. The gods were regarded with scepticism, their motivations and behaviour considered rather uncouth and not taken very seriously by the sophisticated.

We may say that in the sixth century BC a rational revolution emerged, particularly in Athens, when the phenomena of nature upon which man depended, the ocean, thunder, earthquakes, winds, rains and eclipses, the earth and heaven and the transformations of seasons ceased to be seen in the form of personalised deities: their causes had to be discovered in order to make them comprehensible as well as predictable. One may say that the earliest conscious and deliberate attempts to arrive at an understanding of natural forces developed during the sixth century BC among the Ionian philosophers who came to be called philosophers of nature: Thales, Anaxagoras, Anaximander and Anaximenes. It is interesting, however, that their works would hardly have become known to us if it had not been for Aristotle's great interest in them as the precursors of his scientific speculations. But as it was men's minds and their rational faculties that determined both their social conditions and their ability to gain understanding of natural processes, they began to investigate the nature of mind. Thus a philosophy of nature, an inquiry into the working of the mind, epistemology and dialectics were born.

When the gods faded, reason had to take their place; when religion ended, philosophy began.

After millennia when men had projected their narcissistic fantasies upon the gods, the Greeks redirected the narcissistic libido upon the self in the image of the free and perfectible human being. The body was just as beautiful and worthy of worship as the mind, and they created a religion of reason which in no way denied the worship of the body. Indeed, the Athenian Narcissus, excelling in sport and articulate in debate, became a focus of worship, an aesthetic ideal that claimed by far to surpass the attractions of the woman. Men came to respect and to acknowledge the self and its perfectibility as a living, knowing and deciding person, the causative agent and creator of his reality. And here the male achieved his highest accolade: the sons took over the powers previously vested in the divine superego. It was they who had all the best arguments, and they claimed the right of free thought and free speech.

'Man is the measure of all things,' proclaimed Protagoras, and 'Man, know thyself' became possibly the most important motto of Greek philosophy. A theory of knowledge was born, devoted to the rational investigation of reason itself. As the intellectuals of Athens became increasingly sceptical of traditional ways of thinking, they attempted to arrive at secure foundations for the correct use of cognitive processes. The Sophists had already spread new schools for the improvement of understanding and the correct operation of the reasoning faculties. They taught the art of debate and the acquisition of as much knowledge as would help in this art; they were prepared to show how to argue for or against any opinion, and to follow an argument wherever it might lead them. Their principal values were a kind of erudition which puts man in possession of all knowledge useful for his purpose and virtuosity which enables him to choose his topics expediently and to present them in a captivating manner.

However, out of this pursuit of the logic of an argument or a proposition, they came to emphasise the sheer virtuosity in debate associated with political and moral cynicism. This resulted – in spite of the great talents of the Sophists – in a conception of the intellectual life guided solely by success. They pursued the truth of logical propositions and ignored any moral consideration, and it led them to a readiness to exploit their knowledge for whatever advantage it might provide. This aroused odium not only among large sections of the population, but also among philosophers, with Plato in the vanguard. Bertrand Russell, however sides with the Sophists (and, as we have seen, with the linguistic analysts) against Plato and his successors; he upholds the notion that the pursuit of truth must ignore moral considerations, and accuses Platonic philosophers of always being concerned to advocate views that will make people, what they think, virtuous. He prefers the 'intellectual honesty' of the Sophists, because they refuse in any way to prejudge the process of logic by its moral consequences. (Bertrand Russell: *History of Western Philosophy*, Routledge, 1991)

However, it was precisely the increasing cynicism and even frivolity of the Sophists (a state of mind which has many similarities with our own time), and their readiness to support any cause or interest irrespective of its moral aims, that evoked the strong condemnation of Socrates and Plato. It was the absence of any kind of moral conviction, or even their deliberate denial of such, which led Plato to consider the importance and significance of moral concepts in rational thought. For him, the concept of the true and the good became intertwined into an indivisible whole, the dual representatives of reason. It was the good thought and the virtuous behaviour which, together with the investigation into the nature of truth, became the focal point of Platonic philosophy.

After Pericles, the leaders of the Athenian Assembly were mostly drawn from successful men of trade, men sometimes of great ability but opportunists; men who, by nature and training, took partial views dictated by self-interest; and they welcomed sophistry as an expedient instrument to serve their ambitions. By the end of the fifth century BC, nobody was sure about eternal verities: the clever were turning everything upside down, and the simple felt that they had become out of date. To speak of virtue was to provoke this response: 'It all depends what you mean by virtue', and nobody knew. While the Athenians found great delight in a well-argued and well-turned speech, and were fascinated by the elaborate style and subtle arguments invented by the Sophists, they became, as Cleon told them, experts and connoisseurs rather than citizens, while the plain man, worsted in debate or cast aside in his lawsuit, grumbled at the way in which justice was being perverted.

Plato was concerned to establish rational principles at a time when traditional values of religion or sophistry no longer commanded respect. He set out to find universal criteria for truth and morality which would successfully replace the lost certainties.

Philosophy for him was the discovery of a new form of intellectual life, the search for truth arising out of disciplined application of reason, but related and applied to society. He was twice called by Dionysius to be his counsellor in matters of social organisation, and twice he failed.

Plato sees the philosopher as the man, on the one hand withdrawn from the world who has purified himself from the limitations of the senses and transcended the boundaries set to the mind tied to appearances, while at the same time, he is the true lawgiver and politician who, on returning from his excursions into the transcendental realm, offers society his wisdom and becomes its leader. While he is the discoverer and advocate of a rigorous logic, he is also the man of enthusiasm inspired by Eros, the begetter of the beautiful. To rational discussion Plato added the dialectic of love, expressed with a lyrical effusion and mystical contemplation. He proclaims a method of philosophy which represents the fundamental forms of the human understanding: the process of analysis and of synthesis. While the analytic process specifies given phenomena into their constituent parts, the synthesising process connects the parts into a homogeneous correlation until the mind arrives at the concept of the whole. It is in the pursuit of both methods of thought, separation and unification, that philosophy can be assured to arrive at true concepts regarding the nature of the world, and at moral certainties. It is particularly by means of the synthesising process that we are enabled to arrive at universals.

The core of existence, the One and the Absolute, the permanent point in the flood of appearances, springs not only out of the very structure of the mind, but comes down to men by Eros, that mainspring of life itself. There is, according to Plato, an eternal essence, the True and the Good, which cannot be apprehended by sensory perception alone.

Whereas all previous thinking had projected the qualities of eternity and absolute reality upon the gods, Plato gave those qualities back to men. It is man's mind, his eternal Idea, the innate ideas of truth and beauty which represent the true nature of things. The eternal Idea is represented by Plato not by a divinity but in human terms, such as goodness and universal purpose and truth,

... AND GOD WAS BORN IN THE MINDS OF MEN

which the human intellect, if properly employed, can rediscover. However, Plato confronted a paradox which continues to baffle men up to our own time. Are beauty and justice innate to the soul, or must they be learnt? Can the just society be established through love for mankind, or by submission to rationally established rules? At best it is understood that the two must go together, but in practice they tend to be divided. His *Republic* and his *Laws*, while being the most exalted manifestations of human rationality, nevertheless became symbols of coercion to later centuries. And the Dionysian cult of passion and love which had inspired Plato in his youth and early maturity, and which he came to relinquish in his later years, lived on in Greece as an underground culture.

After Plato we find a decline in the level of rational speculation. However, there was still the great, the phenomenal figure of Aristotle, Plato's disciple, who upheld the pride in men's reason. But he no longer had Plato's trust in pure speculation. It was, however, precisely for his reliance on the application of reason to experience, mediated by sensory perception, that he came to be the founder of the scientific method of enquiry. The difference between the two was said by Schopenhauer to consist in the fact that Plato was a philosopher of depth whereas Aristotle was a philosopher of width. 'Give me the findings gathered by the scientists and observers of nature, and I shall co-ordinate them into a theoretical edifice that will reveal the truth about the world,' proclaimed Aristotle. But the seeds of Aristotle's genius had to wait two thousand years to ripen; they began to blossom with the genius of Newton, whereas it can be said that it was Kant who first brought Plato's genius to fruition and laid the foundations of modern philosophy.

Chapter 6

Towards a Rational Morality

1. Some Basic Questions

At a meeting of the leaders of the Western powers dedicated to the 'third way', the Italian prime minister Massimo D'Alema said that one should not be afraid of the word 'socialism'; President Clinton and, following him, Tony Blair and Gerhard Schroeder burst out laughing. They knew the meaning of socialism, the belief in *Liberté, Égalité, Fraternité*, but could not help but laugh that anybody could still believe in it. While they call themselves social democrats, providing a synthesis between the dialectic opposites of communism and unrestrained capitalism, they accept the inevitability of a market-orientated economy.

While there is no argument left for the justification of communism after the horrors of its rule, the apologists of capitalism with a 'human face' maintain that the pursuit of profit, which is enshrined in the tablets of free enterprise, ensures the growth of the wealth of nations for the benefit of all, and once its lessons penetrate to the backward world and break down their pre-capitalist and anti-democratic systems, they too will enjoy the benefits of the advanced nations of the West. Freedom of enterprise which is taken as synonymous with democracy and liberty releases the creative energies of mankind to produce ever new commodities and the machinery necessary for the well-being and happiness of the 'greatest number of people'.

Indeed, they argue that the excitement of the hunt which is an important part of human nature can now find legitimate satisfaction in the competition for wealth and prestige and provide not only material but also psychological satisfaction in which everybody can participate. If one were to point to the large pool of poverty and deprivation endemic in capitalist society, to the inequality of opportunities, they would argue that with the advance of technology and with the advent of computerised information and planning now widely available, everybody would be able to join the hunt and provide sufficient wealth. Thus the progress of humanity would be assured and does not need a change in the socio-economic structure but would increasingly become a capitalism with a human face. We, therefore, have come to an end of politics, as some writers proclaim, and make moral and ideological aspirations irrelevant; the future is the way things are and it will become progressively better under the existing systems of production and distribution, signalling the end of history, meaning that capitalism is the answer to all utopias. But this kind of grand theory, which makes any vision of alternatives obsolete, can be shown to be an illusion upon a critical examination of the facts.

In their concept of human nature, by which they justify the relentless pursuit of wealth, they ignore the main characteristic of the human intellect, namely the capacity and indeed the need for anticipation and foresight, the awareness of the consequences of our actions and beliefs. They are blind to the effect of free enterprise upon the natural environment upon which we ultimately depend, adamant in their belief that the more we hunt the richer we get, without considering what happens to the prey and the planet's natural resources if we go on hunting with the ever more efficient weaponry and tools made available by modern technology. It is now well known that we are killing animals to the point of their extinction, pollute the sea and rivers with the excrement of industry, damage the biosphere, the air we breathe, and deplete the ozone layer with the likelihood of catastrophic consequences for life on this planet.

But does the ruthless pursuit of wealth for the satisfaction of personal greed without regard for the needs of others, does the manic obsession with power and self-aggrandisement really express a true picture of 'human nature'? Is there not a moral dimension in humankind endowed with empathy and consideration for our fellow humans and for the animals around us? Is the denial of these sentiments not due to the neglect and subsequent dysfunction of the higher cortical areas of the brain? Is there not a need to constrain the primitive, narcissistic and aggressive drives, and is the altruistic sense of fellowship not a primary characteristic of humanity enshrined in the models of *civitas* and civilisation?

We can see that these questions have a new urgency, for they concern the very survival of humanity, and moreover cause us to be concerned with the fate of the human mind, for if we cease to exercise the prefrontal areas of our brain or even deny their importance we regress to the more primitive drives and allow them to gain dominance over our thoughts and actions. We have observed earlier that the loss of trust in the grand ideas of the Enlightenment and the metaphysical constructs related to various religions and our inability to form new alternatives, produced a 'breakthrough of the repressed' with an outburst of civic violence and corporate aggression. Since I wrote about them in the early parts of this book, the incidences of brutality and greed have multiplied and their reports in the media become ever more lurid. I do not wish to add to the examples I have given, for every person has no doubt read and heard about them and may have experienced them in his own life.

It is not merely the breakthrough of those previously repressed drives which affect our social existence but also the danger to our intellectual and rational capabilities which must concern us, a kind of stupefication process, of which Theodor Adorno has written in his critique of 'organised capitalism'. It is usually called 'dumbing down', all too obvious in the media with their emphasis upon violence and aggression, as well as their focus upon the rich and famous, giving them prime time on the television and prime space in the newspapers and weekend supplements in particular. In order to catch a large slice of the market for their 'product' they appeal to the lowest common denominator which they think appeals to the majority.

Mankind is a many-faceted organism and its brain contains an enormous number of drives, instincts and fantasies intent upon dominating the mind. We have become aware of the many strands which operate in societies, and psychoanalysis has made us aware of the multiplicity of drives and obsessions which operate in individuals, frequently in conflict with each other. We can say that in each individual as well as in every society there is a multiplicity of psychic processes, most of which are withheld from consciousness or, as we say, are repressed, but which are held in reserve, so to speak, and can erupt to the surface and claim dominance over the ego or a culture. It is the task of the ego to select and choose between those drives which affirm and enhance life – we may call it Eros or the life-force – and those which threaten it despite the momentary satisfactions they afford. Beauty and goodness, psyche and soul, can no longer be considered the work of God, our moral and aesthetic capacities, love and creativity – all the best things about humans – no longer need a superhuman or supernatural source. They are every bit as human as the stupidity, greed and cruelty they oppose. Humanity is now obliged to ask what creates violence, greed, the urge for destruction, sadism and masochism, the so-called dark side of the soul, which manifests itself in the behaviour of nations. Philosophers, psychologists and sociologists have attempted to arrive at an understanding of those destructive aspects of humanity, and psychoanalysis has made considerable advances in our understanding of neurotic and psychotic symptoms.

But when the world of man is split into innumerable separate compartments and a sense of meaning of life and a vision of the future is lost, then the co-ordinating functions of the ego are thwarted and we are confronted by a kind of atomic explosion of previously restrained impulses of primitive energies demanding immediate fulfilment – here and now. There is so much information available in our computerised world that all we can do is catch up with it and there is no time to reflect how we are to evaluate it. Any interest or enterprise has the information available to ensure its success. It helps us not only to improve our product, to rationalise production, to beat the competition in the market place, but also to know what to buy among the plethora of goods available, persuading us that they are just what we need and desire. Buying and selling, the unceasing stream of emotional arousal of our desire for possessions, for easy profit and wealth, for health and beauty obsesses our minds and abuses our intelligence. While we are given the impression of having the freedom to choose between the many sources of satisfaction and happiness available, we are enslaved by the exploitive and cynical world of salesmanship. Everything is speeded up and there is no time or inclination to transcend this reality, to consider wider, long-term issues.

2. The Need for Morality

Let me recap for a moment. When our early ancestors emerged in the world as human beings they had to face an instinctual void which gave them the distinction of being able to make choices and adjustments to the demands of their environment; and they acquired a tremendous advantage over all the other animals, the most important transformations in the life of the planet; but by their new capability they had to pay the price of constant uncertainty, for how would they know the right choices they had to make, the right adaptations to the world in which they lived? They needed guides to teach them. Indeed, they became teachable, not merely by means of conditioned reflexes but by forming precepts and visions as to how they should behave and how they should think. We have seen how among Homo erectus the mature males acted as leaders and teachers to the young males when they went out into the strange and dangerous world to hunt for prey and bring home food and nourishment to the cave home and share it with the women and children. The young hunters had to learn the skills vital to the success of the hunting expedition, and the grown males not only participated in the hunt but taught the youngsters. They set an example to them and became a role model. The conflict between the fathers and the sons did not occur for the reasons I have tried earlier to make clear. Not only as a teacher of skills but also by his love and concern for the community and its members he represented the spirit of morality.

Just as we never forget a good teacher, the leader of the hunt entered into the memory of the young, and they adopted his skills as well as his moral concepts; he became a prescriptive model, not a stranger or frightening father figure or despot but as a friend whom they could admire and love. And as they imbued his spirit it became part of themselves, never forgotten, and in turn projected outwards – externalised – as the eternal spirit which guided their lives. And the sense of continuity, of eternity, was reinforced by the old men of the family or tribe who gave them a sense of their history and tradition, when past and present were unified and gave meaning to their daily encounters with the world they experienced, and inspired them with a vision of the future. Thus a moral concept, a universal purpose, provided them with an individual as well as collective sense of identity, and with it a feeling of duty, obligation and responsibility, not born of guilt but of the need to fulfil their role as grown up members of their society, assuring them of affection and love and a sense of belonging. No doubt they thought that their perception of what life was about was eternal and secure, and it replaced instinct-dominated behaviour – genetic programming – or whatever fashionable name you want to give it. They came to project their sense of purpose upon all living things and thought them to be animated by a spirit, with feelings and emotions like themselves.

Even quite recently the people of the Kalahari ceremonially apologised for the suffering they caused to a tree when they had to cut it down. So primitive men would try to restitute the spirit of animals whom they had to kill and ask for their goodwill and for them not to be angry with them but be their allies.

If one were to allow oneself to engage in a little simplification we might call their world-view a metaphysic which co-ordinates the many skills and activities as well as moral duties into a unified image of men's purpose in the world. This was a very long time ago, but the foundation of human cultures is still implanted and resonant in our souls. Eros bound individuals to each other while the aggressive drives were directed outwards to a hostile and often dangerous environment. It was aggression which served Eros and the preservation of life, not only of the individual but of his community: benign aggression, as Erich Fromm called it. Evolution, however, brought with it a multiplication and diversity of skills with the variety of tools which became available, and disrupted the relative simplicity of the foundation culture. People became specialists in the use and production of tools as well as in the knowledge of the world around them. As specialists and experts intent on pursuing their own field, people are increasingly isolated from the expertise of others and understand only a fraction of the knowledge available to their culture. While we are intent upon the pursuit of our own particular activities and our interests associated with them, we become strangers to the other specialists, their skills and their knowledge. But mankind needs a unified concept of the reality around and the reality within by the very nature of its brain and its psyche. 'Connect, always connect,' said Goethe; 'Co-ordinate and integrate the millions of impressions and sensations into a unified whole,' says the ego.

It is interesting to note that in the feudal societies of the Middle Ages the division of labour with its threat to people's sense of identity was counteracted by the guilds of craftsmen who produced a sense of tradition and identity for their members and in some cases gave them the right to elect or censor kings. With the growth of industrialisation, craftsmanship was undermined as craftsmen were turned into labourers who would be hired and fired by the barons of industry and the guilds lost their powers. Karl Marx intended to resuscitate the dignity and power of the working class by proclaiming the metaphysic of the class war as a dominant force of history and the workers' role as an agent of progress towards the utopia of the classless society. It is not so strange after all that Marx, as a descendent of rabbis from whose commands he wanted to free himself, projected the Jewish role as the agents of God's purpose upon the working class, with himself – Marx – as their prophet. We can find many parallels with the teaching of Jesus, who identified himself with the ordinary people, the poor and the oppressed, against the privileged and arrogant, the priests and rulers of this world, and proclaimed those who had suffered from the ignominies of power to be the true inheritors of God's kingdom. The Christian churches, however, preached the virtues of compassion and charity but took care not to disrupt the *status quo*. Marx's metaphysical imagination was exploited by a megalomaniac psychopath to justify his tyranny, and the working class ceased to believe in the revolutionary transformation of society. The atomisation of the productive process progressed and people who actually make things became anonymous units in a statistical universe, and the dignity of craftsmanship was further diminished by the tidal wave of the profit motive in the market-orientated society.

As people have lost the belief in a socialist transformation they only appear concerned with the improvement of wages and working conditions. The political leaders no longer dare to speak in terms of ideology, and ideas have been replaced by slogans which upon examination have little rational foundation and frequently defeat the objectives they intend to pursue. The philosophers who since Plato were to guide the politicians by their wisdom and their vision of the good society are now divided among and against each other and, as we have observed, have retreated into hair-splitting analysis of syntax and the meaning of words, shying away from grand ideas and declaring them anathema to the scientific spirit. Thus the synthesising function of the most human part of our brains is being denied and the more primitive areas gain preponderance and dominate not only the thoughts and behaviour of individuals but our culture. The misuse of the all-embracing ideas of religions as well as the Enlightenment has made it inevitable that we have come acutely to mistrust them. But it is now time to reactivate the synthesising and unifying processes of our minds, and at the same time examine them for their rational as well as psychological merits.

I intend again to refer to Kant, the philosopher and teacher who more than any other modern philosopher – by modern I mean post-Cartesian – has undertaken to analyse the innate faculties of our minds, both in their cognitive as well as moral aspects. In his thorough and rigorous investigations of the properties of our mind, he found that for all our perceptions as well as for our understanding there must be a stimulus from the outside impinging upon our senses, and there must be mental faculties which transform sensations into perceptions and understanding of objects. These innate faculties of our minds he termed *a priori* – before experience – and defined them in his categories of cognition. Besides these categories which are fundamental to theoretical as well as empirical reasoning, he analysed the innate categories of morality as the framework for moral concepts which he called the categorical imperatives. As he put it in his introduction to the *Critique of Pure Reason*: 'Though all our knowledge begins with experience, it by no means follows that it all arises out of experience. For, on the contrary, it is quite possible that our empirical knowledge is a compound of that which we receive through impressions or sensations, and that which the faculty of cognition supplies from itself (sensuous experience providing merely the occasion).' He declared that philosophy stands in need of a science which shall determine the possibility, principles and extent of human knowledge *a priori*. What we experience, perceive or know, depends upon the mental apparatus we have for experiencing and knowing.

The idea that we do not merely encounter and experience facts as such but that there exist in our minds innate properties which make experience and knowledge possible was Kant's fundamental and original contribution. We have seen evidence for it in the structure and function of the brain, where the prefrontal lobes coordinate the manifold of impulses and sensations into a unified concept and image (*Vorstellung* – placing it in front of our minds – as the German language puts it more succinctly). It also complies with the psychoanalytic concept of the ego functions whose task it is to unify the multitude of desires and instincts into a coherent whole and provides a sense of self which experiences and thinks.

Kant defines the cognitive processes of our minds by their innate concepts which make perception and understanding possible and calls them the categories of space and time, causality, mass, extension, totality and unity.

3. Kant's Categories of Cognition

i. Space

Space is a concept or image which is not derived from outward experience but precedes it. For in order that certain sensations relate to something outside me, separate from each other in different places, the inner representation of space must already exist. Therefore the perception of an outside object is only possible through the antecedent representation of space which we have in our minds.

ii. Time

Time is a condition *a priori* of all phenomena as we experience them in the world outside, for neither co-existence nor succession would be perceived by us if the concept of time did not exist in our minds, by which we perceive things either as existing at the same time or at different times in succession to each other. The spatial-temporal reality in which all things are perceived is a primary condition of experience. The category of time therefore is the framework for the sense of past, present and future and the foundation for the way things change and develop, how one emerges out of the other, how things follow each other, and also provides the inevitable ground for the category of causality. All phenomena in the world around us are in space and are related to each other according to their position in space. And we can also say that all objects perceived as real are in time and necessarily related to their position in time. Thus the *a priori* concept of the spatial-temporal nature of the world is a condition *a priori* of all phenomena whatsoever, not only for our perception of them but also for our understanding of the way things change and develop.

iii. Causality

While the category of time is the necessary framework in which past, present and future can be conceived, the way things change and develop and what makes things happen provides the inevitable ground for the concept of causality. Whatever takes place in the world, all the phenomena we recognise and experience, the sense of history and the way things change leads to the inevitable idea that everything that exists must have a cause. The concept of causality has been formulated by many philosophers as the sentence of sufficient reason: everything that is must have a cause for its being – *Nihil est sine ratione cur potius sit, quam non sit.* Schopenhauer calls the question 'Why?' the mother of all science.

That this is a universal *a priori* condition of our thinking is shown in the images of deities who are represented as the cause of a variety of natural phenomena or states of mind, culminating in the God of monotheism who is creator and cause of everything – the first cause – the *causa prima*. However sophisticated the modern mind, ready to dismiss God before the altar of science, the cause that made the universe has been traced to the big bang some 14,000,000,000 years ago, even while those self-same scientists maintain that the principle of causality does not operate on the level of elementary particles which the physical universe is made of. There is no doubt, moreover, that the conception of causality is the inspiration of curiosity to find out what makes things the way they are in the world outside us, as well as in the mind of men, and how the brain itself has become the way it is.

iv. Mass and Extension

If we speak of the phenomena which make up our world as we know it, we must also consider the categories of mass and extension. Everything that is must be perceived and thought of as having mass and extension, for without it we could not perceive it, even with the help of the most sophisticated microscopes. The same applies to extension, which means that everything occupies, however minutely, a part of space. If space is the intrinsic *a priori* principle then every object has spatial characteristics, for without them it would not impinge upon our awareness. It is true that quantum physics posits a whole range of subatomic particles which are not directly observable – nobody has as yet actually seen or touched an elementary particle, but its existence is inferred by its impact upon very small or very large-scale aspects of the physical universe. We may speak of sub-atomic particles as wave particles or of energy, but we can neither directly observe them nor understand the way they operate. It is a categorical assumption that every object that exists can be weighed and measured, that by its mass it must have some weight and by its extension must occupy some space which can be measured, however small. As Niels Bohr has exclaimed: 'Anybody who thinks he understands quantum mechanics does not understand it.' We may know something about the unbelievable complexities of the sub-atomic foundations of the natural world, but we can neither understand nor imagine them. Nobody has yet weighed or measured them;

they can only be recognised by their effects, and their existence and characteristics inferred by mathematical and statistical calculation. Indeed they are outside the categories of the understanding and of perception, and we seem to be entering here an area of nature which has the characteristics of a noumenon or, as Kant has called it, *das Ding an sich* – 'the thing in itself', beyond the way in which we understand things. This does not invalidate Kant's propositions but rather proves them. (This is a subject that demands a thoroughgoing investigation which is outside the field of the present book, and I hope to write about it in a different place.)

v. Totality and Unity

The whole area of the *a priori* categories of knowledge follow the principle of unity. What connects all the *a priori* conditions of knowledge is the concept of unity by which the multitude of sensations and impressions are connected into a meaningful whole by the prefrontal areas of the brain. Unity or totality, as I have mentioned, is plurality contemplated as unity. This fundamental human need to integrate the multitude of sensations, impressions, feelings, drives, as well as instinctual urges into a unified, all-embracing image of life is presented by an omnipotent deity, or the laws of physics, of history, the economic foundations of social existence and other metaphysical concepts. It can be said that we all think we are at the centre of the universe, but we have to see ourselves in it and adopt a position in the world. But in order to do this we need to have an image or idea of the world. The unification of all the diverse impressions into a meaningful whole is a condition of the understanding which we do not merely acquire by observation of phenomena. Without the process of unification or synthesis we could neither recognise nor understand the specific character or form of an object.

The concept of unity or totality arising out of the synthetic *a priori* considers that everything that exists follows a universal law and if we discover the law which governs the empirical universe we can understand the singular-specific character of phenomena. To give an example: three hundred years ago Galileo used a telescope to observe the heavens and noted that Jupiter has several moons which clearly orbit that planet. At a stroke, this observation demolished the concept of the earth-centred universe which was upheld by Ptolemy and by the church as God's will. Newton's investigation of the planetary motions showed how the movements of planets could be explained by the universal law of gravity, and the universe was seen to be sun-centred. The sun pulls the earth towards it and the earth moves around the sun so that the centrifugal force balances gravity. As it is now known, millions of stars exist in our galaxy of the milky way which is only one of thousands of other galaxies known to exist in the universe. And here we encounter the two necessary forms of all understanding of objects, namely the analytic and the synthetic *a priori*.

The analytic and synthetic *a priori*

The presupposition of any analytic operation is that from the examination of the whole we arrive at parts of the whole. The parts, as Kant says, are in an analytic concept contained in the whole and we arrive at the parts of the whole by the method of specification. This proposition is fundamental to logical analysis as well as to spatio-temporal investigations, in which case we speak of science. For instance, all judgements in which the relation of the subject to a predicate is thought are possible in two ways: either, the predicate B belongs to the subject A as something contained in it; or B lies outside the subject but is connected with it. In the first case we call the judgement analytic, in the second synthetic.

In the judgement that a rainy day is a wet day the predicate 'wet day' is contained in the subject 'rainy day', and therefore is analytic. Thus the concept of the predicate helps to break up the subject under investigation into those constituent parts that all along have been thought in it; being a square includes being rectangular, or that the constituent concept of being a square is being equilateral and rectangular. Therefore, the predicate of the judgement that all squares are rectangular may be said to analyse out what is already contained in the subject. Another example: the proposition that a forest consists of many trees is analytic *a priori* because 'many trees' is inherent in forests, and the denial of this proposition would be a contradiction in terms. A synthetic judgement can be considered *a priori* if a subject connects with one or more characteristic, and those connections make it possible to relate it to other subjects with similar characteristics. For instance, the proposition that all trees are made of wood is synthetic because the general factor of wood is common to all individual trees, wherever they may be.

The connectedness or unity of the manifold of impressions is the result of the process of unification, and this is the work of the active understanding. All connection, Kant maintains, whether we are conscious of it or not, is the root of understanding, which we might call by the general name of synthesis.

4. The Equivalence between the Categories of Cognition and the Categories of Morality

The reader may wonder why in a treatise on morality I introduce the complicated arguments of Kant's philosophy of knowledge, but, as we shall see, the foundations of cognition can be applied to moral concepts. If we can establish that the categories of cognition are fundamental to our understanding of the world of the phenomena, then we can also assume that they govern our moral concepts. This would enable us to arrive at correct assessments of moral propositions and to judge whether they are valid or nonsensical, self-contradictory or motivated by destructive or aggressive drives, which, as we have found, is all too often the case in religious or ideological convictions where what they claim to be moral merely serves immoral goals. If, for instance, we consider the category of unity as the supreme principle of rational and empirical thinking, we can apply it to moral ideas which relate to all human beings and in various ways to all living things. Equally the definition of the analytic and synthetic introduces logical rules to moral propositions.

i. Space and Time

Space means the extension and the relation of the self to the world around it. The individual is in the world; his dealings with it, the way it affects him and how he acts in it represents his reality. No person is an isolated entity but constantly interacts with the events of the real world, not only on a cognitive but also on an emotional and moral level. He is judged by the world and he judges the world; his interests, drives, desires, ambitions and hopes are acted out on the public stage which is his world – 'He sits in the world', as Heidegger liked to remind us.

Time means that men's actions, attitudes and judgements are related to the past. The world has a history which plays a decisive role in the way contemporary political, economic and ideological constructs have developed. It is equally related to the future upon which we project our aims and aspirations; our present values are not only influenced by the memories of the past but are largely determined by our visions of the future. For instance, the consciousness of the working class and their political aspirations always relate back to the hardships and miseries which their parents and grandparents had to endure in the past. Their struggles for social justice and their judgements of the present state of society are motivated by the kind of society they intend to create in the future.

Time past and time future are present in the consciousness of a culture and the moral consciousness of individuals. We could of course expand the conception of time past and time future if we consider the findings of psychoanalysis, where neurotic symptoms as well as a person's character – his values and perceptions – are traced to his experiences in the past from earliest childhood, which while largely forgotten, or repressed, influence his present judgements and values. Patients seek treatment in order to be freed of their disturbances in the future.

ii. Mass and Extension

The phenomena presented to our senses and perceived as objects can be weighed and measured as empirical data, whereas states of mind are data provided by our own subjective experiences.

Humans are distinguished by a wide range of psychic activities, impulses, conflicts, desires and drives which find expression in their behaviour. By the way they act they can be seen as objects and their behaviour described empirically. We are both subject as well as object which can be observed internally or externally. We can thus perhaps be justified in paraphrasing mass as man's mental substance, the energy invested in mental processes, thoughts and ideas.

While the size and weight of a person's brain can be empirically observed, it is not its weight or size which reveals his mental processes, but the power of his intellect, the intensity of his thoughts which arouse our interest. While Kant's brain – reputed to be the largest ever observed – is of interest to the neurologist and arouses our curiosity, it is the mind of Kant and his intellectual energy which has radiated – and continues to do so – out to the world and has influenced people's thinking. All energy radiates and so do ideas. The equivalence between mass and energy, which Einstein revealed in the physical world, can also be seen to operate in the mental world. We might also say that while mass represents the energy of mental processes, its extension represents the range of its ideas and thoughts.

All energy radiates, but there can be good or bad energy – life-promoting or life-destroying. There is love and there is hatred, life affirmation or life denial or destruction. Who can doubt the destructive energies of a psychopath, as distinct from the life-affirming person who radiates love and goodwill. Whereas the world of the psyche does not have extension or weight, and therefore cannot be weighed or measured, our behaviour is part of the empirical world, characterised by extension, manifest forms in space. One cannot weigh or measure a person's soul; one can, as they say, weigh up a person by his character, his values and his attitudes.

Humans, therefore, are both objects as well as subjects, and one can look at them from the outside as physical entities – their bodies, their chemistry, their anatomical and physiological characteristics, including their genetic endowment as well as their manifest behaviour – or from the inside, so to speak, namely their mental and emotional experiences as well as their values, goals and judgements, both on the conscious as well as the unconscious level. Empirically orientated psychiatrists, psychologists and physicians pride themselves on their scientific approach and give credence only to what can be observed, and focus exclusively upon organic or behavioural disturbances, both in mental as well as physical diseases.

iii. Causality

If we consider that mind and psyche have the power to influence the body, its physiological, chemical and metabolic functions, we might be inclined to think that we are not merely subject to causation but are ourselves causative agents. Humans create their own conditions, frequently without knowing that they are doing so, and then have to adjust to the conditions they have caused. We have acquired the power to transform our natural environment by our instincts, by our will, by our religious or ideological convictions, as well as by technology and science. But all too often our powers tend to bypass the cortical endowment of foresight and anticipation of the consequences of our beliefs and actions, which can be destructive or productive.

I have mentioned the category of mass as substance, as man's fourth dimension of depth. For human beings, their substance is in their subjectivity, and for a rational judgement of the nature of humans we have to approach their subjective essence as well as their objective existence, which means that for the rational intellect man is both subject as well as object. And, moreover, we have found that his subjectivity is the causative agent for the objective world, which he has created and in which he lives.

While on the level of existence man's encounter with his environment and his reactions to it can be observed empirically, we must bear in mind that his manifest behaviour is itself caused by his psyche, his 'essential' self. But we must also ask what it is that causes our psyche, our soul, to be the way it is. But that is the task of psychoanalysis which investigates man's own experiences of his mind as valid data, not from outside but from the inside, in order to understand it.

iv. The Freedom of the Will

As we have seen, the higher cortical functions of his brain oblige man to be free to create his own guidelines for action. Indeed, it is the freedom of the will which is the condition of morality. For if the will were determined by instinctual drives, reflexes or conditioned reflexes, there would be no freedom of choice and no ground for moral concepts. But we must remember the paradox that man can be motivated by paranoid and aggressive fantasies and drives, which exclude reason and matters of fact, and what they proclaim to be moral duties can serve immoral aims. Thus men become slaves to coercive rule which prohibits the exercise of their moral faculties – the feeling of altruism and consideration for their fellow men – when the instinct of love and care for others is denied and gives way to fear and hatred. Thus we can speak of the good will and the bad will. But while the moral feeling is rooted in the need to receive love and to give love, it still needs the reassurance that it has rational validity, for otherwise it is all too easily corrupted or ridiculed, and it is here that the category of unity acquires a decisive role in moral concepts.

v. The Category of Unity

I have mentioned earlier in reference to the synthetic *a priori* that in all our thinking about matters of fact, including scientific thinking, a synthetic concept operates, for without it there could be no unity of consciousness of a law which determines the nature of objects and their relationships; there would be merely a stream of impressions without order or significance. It can happen that what we regard as a permanent feature of the world is merely transient and shown to be erroneous. Unlike analytic *a priori* concepts, synthetic concepts are capable of change, and our basic idea of the law which governs facts would have to change. But while the content of the law can change, the need for a unifying concept of a general law remains.

As Kant's category of unity is the ultimate and most important aspect of theoretical reason, his categorical imperative of unity is the necessary foundation of all moral thinking: 'Act only on that maxim whereby you can at the same time will that it should be a universal law.' It requires the good will as the creative agent to make it possible. Even if it has difficulties in fulfilling its purpose, it is nevertheless the most important force in the pursuit of the *summum bonum* – the highest good. Without the good will the categorical imperative remains a formal law without real impact upon man's activities, his beliefs, politics, economics and social relationships; it would not advance mankind's moral purpose, but would be defeated by the imperatives of self-interest, the interest of family, nation, race, religion or class, against the others, the outsiders, the enemies. The unity of aims shared by mankind will be considered a chimera, an impossible dream of romantics, poets or philosophers, which has no bearing upon the real world. Thus the categorical imperative of unity cannot only be judged by its logical or rational significance or necessity but also by its possibility.

The Categorical Imperatives

Kant formulated only one categorical imperative which as he said, conforms to the law of unity, has universal application and is therefore necessary. I shall specify a number of moral imperatives which are contained in the universal law and follow from it. This, I believe, would bring us a step nearer to an understanding of how the categorical imperative can be applied in the real world.

1) Kant's formulation of the imperative of unity as the categorical imperative: 'Act only on that maxim whereby you can at the same time will that it should be a universal law', so that 'your actions confirm, and are in keeping with, the universal law of morality' and contribute towards its realisation.
2) The imperative of freedom and human dignity: 'Never treat a human being as a means to serve your ends but always as an end in himself'.
3) The imperative of the good will: 'Do not do unto others what you would not want them to do unto you'. As we do not wish that others should hurt or ignore our feelings it implies that equally we should consider the feelings of our fellow men.

4) The imperative of congruence: Act in such a manner that the facts created by your actions are in keeping with your concepts of ends.
5) The imperative of honesty: Conceive moral ends in such a manner that it is possible for yourself and for humanity to follow them. Consider whether universal morality which embraces all humanity is possible.

We can add that the imperative of honesty also demands of us to consider whether the propositions of a universal morality express our own feelings and whether we can truthfully say that we desire and look forward to their realisation; whether we really want the transformations in life and in society as envisaged by the categorical imperatives, and whether we welcome the intellectual and emotional orientations it demands.

5. Reconstructing God

We must once again try to hear the voice of the old teacher, the spirit, the superego, the God, who by his presence and immortality created a sense of unity, of past, present and the future, cohesion and belonging among his fellows. And we must reassess his message and his instructions in the light of our experience and the conditions of our time. For the history of culture has produced the indelible impression that it does not take long before a God of love who cares for his children, understands their foibles and is ready to forgive them and is always there to help, turns into a God of war, encouraging his followers to exercise revenge upon those who are taken to be the cause of their hardships. When his promises for happiness and prosperity fail to materialise, he blames the non-believers, the aliens for his people's disappointments. Gods and kings have all through history employed the old tactic of projecting their failures and people's anger upon the enemy, so that they need God's protection and worship him to ensure victory. If the God and the kings fail, they need an enemy to blame in order to ensure their status in people's mind and to hold on to their powers.

FOUNDATIONS OF MORALITY

The supreme God of monotheism wants mankind – his ultimate masterpiece – to acknowledge him and to show him their gratitude, their appreciation for what he has done and to explore the wonders of his creation, of life on earth and the mysteries of the universe, and above all that they fulfil his purpose and to ask for his approval. As Kant has put it: 'It is impossible to cherish morally pure dispositions without at the same time conceiving that these dispositions are related to the supreme Being.' For God knows how we think and act, and therefore the concept of morality relates to His expectation and our behaviour is recognised and judged by Him. In all our choices we relate them to some real or imagined judgement by which we evaluate our actions or intentions. In psychoanalysis we call it the superego, that internal watchman who knows what we think, what we do, condemns or approves, makes us feel guilty or praised, and is the root of our conscience, good or bad. Freud, speaking from the point of view of patriarchal society, considers the superego as the father figure who judges us according to his expectations and plans and imposes taboos upon impulses or actions which contradict his intentions or threaten his authority.

In a culture dominated by the Oedipus complex, which Freud considered to be universal, it is the taboo upon the boys' as well as the girls' sexual drives or narcissistic assertiveness which rivalled the father and aroused their bad conscience which patriarchal religions considers to be man's state of sin, which can only be overcome by submission to the heavenly father and begging for his forgiveness. We can therefore speak of the good and loving superego or the bad and angry superego, and Freud maintains that the taboos imposed upon man and submission to the social authorities are the universal foundation of civilisation in its various forms, the reason for civilised man's neuroticism and discontent. Indeed, most civilisations uphold a rather pessimistic view of human nature, but men continue to invoke God's help to overcome their bad conscience, they ask for God's forgiveness for their sins, and beat their breasts and bow to him and glorify him in song and prayer and hope to evoke his goodwill and restore his love for mankind. We pray for peace but endlessly make war against each other; we tyrannise, oppress and exploit our fellow men and threaten the life of this planet. But we still think that God harbours a good will and love for mankind, and beg him to help us to overcome our sinful nature.

God no longer answers our pleas. He has disappeared from our view, and while we can read the words pronounced by the prophets we do not understand them. But we must remind God that he has promised that there will be a time when we would be able to speak and to 'discuss together', and it is now the time to speak and to ask why he has forsaken us in the terrible twentieth century when millions died in the trenches, the atrocities of the holocaust, Stalin's terror and Hitler's maniacal creed of hatred, and when rage and violence continues to visit large parts of humanity.

As we speak to him he responds, and says, I have loved you and I still do, and I want to be proud of the species I have endowed with reason and morality, but you have forsaken me. Whether you recognise me as God or the life force or the cosmic energy makes no difference for you can only see me in terms which you understand, but the love which I have given you and which is in you seems to have been defeated by primitive drives of aggression, destruction and sadism, and the pleasures they afford you. While your mind is dominated by these perversions I cannot help you, and you have to show your goodwill and the determination to overcome them. It is now up to you to employ your rational faculties to understand the causes of these perversions; you have to analyse why Eros, my messenger, is constantly defeated by his adversary Thanatos. And now it is time to give Eros – the life force – the chance to emerge victorious if you want to survive.

Well, it is good to hear God, that image by which we represent to ourselves the life force, encouraging us to affirm it.

As a psychoanalyst, I understand what he means by the innate love that is in us, for in my work I have discovered that people are not born with anger or hatred, they are not born evil but with a need for love. But what turns love into aggression, mistrust of their fellow men, jealousy, envy, the manic need for power or the passive despair, what makes them feel inadequate, unrecognised, afraid of life, paranoid or psychopathic criminals? I have described the processes by which love turns into the many forms of hate and destruction in previous books, but want here to give a short overview of these processes.

6. The Origins of Thanatos

I want to remark first of all that the negative qualities which in different ways dominate the life of individuals and of societies are secondary reactions to love denied. From earliest infancy the individual reaches out for love, warmth and attention. Its lips are highly libidinised and sensitive, an orientation and explorative organ which immediately makes the infant aware of its mother's responses. The mother's breast is indeed the baby's first encounter with the universe. Nature has provided us with a signalling system for the communication of love in the form of pleasure. We reach out with the desire for warmth and love, and are made aware of it by the feelings of pleasure. If we feel that the primary object, the mother – for the infant the embodiment of the universe – responds with pleasure to our desire, than our desire is good, then we are important and wanted by the world. The pleasure sensations of the loving mother arouse a wide range of erotic feelings often accompanied by vaginal sensations, and we can also observe genital sensations and even erections in male infants.

However, this fundamental process can be subjected to many disturbances, particularly by mothers who suffer from erotic inhibitions and various degrees of pleasure anxiety. This in turn will affect the mother's libidinous communion with her baby, and her nipples and her bodily contact will be devoid of pleasure sensations, empty of libido and warmth. She will appear to be indifferent and guarded, her body tense, anxious and armoured, and the infant will become aware of this and become very frightened. The social life of a woman, particularly her relationship with her husband, the quality of love or indifference between them, her feeling of being unwanted or in turn not wanting her partner, will greatly affect her capacity to give out the warmth and love which the child craves for. Her own upbringing will largely influence her capacity to relate with love to her child. But beyond that there is the general attitude of a culture towards Eros and sexual pleasure, whether it affirms and validates mankind's erotic needs or condemns them as sinful.

The child experiences, as it were, the social taboos upon the libido in its contact with the mother, and becomes afraid and quite desperate. Its reactions to the world and the armoured breast will be to attack the breast in order to penetrate her non-giving armour and get through to the libido underneath it. It must also be realised that the quality of the milk, its chemistry will be affected by her erotic attitudes in general and to the child in particular. The taste of the milk will feel sour, bitter, unacceptable or hostile, or it will feel sweet and pleasant, reflecting the mother's attitude to the child and to herself. If it feels bad the child's lips and jaws will tense up, as well as its whole body, its throat, stomach and genitals, its limbs, respiratory and digestive system, will become tight in a defensive, rejective manner. In its anxiety – frequently amounting to terror – it will start kicking, screaming, stopping itself breathing, and a whole lot of other reaction-formations which every mother can observe without understanding their meaning.

The child cannot speak to communicate its needs and its feelings, and will do so with its body. On the oral level its jaw muscles will tense up as manifestations of fear and anger, and it will attack and bite, partly as a release from the tension but also to penetrate the mother's armour and to release the libido which she has hidden and denied. It is quite natural, therefore, for it to become aggressive, for otherwise it would remain isolated, with a feeling of being unwanted, unloved, its existence unrecognised. Unless it attacks nothing ever happens, nothing flows and it ceases to exist. The death of the libido means the death of a person, which is literally true for the infant and also true for grown-ups, and we can understand that such people will become aggressive in order to alleviate their anxieties. If, however, the mother senses the child's needs and allows herself to respond to them, its anger will either recede or remain a part drive, a sensitive reaction to perceived neglect, which however can be reassured by love. But if the mother cannot respond and the child does not feel able to make her, then it feels helpless and anger turns to rage – as we say – helpless with blind rage – and destructiveness. To put it colloquially, if we are surrounded and imprisoned by a blank wall then there is nothing we can do to make it disappear, then we have to attack and destroy it with all our power.

We can see here a similarity with the condition of many young men or women who feel that the world ignores them and will not respond to their needs, is indifferent to their very existence, and then they respond with rage and see the world around them as their enemy. This frequently leads to the primacy of sadism and the pleasure it affords as an end in itself. They feel helpless and see no way to change their condition, and sadism is the only outlet for their needs to be recognised. Violent criminals or psychopaths are to a large extent fixated upon this reaction-formation, and it dominates the thoughts and actions of many nations or tribes, driving them to the most brutal crimes.

While an individual's encounter with his primary environment during the first moments, months and years of his development exercise a decisive influence upon his psyche, it will extend to his narcissistic need to love himself and to be loved by his environment and by the society he lives in, or his needs to be properly recognised as a person. If he can as a young person or as a grown-up achieve by his own efforts a positive relationship with the people around him, he can repress or sublimate the traumas of his first months or years. An important aspect of his narcissistic restitution is the work he engages in, and the things he produces to gain recognition and rewards. In his productive work he can identify himself with what he produces; he reproduces himself and recognises himself in what he has made. His work is not merely a means but in many respects an end in itself. He contributes something to the world, to the culture, to his community, and gains respect and acknowledgement. Therefore, the imperative never to treat a fellow man and his work merely as a means for your ends but as an end in itself is correct, for if men's labours become merely a means, they rob a man of his self-respect, he is denied his image as a distinct person who is appreciated for what he is; he becomes a slave or a robot.

We might say that we cannot build pyramids without thousands of slaves, or cathedrals and palaces without a multitude of labourers; even while some of them are highly skilled, as citizens they are subjected to the coercive powers of priests and kings, are exploited and are not seen as persons. The capitalist entrepreneur who has, in Adam Smith's words, set himself apart from the rule of the guilds of craftsmen, and of the culture of the community and therefore has been free to explore and exploit the potential market for their goods, has no doubt created an abundance of products and developed industrial mass production, but in doing so he has enslaved his workers in order to serve his ends, and forced them to become anonymous units in industrial mass production. No wonder the labouring classes would occasionally be overwhelmed by a collective rage and want to destroy the system which had controlled their lives. The revolutionary rage has all too often, even in recent times, been primarily motivated by the desire to destroy capitalism, without knowing what to put in its place.

It is significant that the Jews regained a sense of their identity by rebelling against the Egyptians who enslaved them, and began their history as a people. They had received the ten commandments which God dictated to Moses, and acquired a moral framework which gave them a purpose and a vision of the future. With God's guidance they no longer felt helpless. Another prophet of the people, of the oppressed and impoverished labouring classes presented an all-embracing image of the laws of history and nature, the universal class struggle, which pointed to the victory of the workers over their oppressors and gave them meaning as well as a sense of purpose and transformed their rage into revolutionary ideology. They need no longer feel helpless, and their anger would be directed to an organised struggle to overcome their dehumanisation in the inevitable coming of the classless society.

While Marx inspired the workers to act in order to regain their humanity, he was wrong in many crucial aspects. His theology, his metaphysical concepts of the nature of history, was flawed. We might also ask whether God was wrong about humanity and the Jews, whether his expectations of the universal unity of human purposes were also flawed. Perhaps he did not sufficiently anticipate that his moral commands were exceedingly difficult for human beings to follow and repeatedly defeated by their psychological conflicts and fixations. No wonder that God himself became angry sometimes and disillusioned by his chosen people, threatening them with destruction, and repeatedly instructed his prophets to warn them. But he had meant well and he loved them and tried again and again to direct them to the right paths.

The Bible tells the story of the conflict between God's expectations, not only of his chosen people but of the species he has chosen to understand and follow his purpose, and the difficulties they experience in fulfilling his aim. So he is right to demand that we should find out what is holding us back and to overcome our resistance and stubbornness. In my work as a therapist I have had ample opportunity to observe the conflicts which beset the human soul, and have written about them in a number of books. We must recognise that God, the personification of the life-force, Eros, is right to demand that we begin to understand and to reconstruct ourselves to enable us to follow his purpose.

I would like to mention here briefly another aspect of men's psychic conflicts which has an important repercussion on the values and behaviour of societies and cultures. The anal libido represents an important aspect of the development and transformations of the libido. Human beings, being meat-eaters, make their faeces poisonous and they are perceived as smelly and dirty. But on the other hand they are, as I have mentioned, a product which comes out of their person, a manifestation of their soul. At first this material is seen by the child as vibrant, alive and golden, and he wants to be proud of what he has made and show it to his mother, but in various degrees he experiences her disgust and repulsion.

If her disgust is too strongly pronounced it makes him feel rejected, dirty and disgusting, and he will feel dirty as a person. If, on the other hand, the mother's reactions are sympathetic and she shows tolerance and continued love, while showing that there is a universal taboo upon playing or smearing himself with it or taking it in his mouth, he can sublimate his forbidden pleasure and replace faeces with other material. He learns to play with things and forms them into recognisable shapes endowed with images of his soul. He learns the pleasures of working and producing things and to offer them to his fellows. But if the sense of being rejected as dirty during his early encounters with his mother is too powerful and becomes a fixation, he will become retentive, stubborn and frequently driven by the compulsion to cleanse himself. Rituals of cleansing become neurotic obsessions and play an important part in religious rituals.

The conflict between the clean and the dirty acquires a paramount role in the hierarchy of societies and cultures. The kings and the aristocrats are the clean ones, they surround themselves with pleasing smelling perfumes and appear to be well-washed and groomed, while the ordinary people, the workers, dirty themselves in their work, are perceived as unclean and inferior. The formal, clean clothes of the favoured classes represent their superiority, while the informal or dishevelled clothes of the ordinary people with their unclean habits are taken to be inferior. It is the task of the priests in their immaculate appearance to clean the people by their purification ceremonies, often immersing them in holy waters or sprinkling them. The orthodox Jews, clinging to their position as faithful adherents to God's commands, mistake God's moral injunctions for ritual obsession.

It is interesting to note that in a culture which wants to show its defiance of the traditional hierarchies many will deliberately walk about like labourers at work, or tramps; or women – protesting against their traditional role of being submissive and demure – will aggressively assert their equality or superiority by being sexually provocative in their dress and appearance. The rebellion against the sexual taboos imposed by patriarchy can find expression in a libertine show of sexual freedom and will consider promiscuity as a virtue, and feminists – the proselytisers of female freedom – will consider the family outdated and even consider males redundant, not only for themselves but also for their offspring. We must remember that for too long sexuality was identified with dirtiness and women were considered unclean. And we encounter therefore a powerful reaction-formation against these traditional judgements. Thus, at this moment of our cultural history we find rebellion and aggressiveness as a kind of standard model for behaviour in all kinds of human activities, but there is no idea what to put in place of the order they want to destroy. Rebellion thus becomes an end in itself and encourages a wide range of primitive drives – previously repressed – to rise to the surface.

While it is important to understand the unconscious roots of our anger and rage, aggression and sadism, which divides mankind as it divides an individual soul, it is not enough.

It is time to reconstruct the old teachers, and the God who speaks to humanity and to bring them up-to-date, so that we can recognise their meaning and their relevance to our time, and teach fathers how to be at one with their children and how to instruct them. For children have to be taught and given models they can identify with, not in anger but in love and affection, and be free to ask questions and to discuss their problems, not only to know what the father thinks but also for the father to know what his children think.

Chapter 7

Towards the Good Society

I shall endeavour to define the objectives of morality by making a number of propositions or maxims of aims, in the belief that they are applicable to all men. A definition of aims must, if it is to claim general validity, be congruent with the normative principles of morality, as well as with the facts of reality. If they meet both these demands, then they can be called true. If they meet only the first, namely the principles of the categorical imperatives they can be called partially true, but if they do not meet either of these requirements then they are bound to be false. I call them maxims because, although I consider them to have general validity, discussion and agreement on them is necessary before they can be called laws. If, however, they can be shown to be true in the way I defined above, then they could be considered as duties, or at least aspirations.

1. The Maxims of Moral Aims:

1) enjoy your feelings of love and of being loved, and don't be afraid of them; nor do you need to hide them in your relationship to others.
2) respond to other people's feelings, and have empathy with their suffering, their grief and pain as well as their joy and happiness.
3) enjoy sexual feelings in yourself and in others without anxiety and guilt, but never use others as a means, as objects for your sexual gratification without respect for their desires and feelings. Never force others to submit to your desires or use violence to gain gratification.

4) participate with others in pleasurable and creative activities without the need to assert yourself over them and diminish their self-respect.
5) cherish your pleasure in your work and productive activity, and in the exercise of your skills to see yourself reflected in what you produce; experience self-realisation and a sense of dignity by what you create and through satisfaction of contributing to the welfare of others.
6) enjoy taking responsibility for your actions and for the purposes which they serve; feel satisfaction in the carrying out of your duty as an active member of society.
7) cultivate your moral and rational capabilities and examine at all times statements and dictates for their rational and moral content and anticipate their consequences, for this affirms your freedom and your autonomy.
8) examine the logic and value of your own propositions and appraise the facts contained in them, and, above all, never let your obsessions and prejudices be presented as universal truths. Never fabricate evidence to justify your beliefs.
9) never submit to the demands and ideas of those who speak in the name of authority without examining their value as well as their logic. Cultivate the ideas and actions which serve the advancement of humanity and find humanity reflected in your own humanity.
10) recognise secondary drives of aggression and sadism as well as greed, possessiveness, the demand for power over others, envy and revenge, and do not adopt a stubborn self-righteousness in order to justify yourself, nor project such compulsions upon others and thereby develop paranoid fears which frequently dominate personal as well as social relationships.
11) promote the virtues of love, empathy and mutual trust as the good qualities of life, the source of the good will, and feel a sense of responsibility for the promotion of these qualities in society.

A society which promotes these maxims merits the name of a good society, and individuals who cultivate them to their best abilities are endowed with good will.

While these maxims relate to the states of mind and values of individuals in their affirmation of freedom and responsibility, with love, beauty, truth and justice as the highest aim, the question of what a good society which follows these ideals looks like in practice immediately springs to one's mind.

One might say that it is all very well to expound the principles of morality, but the test is surely how they could be enacted in the practical world, in politics, legislation, the prevailing economic system with its mode of production and human relationships, and how peace and goodwill can be assured among nations, races and religions.

Plato intended philosophers to guide people and their social organisation to an understanding of the truth of the nature of reality, and to rediscover their innate knowledge of the beautiful and the good, and affirm it in their existence. When he was asked why in his old age he undertook the long and arduous journey to the court of Dionysius II to be his adviser, he replied that he had to do this, otherwise he would be considered to be merely a man of words. Shelley maintained that poets are the unacknowledged legislators of mankind.

I want, therefore, to show just a few examples of how moral principles could be applied in our present societies.

2. Work as Creativity

Work which gives satisfaction and is carried out not only as a means, but to a significant extent as an end in itself, is good work; it makes a good product and satisfies not only the worker but also the consumer. What type of society would once again refurbish the sense of pride in skill and craftsmanship, and encourage people to identify with what they have produced and see it as a mirror of their own soul, Narcissus reborn in the product of his labours?

'They shall build houses and inhabit them; they shall plant vineyards and eat their fruit. They shall not build and another inhabit; they shall not plant and another eat; for like the days of a tree shall the days of my people be, and my chosen shall long enjoy the work of their hands. They shall not labour in vain' (*Isaiah* 65: 31).

The consumer of another man's product will not be grateful and appreciative of it if the producer is not appreciated or is unknown – has no place in our mind. The mass of commodities which now fill the shops and are made available by machines and computers turn the producer into an anonymous non-person alienated from his product.

Work is without doubt one of the most important activities for the preservation of life and its enhancement. Without work we would starve and be oppressed by a sense of failure. This applies in various ways to all living things. In humans it not only serves the instinct of self-preservation but also of self-realisation, as in the exercise of one's skills one sees oneself reflected in the product one has created, and we derive a sense of personal dignity and a sense of satisfaction of contributing to the welfare of others (5th Maxim). However, in our world of industrial computer controlled mass-production, sometimes called post-industrial, this maxim is ignored and contradicted in practice. The producer is forced to serve high-tech robots, and becomes a depersonalised robot himself, a number in the statistic of capitalist economy, when factories serve the financial interest of industrial conglomerates dependent upon banking houses, financial corporations and investment companies, all chasing for profit and prominence on the stock exchange.

The depersonalising influences which operate in the production of commodities is further intensified by the enormous proliferation of the professions serving the promotion of sales – advertising, public relations and the media – reducing still further the consumer's contact with the actual producer. The product is as impersonal as the producer, and fails to give the consumer a sense that it is made for him.

Very few children, and indeed grown-ups, have any idea where the food displayed in the supermarkets comes from. They have never seen a living cow or pig, nor the farmer milking cows or rearing his pigs, nor how wheat grows and is made into the bread they eat. They are equally unaware how the innumerable goods available in the shops and advertised on television, through the internet and in newspapers are made, and by whom. As there appears to be no connection between the product and the producer, there is nobody one can be grateful to for providing these things for us, and if we cannot feel grateful, we are not gratified.

We have seen that the infant needs not only the physical nourishment but the good libido of the mother, in order to feel good. But if the mother does not communicate her love and her pleasure in the act of giving, it will feel unsatisfied, unwanted and excluded. These primary experiences continue to operate in the grown-up person on the unconscious level. He will want to see or at least imagine the person who provides the product, so that the act of consumption is a special experience which makes him feel special, not just for the moment but as a continuing feeling which pervades his personality. Otherwise he will be driven by a ruthless and frantic search for gratification without being able to still his hunger, like a bulimic person who has to fill his stomach up till it bursts and then throws up and starts again without ever feeling a sense of gratification. We can speak of a collective bulimia in our mass-production culture, where its citizens never seem to reach the limits of their always proliferating desires.

If the commodity he consumes is empty of love and affection, it will cause him to feel empty, however much he acquires and consumes what is offered, and he will want to reject it, get rid of it, throw it away, to look for another object of consumption, to find that special experience he craves for. Getting rid of it symbolises throwing it up, vomiting it out, in order to make room for the new and promising multitude of objects. It is a world of refuse and discards, there is nothing that is special for more than the moment; for instance, the fashion industry now provides people with dispensable garments which symbolise rubbish, which defy innate images of beauty, indeed, the more outrageous they are the better. There is an inbuilt obsolescence in their product which of course increases their sale in a market which constantly chases for something new and different.

If anybody thinks that I am exaggerating, just let them look at the endless photographs in newspapers and coloured supplements of models on the catwalk and the enthusiastic reporting of fashion designers and moguls of fashion houses. It is also noteworthy that the models parade without any expression of pleasure and look disgusted with what they are wearing, and with the public stupid enough to buy it. Many models appear to be anorexic, the other side of bulimia, both part of the syndrome of rejection. Their studied sexuality is provocative and joyless.

People are beginning to ask why our world is devoted to the worship of consumerism and why, when there are many more rich people than at any other time in history, there is such an absence of optimism, a sense of disenchantment bordering on melancholia, or what is called miserabilism.

I have diverted from my original question: what we can do to put some pride and pleasure into the act of production and make work truly creative.

3. Training and Education

It is self-evident that every worker should be able to acquire the skills of his craft to make him feel proud and pleased with his ability to be a creator of goods and feel a sense of satisfaction in their quality. But it is not only the producer of commodities but every human being as he grows into adulthood must acquire the necessary skills in whatever field he chooses to become a valuable and esteemed contributor to the nation's welfare. A decent society would make sure that every individual acquires a skill, with a diploma or degree according to their talent, and that there would be no unskilled individuals deprived of self-respect and unable to earn a proper living. Every human being possesses a variety of talents, but some of these are predominant and determine the role he wants to play in life.

The recognition of a child's talents should play an important role in its education. Teachers should encourage children to communicate what they want to be when they grow up, even though young children would at various stages of their development express different ideas of what they would want to do. What is important is that they know that society is interested in their feelings and expectations of their future. More accurate assessments of their abilities and talents would also help the educationalists as well as the children to guide them in the most rewarding choices of profession, a kind of positive reinforcement, encouraging their best qualities, as against the negative kind of reinforcement which is now fashionable in aptitude tests which are felt to discriminate against them by emphasising their limitations and excluding them from the 'best jobs'.

It is in the interest of society to emphasise and promote the best qualities of its citizens and to show appreciation of their talents, for we know all too well that many people, having their talents unrecognised, become discontented or even hostile, and society loses a vast reservoir of abilities to its detriment. Those who want to exercise their skills in making material objects must be encouraged to be masters in their trade, to undergo apprenticeship and training in the process of becoming craftsmen. They should not be forced to stay at school longer than they need, for they would come to resent having to be stuck for years in classrooms which they no longer find interesting, making them restless and frequently rebellious. At the age of about fifteen they should enter into the productive environment of workshop or factory as apprentices to learn the skill required of a competent workman and receive a diploma for it, and eventually have the title of master of their trade, and, if they wish, be able to start their own company, or become managers of large enterprises.

Every workshop or factory should be obliged to employ a number of apprentices and pay them a certain wage. On the other hand, adolescents should have the option to enrol in a trade school or academy where they could be trained in their chosen profession. Young people who have a call for more intellectually orientated activities would stay longer in schools and be prepared for university.

While the producers of commodities would have a diploma of craftsmanship or masters of their trade, the others would acquire degrees in the field they choose to study. All these titles should give public recognition for people's talents and abilities in their different roles in society. This would help to break down the snobbish image of elitism in the social hierarchy, and everybody who has achieved competence in their chosen fields would be recognised as valuable members of the community.

Boys and girls who leave school early, as they don't want to have their minds choked with a lot of information that seems irrelevant to them, should have the opportunity to become familiar with the intellectual dimensions and traditions of their culture. At least once a week they should attend a polytechnic (whose proper role in society should be re-established), or a workers' university to stimulate and to enrich their minds.

The number of actual producers of goods has been greatly reduced due to the demographic changes of modern societies which have seen an enormous proliferation of middle men engaged in the promotion and sales of commodities. A whole new industry engaged in advertising, public relations, market analysis and accountancy, all specialists and experts in their field, has still further enlarged the gulf between the actual producer and the customer. This vast and growing regiment of specialists are concerned to ensure the success of the tasks set before them and increasingly lose sight of their impact upon the community as a whole. They are intent not only to promote the interests of the industrial corporations they are meant to serve, but to promote their own interests, their importance in society and the maximalisation of their profit (see 6th Maxim). They should be encouraged to see their work as an active contribution to the welfare of society, and their role defined with this end in view.

This process has been dramatically compounded with the emergence of computers which have become an integral part of our economy.

4. The Humanisation of Machines and the Dehumanisation of Man

We have seen that in our evolution we have externalised our motor senses upon tools and machines to increase our capacity to work and to produce things. Tools developed into machines which in industrial modes of production came to dictate the work process as they acquired more and more of the human skills and reduced the skills of the workers, leaving them to be servants of the machine system. With the 'progress' of technology we have externalised not only the skills of work but also our minds into the humanisation of machines, which not only dictate the process of production but also dictate the way we think. The so-called thinking machines have acquired many capabilities which were unique to man. They not only have appropriated the work process but also our logical faculties, our foresight and anticipation, our ability to judge and discriminate between what is correct or wrong in the way we do things. They have come to be superior to the human mind in many of its attributes, and men feel increasingly dependent upon their instructions.

Computers, however, do not possess the most important qualities of the human mind, although they can outpace by far its speed of decision making. They have no commonsense, they do not know that the rain is wet or that mothers are older than their daughters, and they cannot relate the factual information they provide to the emotion which we associate with facts; they don't know what makes people happy or miserable. They can only present and calculate quantitative relationships, mathematical and statistical information available at any given time, they help accountants, managers and financial speculators by providing them with the facts they need and statistically based prognoses of what is likely to be of profit. Their world is one of numbers and symbols and it does not understand what motivates people to seek the information they want. In a world of instant information and instant decision making there is no time for reflection, no time to question one's motivation or consider the long-term consequences of decisions we are making; one does not arrive at decisions – they are instantly given. It is a reflex-dominated world, as we imitate the reflexes of the computer. And time is short, there are so many things we can do, and are therefore compelled to do them, in order not to miss out on any opportunities available. Instant gratification by instantly available information, instant availability of commodities through the internet website and e-mail, and we cannot resist their instant acquisition for ourselves as well as for our children. Greed and possessiveness dominate.

Our minds and our psyche as well as our physiological behaviour regress to reflex-dominated impulses. We find this in so many aspects of our culture, from the arts, theatre, literature and young people's idea of having a good time – raves, acid parties, drugs – and the constraints of what used to be civilised values are discarded. There is an explosion of energy which gives free rein to the primitive areas of the mind, by-passing or neutralising the prefrontal lobes of the cortex. This can be seen in the explosive and disjointed images in films and television, and in advertisements. Computers know nothing of beauty and moral considerations, and in the analysis and information they provide do not consider the aesthetic qualities.

Governments, whose idea of a good education consists in teaching young people the skills of computer manipulation, will undermine their intellectual capabilities by deferring to the computer's superior logic and speed of information; they relinquish their responsibility by handing it over to the machine.

Computers can be very useful for providing quick information for all kinds of purposes, such as finding a plumber in an emergency, or the name of an author of a book you want to read, or getting a theatre ticket at the last moment, and so on. These can be considered as useful and morally neutral. But there are other types of information which have a profound moral implication and can be used for all kinds of aggressive and destructive ends, such as how to find the best way of perfecting chemical weapons, or making nano-robots which have the power to reproduce and multiply themselves, or cloning animals or humans without considering the long-term consequences. Thus information always serves a purpose, and we must learn to ask what purpose it serves, for it can be good or bad. It can serve our greed, our desire for riches, our lust for power or the extermination of people whom we regard as enemies, or does it serve our goodwill and the enhancement of life? Thus the computer inevitably engages our moral conscience, whether we are aware of it or not. What do we want their information for, what purposes does it serve? It sounds simple enough and may be obvious; but at a time when we have lost the sense of a moral purpose, which I have called the moral vacuum, and one impulse or desire appears to us as good as any other, there is a real danger that we use the information computers provide indiscriminately.

We confront the further question how we can make ourselves conscious of the moral imperatives, not only in the use of the mass of information available to us, but also in our personal and social relationships. This, as I have tried to show, is an integral part of education, both of children as well as grown-ups. In the first instance, it is the responsibility of parents to teach children some basic moral precepts, to speak to them of right and wrong, and to listen to them and learn how they respond and to 'discuss with them'. The parental role is then expanded and transferred to school which must not only provide information about all kinds of facts but also about the values predominant in our culture and its moral ideas. It is the duty of teachers in our time, when, apart from religious schools which inculcate their dogmas, there is an implied belief in freedom of opinion, to teach the values of our humanistic moral concepts as a duty which upholds consideration and care for our fellows.

It is also time for us in the West, responsible as we are for the technological progress which has made industrialisation and automation possible and has spread them across the globe, to consider when to put a break on its further 'progress' before it becomes a real danger to man's survival. The ideas of the Enlightenment which gave birth to science and technology have to be brought back and re-examined in order to guide us in the way we can apply them in practice. The unreflecting pursuit of technological advance is 'blind progress', and we have to open our eyes and visualise where we want to go, to contemplate our future and ask ourselves to what kind of world we wish to progress. We have to question, examine and discuss our future as a species, particularly as we are responsible not only to ourselves but also to the fate of the planet and to the life as we know it. And we must discover how to modify our ways of thinking and our habits to avoid committing ourselves to catastrophe. This is not only a question of future survival but also of man's dignity as the most advanced form of life.

I have observed a few signposts of danger in our evolution of the positive as well as negative aspects of human nature. There are of course many other manifestations of crisis, and they have to be connected into a unified understanding of the problem we face. Our freedom to choose makes us responsible for how we choose, for we are free to destroy life or to enhance it.

It is now time to activate the highest part of our brain and call upon its full potentials so that humanity can be born at last. It may not be easy, but then no birth is painless, but, once accomplished, it is a source of great joy and celebration.

Bibliography

Atkins, G. Douglas & Morrow, Laura, eds: *Contemporary Literary Theory*, Macmillan, 1989
Andreski, Stanislav: *Social Sciences as Sorcery*, Deutsch 1972
Andrewes, A: *Greek Society*, Penguin, 1991
Austin, J. L: *Sense and Sensibilia*, OUP 1962
Ayer, A. J: *Language, Truth and Logic*, Penguin, 1990
— *The Problem of Knowledge*, Penguin, 1990
Bachofen, J. J: *Myth, Religion and Mother Right*, Routledge, 1968
Barthes, Roland: *The Death of the Author*, Hill & Wary, 1977
Bell, Daniel: *The Coming of Post-Industrial Society*, Heinemann, 1974
Benedict, Ruth: *Patterns of Culture*, New American Library, 1959
Bowra, C. M: *Ancient Greek Literature*, Butterworth, 1933
Boyne, Roy: *Foucault and Derrida: The Other Side of Reason*, Unwin and Hyman, 1990
Brehier, Emile: *The Hellenic Age*, University of Chicago Press
Breton, André: *Manifestoes of Surrealism*, University of Chicago Press, 1969
Briffault, Robert: *The Mothers*, Macmillan, 1927
Bronowski, J. & Mazlish, B: *The Western Intellectual Tradition from Leonardo to Hegel*, HarperCollins, 1960
Burckhardt, J: *The Civilisation of the Renaissance in Italy*, Penguin, 1990
Cambridge Ancient History, The, Volumes 1 & 2, CUP, 1980

Calvin, William H: *How Brains Think*, Weidenfeld & Nicolson, 1997
Campbell, Joseph: *The Hero with a Thousand Faces*, Princeton, 1968
— *The Masks of God: Primitive Mythology*, 1973
Carnap, Rudolf: *Logical Foundations of Probability*, University of Chicago Press, 1962
— *Theoretical Questions and Practical Action*
Chadwick, Owen: *The Reformation*, Penguin History of the Church, 1970
Chalmers, D: *The Conscious Mind*, OUP, 1996
Childe, V.G: *Man Makes Himself*, Watts, 1936
Clark, Grahame: *World Prehistory*, CUP, 1969
Clark, W. E. Le Gros: *The Antecedents of Man*, Edinburgh UP, 1962
Cohn, Norman: *Warrant for Genocide*, Serif, 1996
Crick, Francis: *The Astonishing Hypothesis*, Pocket Books, 1995
Crook, J. H: *Gelada Baboon Herd Structure and Movement*, Symposium Zoological Society London, 18, 1966
Damasio, Antonio: *The Feeling of What Happens*, Heinemann, 2000
Dart, R.A: 'Australopithecus Africanus' (*Nature*, London, 1925)
— *Adventures with the Missing Link*, Viking, 1961
Derrida, Jacques: *Positions 1972*, Athlone Press, 1981
— *Structure, Sign and Play in the Discourse of the Human Sciences in the Language of Criticism and the Sciences of Man*, John Hopkins University Press, 1970
Descartes, René: *'Discourse on Method' and Related Writings*, Penguin 1999
Ditfurth, Hoimar von : *Der Geist fiel nicht vom Himmel*, Dtv, 1991
Dobb, M: *Studies in the Development of Capitalism*, Routledge, 1963
Dobzhanski, T: *Mankind Evolving*, Yale University Press, 1968
— 'Cultural Direction of Human Evolution' (*Human Biology*, 1963)
Dubos, R: *So Human an Animal*, Transaction Pub., 1998
Einstein, A. & Freud, S: *Why War?* 1933
Ellul, Jacques: *The Technological Society*, Random House, 1967
Erikson, E. H: *Childhood and Society*, Vintage, 1995

BIBLIOGRAPHY

Farrington, B: *Francis Bacon, Philosopher of Industrial Science*, Macmillan, 1973
Finley, M: *Early Greece*, Chatto & Windus, 1981
Foot, Michael: *The History of Mr Wells*, Doubleday, 1995
Fox, R: *In the Beginning – Aspects of Hominid Behavioural Evolution*, London, 1967
Frank, Philip: *The Validation of Scientific Theories*, Beacon Press, 1955
Frankfort, Henry: *Kingship and the Gods,* Chicago, 1948
— *The Birth of Civilisation in the Near East*, London, 1951
Frankl, George: *The End of War or the End of Mankind*, Globe Publications, 1955
— *The Failure of the Sexual Revolution*, Kahn & Averill, 1974
— *The Social History of the Unconscious*, Open Gate Press, 1990
— *Archaeology of the Mind*, Open Gate Press, 1992
— *Civilisation: Utopia and Tragedy*, Open Gate Press, 1992
— *The Unknown Self*, Open Gate Press, 1993
— *Exploring the Unconscious*, Open Gate Press, 1994
Frankl, Viktor: *The Will to Meaning*, Plume Books, 1989
Frazer, Sir James: *The Golden Bough*, Macmillan, 1922
— *The Magic Art*, 1911
Freud, Sigmund (see Standard Edition, Pelican Freud Library, Hogarth):
— (1905) *Three Essays on the Theory of Sexuality*
— (1913) *Totem and Taboo*
— (1915-17) *Introductory Lectures on Psychoanalysis*
— (1921) *Group Psychology and the Analysis of the Ego*
— (1927) *The Future of an Illusion*
— (1930) *Civilization and its Discontents*
— (1933) *New Introductory Lectures on Psychoanalysis*
Fromm, Erich: *Psychoanalysis and Religion*, Yale UP, 1950
— *The Sane Society*, Holt, 1990
— *The Crisis of Psychoanalysis*, Jonathan Cape, 1970
— *The Anatomy of Human Destructiveness*, Pimlico, 1993
Gimbutas, M: *The Goddesses and Gods of Old Europe*, Thames & Hudson, 1974
Goldman, Lucien: *The Human Sciences and Psychology*, Jonathan Cape, 1969
Goodheart, Eugene: *The Sceptical Disposition*, Princeton University Press, 1984

Gould, Stephen Jay: *Ontogeny and Phylogeny*, Harvard UP, 1985
Guittari, Félix: *Chaosmosis: An Ethico-Aesthetic Paradigm*, Bloomington, Indiana University Press, 1995
Hammond, N. G. L: *The History of Greece to 332 BC*, OUP, 1959
Harrison, J. E: *Prolegomena to the Study of Greek Religion*, Princeton, 1991
Harth, Erich: *Windows on the Mind: Reflections on the Principal Basis of Consciousness*, Harvester Press, 1982
Helbaek, H: 'First Impressions of the Çatal Hüyük Husbandry' (*Anatolian Studies XIV*, 1964)
Hilton, Anthony: Article from *Evening Standard*, 3.4.96
Howells, William: *Mankind in the Making*, Secker & Warburg, 1961
Hudson, Christopher: Article from *Evening Standard*, 14.5.96
Hudson, Liam: *The Cult of the Fact*, Jonathan Cape, 1972
Hutton, Will: Article from *The Observer*, 12.12.99
Irigaray, Luce: 'A Chance for Life': in *Sexes and Genealogies*, Columbia University Press, 1993
James, E. O: *The Cult of the Mother Goddess*, London, 1959
Johnson, Paul: *A History of Christianity*, Weidenfeld, 1976
Kant, Immanuel: *Critique of Pure Reason*, Everyman, 1993
— *Critique of Practical Reason (1788)* in *Practical Philosophy*, ed. Mary J. Gregor, CUP 1999
— *Idea for a Universal History (1784)* in *On History*, Indianapolis 1963
— *The Metaphysics of Morals (1797)* in *Practical Philosophy*, ed. Mary J. Gregor, CUP 1999
Kerényi, C: *The Gods of the Greeks*, Thames & Hudson, 1982
Kitto, H. D. F: *The Greeks* Pelican, 1972
Klapp, Orinn E: *Collective Search for Identity* Holt, Rinehart and Winston, Inc.
Kristeva, Julia: *Desire in Language*, Columbia University Press, 1980
— *Revolution in Poetic Language* (French edition 1974), Columbia University Press, 1984
Jacques Lacan: *Écrits*, Routledge, 1990
Larousse Encyclopaedia of Mythology, Paul Hamlyn
Lasch, Christopher: *The Culture of Narcissism*, Norton, 1991
Leakey, L. S. B: *Adam's Ancestors*, Harper & Row, 1960

BIBLIOGRAPHY

LeDoux, Joseph: *The Emotional Brain: The Mysterious Underpinnings of Emotional Life*, Weidenfeld & Nicolson, 1998
Leroi-Gourhan, A: *The Art of Prehistoric Man in Western Europe*, Thames & Hudson, 1968
Lévi-Strauss, C: *The Savage Mind*, University of Chicago Press, 1967
Lodge, David and Woods, Nigel, eds: *Modern Criticism and Theory*, Addison Wesley Longman Higher Education, 1999
Mach, Ernst: *The Analysis of Sensations*, Thoemmes Press, 1999
Malcolm, Norman: *Ludwig Wittgenstein. A Memoir*, OUP, 1984
Malinowski, B: *Sex and Repression in Savage Society*, Routledge, 1960
— *Sex, Culture and Myth*, Mayflower-Dell, 1967
Mandel, C. W. K: *A Critique of Linguistic Philosophy*, 2nd edition, 1979
Marcuse, Herbert: *One-Dimensional Man*, Routledge, 1991
Marx, Karl and Engels, Friedrich: *The Communist Manifesto*, Penguin, 1985
Mead, Margaret: *Coming of Age in Samoa*, William Morrow, 1961
Mellaart, J: *Çatal Hüyük: A Neolithic Town in Anatolia*, Thames & Hudson, 1967
— *The Neolithic of the Near East*, Thames & Hudson, 1975.
— *Earliest Civilisations of the Near East*, Thames & Hudson 1978
Midgley, M: *The Ethical Primate*, Routledge, 1994
Mitchell, J & Rose, J: *Jacques Lacan & the École Freudienne: Feminine Sexuality*, Macmillan, 1985
Mumford, Lewis: *The Myth of the Machine*, Harvest Books, 1971
Nagel, Ernst: *The Structure of Science*, Hackett, 1987
Napier, J: *The Roots of Mankind*, Smithsonian Institute, 1970
Neurath, Otto (ed.): *Foundations of the Unity of Science*, University of Chicago Press, 1971
Newton, Isaac: *Optics*, 1755
Nolte, John: *The Human Brain: An Introduction to its Functional Anatomy* Mosby, 1999
Oakley, K.P: *Man the Toolmaker*, Chicago, 1961
Oparin, A. I: *Life – Its Nature, Origin and Development*, Oliver & Boyd, 1961
— *The Qualitative Change from Natural to Mental Phenomena*

Parrot, A: *Sumer*, London, 1960
Piaget, J: *Origins of Intelligence in Children*, International Universities Press, 1992
Pilbeam, D: *The Evolution of Man*, Thames and Hudson, 1970
Popper, Karl: *Conjectures and Refutations*, Routledge, 1969
Pfeiffer, John E: *The Emergence of Man*, Thomas Nelson, 1970
Reed, Bika, (ed.): *Rebel in the Soul: An Ancient Egyptian Dialogue Between a Man and His Destiny*, Inner Traditions International, 1997
Reich, Wilhelm: *Character Analysis*, Farrar Strauss Giroux, 1980
Reichenbach, Hans: *Modern Philosophy of Science*, Humanities Press, 1959
Reik, Theodor: *Ritual – Psychoanalytic Studies*, Farrar, Strauss, 1957
Rickman, H. P: *The Challenge of Philosophy: from Modernism to Deconstructionism*, Open Gate Press, 2000
Roberts, Catherine: *The Scientific Conscience*, Open Gate Press, 2000
Roheim, Geza: *Psychoanalysis and Anthropology*, International Universities Press, 1971
Rorvik, D: *As Man Becomes a Machine*, Souvenir Press, 1973
Rose, Steven: *The Conscious Brain*, Penguin, 1978
Rose, Steven, ed: *From Brains to Consciousness* – Essays on the New Sciences of the Mind, Penguin 1999
Roszak, T: *The Making of a Counter Culture*, University of California Press, 1995
Russell, Bertrand: *History of Western Philosophy*, Routledge, 1991
Ryle, Gilbert: *The Concept of Mind*, Penguin, 1990
Sandars, N. K: *Prehistoric Art in Europe*, Penguin, 1968
Schaller, George: *The Year of the Gorilla*, University of Chicago Press, 1988
Schlick, Moritz: *Philosophical Papers*, Kluwer Academic Publishers, 1979
Searle, J. R: *The Construction of Social Reality*, Penguin, 1996
Simmel, Georg: *The Philosophy of Money*, Routledge, 1990
Simmons, L. E: *The Early Relatives of Man*, 'Scientific American', July 1964
Sokal, Alan and Bricmont, Jean: *Intellectual Impostures*, Profile Books, 1998

BIBLIOGRAPHY

Strachey, A: *The Unconscious Motives of War*, Allen & Unwin, 1957
Sweezy, P. M: *The Theory of Capitalist Development*, Modern Readers Paperback, 1970
Tawney, R. H: *Religion and the Rise of Capitalism*, Pelican, 1940
Thomson, G: *Studies in Ancient Greek Society*, Weidenfeld & Nicolson, 1980
Ure, Andrew: *The Philosophy of Manufacture*, London, 1835
Vaisey, John: *Capitalism and Society*, Weidenfield & Nicolson, 1980
Virilio, Paul, ed. Derian, James Der: *The Virilio Reader*, Blackwell, 1998
Washburn, S. L: *Mankind in Amnesia*, Sidgwick & Jackson, 1982
Washburn, S. L. & Lancaster, C. S: 'The Evolution of Hunting' in *Man the Hunter*, Chicago University Press, 1968
Weber, Max: *The Protestant Ethic and the Spirit of Capitalism*, Routledge, 1992
Wells, H. G: *The Mind at the End of Its Tether*, Heinemann, 1945
Wittgenstein, Ludwig: *Tractatus Logico-Philosophicus*, Routledge, 1990
— *Philosophical Investigations*, Blackwell, 1997
— *Blue and Brown Books*, HarperCollins, 1980
Wheen, Francis: *Karl Marx*, Fourth Estate, 1999
Yerkes, R .M. & Yerkes, A.V: *The Great Apes*, Yale, 1929
Young, J. Z: *Doubt and Certainty in Sciences: A Biologist's Reflection on the Brain*, OUP, 1960
Zweig, Stefan: *The World of Yesterday*, University of Nebraska Press, 1964

Index

A

a priori 37, 44, 45, 47, 80, 173, 174, 175, 176, 177, 178, 179, 183
Abraham 157
Abraham, Karl 15
Abrams, M. H. 77
Adorno, Theodor 13, 168
alienation 20, 108
all-male group 122–3
Altamira 141
altar-like edifice 130
Anaxagoras 161
Anaximander 161
Anaximenes 161
Anderson, Danny 74
Andreski, Stanislav 73, 74
Aristotle 6, 165
Athenian culture 161
Attlee, Clement 63
Aurignacian tool-making 134,
Aurignacian culture 134, 137, 138
Auschwitz 7, 8, 13
Austin, J. L. 60, 64, 65
Australopithecus 108, 116

B

Bachofen, J. J. 148
Bacon, Francis (artist) 31
Bacon, Francis (philosopher) 55
Bacon, Roger 49
Barthes, Roland 75
Bauer, Otto 56
Bayle, P. 54
Beethoven, Ludwig van 13
Beginnings of Agriculture 145
behaviourism 82
Belsey, Catherine 75
Berg, Alban 29
Berkeley, Bishop 53
Blair, Tony 166
Bohr, Niels 176
Bolshevism 6
Boyne, Roy 76
Breton, André 28
Breuil, Henri 140
Bricmont, Jean 67, 69, 73
Bridges, Lucas
burial rites 127–31
burin 134, 135
Byron, Lord George Gordon 13

INDEX

C

Calvin, W. H. 98
Campbell, Joseph 129, 144
Capsian people 146, 147, 149
Capsian culture 147
Carnap, Rudolf 35, 42, 44, 59, 60
Çatal Hüyük 157
Categorical Imperative 184
categorical imperative 80, 173, 183, 184–5, 195
causa prima 53, 104, 176
— First Cause 51, 52, 176
cave-bear 130
Chirico, Giorgio de 29
Christian Middle Ages 48
Clinton, Bill 166
Combe-Chapelle 133
Communist 77
— communist Utopia 43
concept of property 148, 151
Copernicus 49
Crick, Francis 84
crisis of morality 1
Cro-Magnon man 133, 134, 137, 139
Crook, J. H. 121–2
cult of cynicism 11
cultural symbol 117, 138
culture *passim*

D

D'Alema, Massimo 166
Dali, Salvador 29
Damasio, Antonio 102
Darwin, Charles 6, 19, 99, 107
das Ding an sich 177
deconstruction 66
deconstructionism 8, 66
deconstructionist 32
defiance of civilised virtues 21
Deleuze, Gilles 67
Derrida, Jacques 67, 76
Descartes, René 50, 51, 53, 103
Dewey, John 62–3
Dilthey, Wilhelm 66
Dionysius II 164, 197
Ditfurth, Hoimar von 105
divinity of kings 152–4

E

early neolithic man 149
ego 12, 13, 14, 17, 29, 30, 33, 41, 50, 51, 52, 53, 54, 70, 79, 89, 98, 125, 136, 141, 155, 160, 169, 172
Einstein, Albert 6, 30, 36, 107
emergence of agriculture 147, 156
Emin, Tracey 31
Enlightenment 1, 2, 7, 8, 10, 34, 35, 41, 46, 47–56, 61, 66, 76, 80, 168, 173, 205
— culture of 11, 13
Ernst, Max 29
Eros 10, 164, 169, 171, 187, 188, 192
eros 32, 33, 114, 124, 141
Escale 120
evolution 48, 55, 82, 83, 84, 85, 89, 94, 97, 99, 100, 103, 105, 106, 107, 108, 111–16, 118, 126, 134, 202
externalisation 108, 110, 111, 112, 117, 125

F

Fascism 6
Fascist 57
Feigl, H. 35, 59, 60
Fertile Crescent 147
Fichte, Johann Gottlieb 55
fire 119–21, 127
Font de Gaume 141

INDEX

Frege, Gottlob 35, 38
Freud, Sigmund 6, 10, 14, 72, 122, 186
Fromm, Erich 171

G

Galileo 6, 177
Gauguin, Paul 27
ghost 117, 118, 125, 127, 129, 130, 144
ghost worship 117–18
God 8, 12, 36, 47, 48, 49, 50, 51, 52, 53, 54, 55, 62, 75, 104, 107, 111, 118, 125, 126, 131, 132, 153, 155, 156, 157, 169, 172, 176, 178, 185, 186, 187, 191, 192, 193, 194
— God the Father 155
god 1, 7, 14, 125, 132, 141
goddess 137, 138, 139, 140, 141, 142–4
Gödel, Kurt 59, 72
Goethe, J. W. von 6, 172
Goodheart, Eugene 75
Gould, James and Carol 99
grand theories 4, 45
Gregory IX, Pope 48
Grey, John 7
Guattari, Felix 67

H

harem group 121
Harrison, J. E. 144
Heckel, Erich 27
Hegel, G. W. F. 3–4, 42, 55, 56, 65, 108, 111
Heidegger, Martin 55, 180
Heine, Heinrich 111
Hesiod 160
Hilton, Anthony 18
Hirst, Damien 31

Hitler, Adolf 6, 56, 187
Hobbes, Thomas 54
Homer 160
Homo 108
Homo erectus 112, 116, 119, 124, 127, 170
Homo pekinensis 112, 118
Homo picanthropus erectus 112
Homo picanthropus 116
Homo sapiens 107, 118, 132–44, 147
Hume, David 52, 54, 55
Hutton, Will 19
hypothalamus 93–5

I

id 14, 17, 19, 29, 30, 33, 79, 155
innate mental faculties 45
Innocent III, Pope 48
instinctual void 79
Irigaray, Luce 67
Isaiah 6, 198

J

James, William 62
Jericho 149, 150
Jesus 6, 172
Jewish concept of God 157–9
Jolly, Clifford 121
Judaism 157–9

K

Kandinsky, Wassily 28
Kant, Immanuel 6, 36, 37, 44–6, 52, 53, 54, 55, 79, 80–1, 157, 165, 173–85, 186
Kirchner, Ernst Ludwig 27
Kokoschka, Oskar 27
Kounellis, Jannis 31
Kristeva, Julia 67, 72–3, 74

INDEX

L

La Ferrassie 128–9
Lacan, Jacques 67, 68–72, 73, 74
Laing, R. D. 3
Laplace 52
Lascaux 141
Lashley, K. S. 82
latency period 124
Latour, Bruno 67
LeDoux, Joseph 99
Le Moustier 128
Lenin. V. I. 57
Les Eyzies 133, 138
Lévi-Strauss, Claude 69
libido 29, 38, 71, 131, 136, 137, 146, 160, 161, 188, 189, 192, 199
linguistic analysis 60, 71, 72
linguistic analyst 32, 63, 71, 77
linguistic phenomenology 64
Locke, John 44, 54, 55
logical empiricism 60
logical positivism 35, 42, 60
logical positivist 32, 42, 58, 59, 60

M

Mach, Ernst 35, 43
Macke, August 27
Magdalenian
— art and artists 139–42, 145–6
— culture 138
— people 140, 145, 149
— period 138–44
Malcolm, Norman 40, 41, 58
Malthus 9, 11
'Man, know thyself' 162
Man Ray 29
Mandel, C. W. K. 63, 64

Marcuse, Herbert 14
Marx, Karl 4, 9, 42, 56, 108, 172, 191
Marxism 72
Marxist movements 33
matriarchal culture 134–8
matriarchy 134–44
— crisis of 142–4
— revolt against 145–6
Mellaart, J. 150
memory store 120
Messianic Age 158
Middle Ages 48, 49, 172
Miocene 113
Mirandola. Pico della 6
Miro, Joan 29
monotheism 157, 158, 176, 184
morality *passim*
Moses 157, 191
mother-goddess 134–44, 156
Mozart, W. A. 13
Mueller, Otto 27
Munch, Edvard 27
myths 43, 46, 47, 117, 120, 125, 143, 145, 147, 156, 160, 161

N

Narcissus 161, 197
Napoleon 55
Natufian
— culture 149
— people 147
— settlements 150
Nazi 44, 57, 59, 76, 77
— anti-Nazi 77
Nazism 6, 11, 43, 59
Neanderthal 126, 127, 128, 129, 130, 131, 132, 133
Neurath, Otto 35, 44, 59
Newton, Isaac 6, 50, 51, 52, 165, 178

INDEX

Niaux 140, 141
Nietzsche, Friedrich 62, 63, 76

O

Oedipus complex 122, 123, 124, 154, 156, 160, 186
Olympic myths 161
Olympic pantheon 144
one-male breeding group 122–3
Oparin, A. I. 82
oral-cannibalism 15

P

Paranthropus 108
Pascal, Blaise 54
patriarchal
— culture 148–56
— family 149
— man 152
— morality 155
— religion 185–7
— society 185
patriarchal paranoia 154, 155156
patriarchy 148, 152, 155, 157, 160, 193
Patriarchy emerges 148
Peche Merle 141
people of the Kalahari 171
Pericles 163
Perigordian culture 138
Pfeiffer, J. E. 113, 137
phallic-assertive drive 147
Picasso, Pablo 29
Plato 6, 49, 50, 109, 162, 163, 164, 165, 173, 197
Pleistocene 112, 113, 114, 119, 123, 127
Popper, Karl 35, 43, 44, 59
postmodernism 66
postmodernist 32
post-structuralism 66

prefrontal lobes 83, 87, 89, 90, 91, 94, 97, 98, 100, 101, 102, 174, 204
Protagoras 162
Ptolemy 178

R

Ramapithecus 108, 113–16
Randell, Peter 91–3
Regressive disintegration of the arts 26
Renaissance 49
Rickman, H. P. 74
Ricoeur, Paul 71
Rose, Steven 83, 86
Rousseau, Jean-Jacques 54
Russell, Bertrand 35, 37, 38, 42, 58, 65, 162–3

S

Sargon of Akkad 152
Sartre, Jean-Paul 103
Schaller, George 115
Schelling, F. W. J. von 66
Schiele, Egon 27
Schleiermacher, Friedrich 66
Schlick, Moritz 35, 42, 44, 59
Schopenhauer, Arthur 6, 44, 56, 63, 165, 175
Schroeder, Gerhard 166
Scruton, Roger 7
Shakespeare, William 6, 13
Shelley, P. B. 13, 197
Simmel, Georg 16
Simmons, L. E. 115
Smith, Adam, 191
social democracy 58
socialism 10, 11, 20, 42, 43, 166
Socrates 163
Sokal, Alan 67, 69, 73
Solutrean culture 138

INDEX

sophist 161, 162, 163
Spinoza, Benedict de 6, 50, 52
spirit 7, 12, 13, 47, 52, 53, 54, 75, 153, 155, 157, 173, 185
— of ancestor 129
— of the Enlightenment 56
— of father-figure 170–1
— 'German' 59
— of modernism 29
— of the mother 136
— of morality 170
— of totem animal 131
spiritual
— authority 7
— capacity 128
— dimension of mankind 101
— freedom, struggle for 53
— meaning of the world 12
— power of the woman 143
Stalin, Josef 42–3, 56, 186
Stalinism 11
Stravinsky, Igor 29
Strindberg, August 29
superego 14, 15, 19, 25, 28, 32, 33, 51, 52, 53, 75, 79, 140, 141, 143, 152, 154, 155, 159, 162, 185, 186
symbolisation 110–11
synthetic *a priori* 37, 45, 92, 177, 178, 183

T

Tanguy, Yves 29
Teyjat 141
Thales 160
Thanatos 10, 187, 188
Theognis 160
tool-making 107–11, 112, 117, 126, 134, 138
tribal paranoia 155

U

universal God 157–8
universal moral concept 159
Urmson, J. O. 64

V

vegetative system 95
Vienna circle 35, 41–7, 56–60
Virilio, Paul 67
Voltaire 6, 54

W

Waismann, F. 35, 44, 59
Warnock, G. J. 64
Wedekind, F. 29
Wells, H. G. 4–5
Western civilisation 5, 28, 32, 145, 157
Wittgenstein, Ludwig 3, 32, 35–42, 44, 57, 58, 64, 65, 75
working classes 19–20, 180

Z

Zabarella, Giacomo 48
Zeus 160
Zinjanthropus 108
Zweig, Stefan 5–6